THE
STAR TREK
INTERVIEW
BOOK

THE
STAR TREK®
INTERVIEW
B·O·O·K

ALLAN ASHERMAN

POCKET BOOKS

New York   London   Toronto   Sydney   Tokyo

An *Original* publication of POCKET BOOKS

POCKET BOOKS, a division of Simon & Schuster Inc.
1230 Avenue of the Americas, New York, N.Y. 10020

STAR TREK is a Registered Trademark of
Paramount Pictures Corporation.

This book is published by Pocket Books, a division of
Simon & Schuster Inc., under exclusive license from
Paramount Pictures Corporation.

ISBN: 0-671-61734-X

First Pocket Books trade paperback printing July, 1988

10 9 8 7 6 5 4 3 2 1

POCKET and colophon are trademarks of
Simon & Schuster Inc.

Printed in the U.S.A.

Charlie's or Boston
508-583-1300

This book is dedicated to Arlene Lo, the woman I love.

ACKNOWLEDGMENTS

Many thanks to all those whose names appear below, especially Gene Roddenberry for starting it all, and to Harve Bennett for extending the frontiers of the STAR TREK universe. Special thanks to Dave Stern of Pocket Books for his counsel, patience, and friendship,

Forrest J. Ackerman, Darrell Anderson Jr., Darrell Anderson Sr., Howard Anderson, Ira Anderson, Bill Andrews, Richard Arnold, Charlene Bergman, Jerome Bixby, Rebecca Brookshire, Robert Butler, Morris Chapnick, Alexander Courage, Gary Crandall, Elaine Dabick, Joseph D'Agosta, Jim Danforth, Marc Daniels, Genny Dazzo, Lawrence Dobkin, James Doohan, George Duning, Carol Eisner, Joel Eisner, Jack Finlay, Robert Fletcher, Michael Forest, Al Francis, Fred Freiberger, Shirley Freiberger, Gerald Fried, Eva Marie Friedrick, Herschell Burke Gilbert, Gail Glick, Michael S. Glick, Murray Golden, James Goldstone, Douglas Grindstaff, Karen Haas, Verna Harvey, James Horner, Jack Hunsaker, Walter M. Jefferies, Greg Jein, George Clayton Johnson, Al Jones, Robert H. Justman, Stephen Kandel, Karen Kearns, Carolyn Kelley, DeForest Kelley, Walter Koenig, Richard Lapham, Paul Mandell, Tasha Martel, Vincent Joseph McEveety, Vincent Michael McEveety, Jim Meechan, Edward K. Milkis, Craig Miller, Arthur Morton, Joe Mullendore, John Newland, Nichelle Nichols, Leonard Nimoy, Gerd Oswald, Joan D. Pearce, Samuel A. Peeples, Gregg Peters, Joseph Pevney, Robert Raff, Majel Barrett Roddenberry, Brigette Roux-Lough, James Rugg, Susan Sackett, Paul Schneider, Bruce Schoengarth, Tom Sciacca, Ralph Senensky, Orri Seron, William Shatner, Peter M. Sloman, Jerry Sohl, Carrie Sorokin, Joseph Sorokin, Norman Spinrad, Fred Steiner, George Takei, Fabien Tordjmann, Judy Walker, Robert Walker, Patrick White, Grace Lee Whitney, Joan Winston, Ralph Winter, Robert Wise

. . . and my parents and everyone else who saw very little of me while I was working on this book.

CONTENTS

INTRODUCTION

There have been an awful lot of books written about STAR TREK over the past twenty-odd years: over that same span of time, there have also been an awful lot of published interviews with its stars and creators. When I originally conceived of The Star Trek Interview Book, I thought of it as not just a chance to collect the thoughts of those most closely associated with the show (Gene Roddenberry, William Shatner, Leonard Nimoy, etc.) but as a chance for the many lesser-known artists who worked both sides of the camera on the original series and feature films to speak about STAR TREK.

Now remember that STAR TREK began production in 1964 . . . a long time ago by movie and TV standards. Not only was I worried that just finding a lot of the people I wanted to interview would be impossible—I was well aware that many simply would not remember or wish to talk about things that happened so long ago in their careers.

I was delighted to find that, with very few exceptions, everyone I located wanted to talk about STAR TREK. Although at first some were concerned that they would not remember much, once I began asking questions, they found themselves reminiscing fondly about the show, recounting stories and opinions they had wanted to share for many years.

The most wonderful moments I had were the initial conversations with artists whose work I have admired for years. I was also elated when the interviews resulted in discoveries never before made public about STAR TREK's formative phases (I knew I had a scoop when I heard something like, "I've never said this before, but . . ." or "Nobody's ever asked me that question"). There were some sad discoveries as well, when I learned that people I had hoped to speak with had died, such as cinematographers William Snyder and Ernest Haller (who worked on "The Cage" and "Where No Man has Gone Before," respectively) and "Shore Leave" director Robert Sparr.

Unfortunately, what started as a search for enough material turned into a challenge to prevent The Star Trek Interview Book from becoming a prohibitively large volume. I regret that some material, including interviews with directors John Newland, Gerd Oswald, Michael S. Glick and Vince McEveety, special effects consultants Gary Crandall, Howard and Darryl Anderson and com-

poser Alexander Courage, actor Robert Walker, Jr., associate producer Eddie Milkis, special effects artist James Rugg, STIV executive producer Ralph Winter and Gene Roddenberry's assistant Morris Chapnick had to be cut from the final manuscript. In order to fit as much material in as possible, the book follows a straight question and answer format, with as little explanatory copy as possible.

I hope that anyone who picks up this book finds it as enjoyable to read as it was to put together. If nothing else, I hope it will give the reader an appreciation for the dedicated work of all the artists who have contributed to STAR TREK.

Mail to Allan Asherman may be sent to P.O. Box 3474, Hoboken, N.J. 07030-4405.

THE STARS

THE NINE PEOPLE WHOSE INTERVIEWS FOLLOW TRULY
NEED NO INTRODUCTION: THEIR NAMES AND FACES
WILL FOREVER BE ASSOCIATED WITH STAR TREK

GENE RODDENBERRY

If someone handed you a motion picture script about a young man who becomes first a heroic airline pilot, then a high-ranking policeman, then a television writer, and then creates the most popular TV series in history . . . you'd probably find it difficult to believe that such a man could exist. And yet all these things are part of the life of Gene Roddenberry.

Roddenberry believes in the potential of the human race to rise above its aggressive, prejudicial tendencies. He believes that someday all the people of Earth will take constructive delight in their differences. Because of this man and his beliefs we have STAR TREK. If anyone else had created the concept, it would bear little resemblance to the phenomenon that we know and love so well.

When I arrived in Los Angeles to conduct my interviews for this book, Gene was in the midst of the many intricate creative challenges of the first week's production of STAR TREK—THE NEXT GENERATION. Thousands of details had to be attended to, meetings held and rewrites done very quickly. Yet when I saw him walking back to his office on the Paramount lot he stopped, smiled, and confirmed that he would find the time to meet with me.

I don't know how he did it, but Roddenberry did find the time. I spoke with him in his office, a room decorated with memorabilia including the framed original artwork of "The Cage" videotape package, presented to him after the 100,000th sale of that Paramount Home Video cassette.

AA   *You created STAR TREK, and your name is known all over the world. How does it feel?*

GR   I feel, as I wake up every morning, "I hope today isn't the day they find me out." I have no feeling of having it "made." My life, I believe, is a life of education and growth, and I desperately hope I have not, and will not, reach a point and say, "Okay, I finally got it," because that will stop the education and growth. I'm still on reading programs, studying programs. I still take 16 or 17 publications a month, so I'm sorry if people think I've got it made. I know different.

AA   *When I was researching your background, I learned that you may actually have been offered the post of police chief of Los Angeles, but that you turned it down.*

GR When I was a police officer, [William] Parker, who was then the Chief of Police, and whom I worked with very closely and personally, wanted me to stay on and become that, but I wasn't offered the job . . . a lot of executives put their eye on certain young men and want to guide them to a position, but what I wanted to be was what I turned out to be. . . .

AA *STAR TREK is also a household word all over the world, and now it has even been shown in the Soviet Union.*

GR Yes, I think that's fun.

AA *Do you have any hopes of STAR TREK actually doing what it depicts for the future, of its being an instrument to draw mankind together?*

GR First of all, I have no belief that STAR TREK depicts the actual future. It depicts *us, now,* things we need to understand about that. But I hope that STAR TREK will encourage other artists and other writers to work in this area. I think that drama is a powerful force we still do not use very well, especially in television. I understand, of course, that we're going to have programs that are frothy and fun. I liked THE BEVERLY HILLBILLIES. I think the ancient American legends of the country boys who outsmart the city slickers are great fun. Mark Twain liked them, too. I don't ask that every program on the air be an exercise in reality, but I would like to see other shows do more, to talk about what we are, where we should be going, and what we lack. It troubles me that there are no programs on television, at least none I've seen, that point out that the world is operating in a very primitive way on the basis of hate. Our own president hates the Commies, and he and his henchmen believe that therefore everything they do to defeat the Commies, whether it's illegal or not, is justified because of their hate. The Ayatollah feels the same way, and in Northern Ireland both sides feel the same way, and in India the same things are happening. If we are ever to turn the corner away from that, we need our artists and poets and entertainers pointing it out.

AA *You wrote one of the first definitive studies on the narcotics problem in Los Angeles for Chief Parker. Do you think that any progress has been made, or are they even going along the right channels?*

GR No, they're not going on the right channels. You cannot stop people from having something they need badly by declaring it illegal. We could not stop alcohol that way in the days of THE UNTOUCHABLES. No, they haven't approached drugs at all the right way. I'm upset, for example, that the MIAMI VICEs of the world look at drug offenders the same way we looked at insane people three hundred years ago. The thing to do is to put them in a cage, punish them. The truth is that drugs actually represent something that's very wrong in our society. I submit it is frightening that when a person reaches adulthood or adolescence they need some sort of help to make life happy. What emotional things are we doing to those people who need a substance to get by? We should be examining that, not the criminal aspect of drugs. It may be that unless our world becomes more perfect some people are always going to need mood changers. It is . . . the nature of the beast in our society at present, but we go at it improperly. We go at it blind. . . . [In regard to] terrorists, many people accept that it was quite all right when the Jews bombed the King David Hotel when the British held it, and some 80-odd people were destroyed, but that's okay, because they were fighting for their rights. Yet when a Moslem bombs someone in Beirut he's a terrorist, a madman. I think we've got to accept that the Moslem has something he believes in, too. Right or wrong, he does it out of some strong belief.

AA   *But both parties are wrong in resorting to violence.*

GR   Yes, of course they are . . . But there are just dozens of such things that artists, playwrights, poets, television writers and movie writers should be addressing through their particular type of communication. So my hope for STAR TREK is that it encourages that in television. I don't think STAR TREK itself is going to create great changes.

AA   *Can you recall the first thing you thought about when you conceived STAR TREK?*

GR   I guess it was the thought that under the terrible restrictions of television it might be a way I could infiltrate my ideas, and that's what it's been all the time. You see, it's difficult for people to understand that even in the barren vineyards of television you might do these things. Actually, you can do them better there because you reach more people with more impact. You don't do it by each of your episodes being a fine HALLMARK HALL OF FAME, or those great shows that are meaningful and deep and advertised as such. The power you have is in a show like STAR TREK, which is considered by many people to be a frothy little action-adventure—unimportant, unbelievable, and yet watched by a lot of people. You just slip ideas into it. I've been very much heartened by the fact that some key people like the Smithsonian Institute take a look at STAR TREK, and they understand. They don't expect it to be more than it is, because what it is is a lot. Other shows can be the same thing. We do love America to be turning out things that are deep and meaningful and sending people staggering out of the theater and away from the television set, but those are special-occasion-type shows. What you need is for the small mills of television drama to do these things.

AA   *Samuel Peeples remembered that when you initially began to research science fiction literature, you were very curious about Olaf Stapledon's writings.*

GR   I still am. As a matter of fact, on my nightstand at this time there's some Olaf Stapledon material I'm rereading, although I think the type of thing he did, the traveler through space and imagination and so on, really doesn't work for mass-audience weekly shows. You've got to put the ideas he talks about into the heads of more ordinary characters, who merely fly a starship that goes places faster than the speed of light.

AA   *Mr. Peeples also remembers one stage of Mr. Spock's evolution, when all you were sure of was that he was an alien, and that he had a metal plate in his stomach through which he consumed energy to sustain himself. Do you recall this early formative time for Spock?*

GR   Vaguely, yes. Series are a process of refining ideas. I'd like to say that all the ideas that I get are bright and eternal and right for all time, but they're not. You do evolve things.

AA   *You once told me that you had an early thought about casting a black man as "Mr. Spock." Was your aim in creating Spock to make someone who was different to some extent, looking at the rest of the series' personnel as an outsider?*

GR   Yes, very definitely. I was also considering Michael Dunn, a dwarf [best known for his appearances as "Dr. Lovelace" in THE WILD, WILD WEST]. I wanted Spock to look different and be different, and yes, to make a statement about being an outsider looking in. I did finally pick the way we went because I was dealing in weekly mass-audience television, and I needed Spock to be attractive even though he was different. I'm afraid Michael Dunn might not have been, and 22 years ago a black man might not have been. It was the right choice for the time.

AA   *TV Guide once ran a short blurb about Martin Landau's being considered for the role of Mr. Spock.*

GR   Yes, but he was unavailable for it; he was a fairly well-known actor who was getting plenty of jobs. Leonard Nimoy was my first choice. Landau, I know, was my second choice, but Leonard agreed and we stayed with him.

AA   *Were there any other second choices?*

GR Well, as I said . . . Michael Dunn, who was a marvelous actor, and there may have been others whose names I don't remember. Dunn was a serious second choice because of his being a dwarf. That seemed certainly to put the stamp of being from another place on it, but as I said I was also dealing in a mass audience, and Spock had to have an attractive look then.

AA *How was Jeffrey Hunter chosen for the lead in the first pilot? Was there anyone else who was under consideration?*

GR Oh, yes. I remember Lloyd Bridges was very much under consideration, except when I approached him with it he said, "Gene, I like you, I've worked with you before in the past, but I've seen science fiction and I don't want to be within a hundred miles of it . . . " I understood what he meant then. I tried to convince him that I could do it differently, but at the time I wasn't that sure that I would treat it differently. I wasn't sure I could manage it.

AA *So this was before "The Cage" was written?*

GR Uh, huh.

AA *Was anyone else considered? You mentioned James Coburn during one conversation.*

GR My wife suggested him for the Captain. I said to her something I've heard over and over for many years since, "No sex appeal." That was a monster of a goof, and I came to realize, though, that there just weren't a lot of actors who would do it. I was talking about what was in many people's eyes a silly show. Leonard, for example, when they were [first] trying ears on him for Spock, tried to get out of it.

AA *You mean he tried to get out of doing the show, period?*

GR Yes, or he just tried to get out of wearing ears, anyway. It was just very difficult to cast.

AA *Did he make his fears known at the time? Was he afraid that people would not be able to take his character seriously?*

GR As we tried them on and began doing camera tests, the crew began chuckling and calling him "jackrabbit," and so on, and he finally started to get a little upset, because he could see [the audience] laughing too, perhaps.

AA *I've also seen surviving frames of a black and white test of Majel [Barrett]. Her eyebrows are pointed upward, and her complexion is dark.*

GR I used Majel for a lot of tests, including the green skin we finally put on Susan Oliver. But she was a close friend and available; [it was] just a case of having a body to paint, and seeing what it would look like.

AA *I think that framed painting on the wall of your office honoring the first 100,000 videocassettes of "The Cage" sold, proves* *how the film is thought of today. How did you feel when NBC rejected it?*

GR I sort of understood. I wrote and produced what I thought was a highly imaginative idea, and I realized I had gone too far. I should actually have ended it with a fistfight between the hero and the villain if I wanted it on television, and so when we did the second pilot, as a matter of fact we did end with such a fistfight. But at least we slipped it by and it got on the air, and then once on the air we began to infiltrate, but it was a good pilot, anyway. It's just that we had to put these things into it because that's the way shows were being made at the time. The great mass audience would say, "Well, if you don't have a fistfight when it's ended, how do we know that's the finish?", and things like that.

AA *I guess Oscar Katz [Desilu executive while both pilots were being made] liked them both.*

GR Oscar Katz liked it.

AA *Did he sell the show to the network?*

GR He was the one who decided that Desilu would make it, and to get a network to cooperate.

AA *I know that you had some disappointing negotiations with CBS. I once heard that there was a time when you were considering selling STAR TREK but not doing it as a line producer, and somebody had approached Irwin Allen to do it. Is that true?*

GR I don't know that story. It may have been, because I don't necessarily know everything that happens in these things. Generally, I was in favor of producing it . . . at least giving it a shot.

AA *Did Jeffrey Hunter want to continue as the Captain when "Where No Man Has Gone Before" was being prepared for production?*

GR His wife of the time didn't want him to, and convinced him that science fiction was beneath him, and so I just had to pick someone else. Shatner was available, he needed a show, was open-minded about science fiction, and a marvelous choice because he did great things for our show.

AA *After Jeffrey Hunter became unavailable, did you ever give any thought to anyone other than William Shatner?*

GR No. I was happy to get him. I'd seen some work he did, and I thought he was an excellent choice, no question of it at all.

AA *And the studio and the network went along with your feeling?*

GR The studio was then Desilu, of course. Yes.

AA *From the beginning, STAR TREK had excellent people— film editors, composers, etc. How did you assemble your production staff?*

GR I realized that we had an impossible production job, and a lot of the people we chose were assistant department heads who wanted a chance at the top. Matt Jefferies, for instance, was a draftsman, not an art director, and we had to cover for him until he got his ticket. We also did similar things in a lot of other areas: set decorators, editors. Our people turned out to be good because we looked for young, bright, malleable people, but they did not necessarily come to us with long shining reputations. I figured older people who were solid in their trade worked at a certain pace, and it might be difficult to change that pace. However, I knew that we would get more creativity and work and imagination out of assistants, because it would have been their only big chance, and indeed it turned out like that. It's easy to look back now and say, "Oh, well, of course you had a proven crew." No. We had some names and recommendations, but it was far from being a proven crew. It became a proven crew because of the way I think we operated. We gave credit to people when they did good work, and cheered, and we very quickly created a family feeling for STAR TREK.

AA *When was the first time you realized that there were a lot of STAR TREK fans out there? How did you feel?*

GR . . . the first science fiction convention that I took our STAR TREK pilots to.

AA *Tricon [the 1966 World Science Fiction Convention], in Cleveland? I was there.*

GR Yes, Tricon. That was it. I was nervous, particularly when I saw them watching other films that were shown before, and booing, and stomping, and laughing at things. I walked out thinking, "They're finally going to show this one." There was a rather loud gentleman surrounded by other people, discussing something at the time my show was starting, and upset already, I turned on him: "For Christ's sake, could you be quiet? My show is on now." And Isaac Asimov said, "Yes, you're perfectly right. We will tone it down." And someone said, "You're dead, you just insulted Isaac Asimov." Well, it turned out that I had not, and over the years we became fast friends. He understood. Then I watched how they accepted this show. I said to myself, "Yes, there *are* people, if we go this way and try these things, who are going to appreciate them." I realized then that we would have fans of some sort and, of course, where that went is insanity. Who expects to have millions of fans? At that time I realized that we'd reached some people. I didn't think it would be anything like it was, but I did realize at that time if I did the show I would be approached by people now and then who would say, "I saw the thing you did years ago, and I liked it." That's enough.

AA *I recall that "Where No Man Has Gone Before" was the first of your films shown, right after THE TIME TUNNEL pilot, which was the film that was being booed and hissed, except for Michael Rennie's performance.*

GR Yes.

AA *People were murmuring throughout the showing, "did he say this was for television?" After it ended, I remember there was a moment of silence.*

GR I didn't know how people were going to react. I think I finally got to my feet and said, "Is anybody going to say whether they liked it or not?," and it was only afterward that the applause began. I remember calling up the studio and saying, "I really think we may have something here," and the studio's reaction was, "Well, so a thousand goofs who go to a science fiction convention like it? That means nothing in television." And they were almost right, because we did get low ratings.

AA *If you were doing the original STAR TREK series now, would you do anything differently from the way you originally did it?*

GR Oh, of course there are literally hundreds of things I would have done differently with the luxury of hindsight, but I'm quite pleased, given the time, the place, the problems we faced, our own lack of knowledge at that time, because we've grown since then, that we did as well as you can reasonably expect. We made lots of mistakes, but obviously we did enough things right that it worked despite the mistakes.

AA *Why didn't NBC see that?*

GR Because network executives, who are hired on the basis of being businessmen, are not creative artists and they did not see those things then, nor do they today. With few exceptions, networks are more interested in the show that represents an established, familiar pattern, and what age group does it play to, and a lot of things that are nonsense. If something seems too risky, they don't want it. They are by nature conservative, and I point out to you, as many people now know, that every show that's ever been a hit came near to being canceled in its first season. "Archie Bunker." Oh, my God, they hated that because it was so different. . . .

AA *That series, ALL IN THE FAMILY, also had more than one pilot, I understand.*

GR Yes. Going all the way back to GUNSMOKE. That was almost thrown out. Dick Van Dyke's first show was at one time canceled, and brought back. So, it's no wonder that

STAR TREK, with spaceships and pointy-eared hobgoblins and so on, was close to cancellation.

AA *Why did you step down as line producer halfway through the first season?*

GR Because it is just impossible for one person to produce, write, and look over a show so extraordinarily complex as STAR TREK. Really, what I became during the first half of the first year was full-time script rewriter, and you just cannot do that and in addition fulfill all producer functions. Becoming executive producer really meant becoming full-time story and script rewriter. Bob Justman was really in charge of the physical side of production. It is impossible to do a science fiction show like STAR TREK, but we managed to do it despite that fact.

AA *Why do you think no other show has come close to duplicating what STAR TREK accomplished?*

GR I think because caring that much about what you do, as most people realize, is an invitation to disaster or tragedy, and they're not willing to do it when you can make a very good living, and in fact you can get much richer, by just doing an ordinary show well. My own attorneys and advisers used to say to me, "Gene, why don't you write a detective, or a police show, or something like that. You are good at writing, you are good at putting in action, excitement, movement, pace, adventure, and forget about really changing the world and talking about things that upset people, because if you just do an ordinary show you can do it eight hours a week, you can make millions of dollars if you do it well, and forget this STAR TREK-type stuff."

AA *What did you answer?*

GR I said, "I'd love to, but if I took on another show, I know my perverse nature. I would start writing extras into it, and whatever it started off as, it would eventually become a very difficult kind of a show, and I'd be right back where I'd started, except I'd be doing it in modern day, or ancient day, rather than in the future."

AA *Have you ever felt typecast because of STAR TREK?*

GR Of course. When I finished doing STAR TREK, I had trouble getting a job. They said, "You're a science fiction type." I said, "Hey, wait a minute, I used to write westerns, I wrote police stories," and they said, "No, you're now science fiction." I don't feel bitter about that. That's the way Hollywood is, and that's the way mediocre people think. It's an easy way to think and television, like movies, like plays, like everything in the world, is staffed by mediocre people with, thank God, a few other extra people who do make things happen. They make the big changes. I never doubted that I wouldn't do reasonably well in television, because all I had to do was keep writing, and rewriting, and rewriting, and eventually I could at least turn out something a little better than average.

AA *Why hasn't Paramount Home Video issued either POLICE STORY or THE LONG HUNT OF APRIL SAVAGE, the other pilots you did at about the same time as "Where No Man Has Gone Before"?*

GR I don't know that they feel anything about those shows would be particularly attractive to the buying audience. STAR TREK is, of course, broadly known, and I think just because a show was written and produced by Gene Roddenberry it would not necessarily have enough audience attraction unless it was promoted. But I think without doubt that if Paramount acquired *The Questor Tapes*, which Universal owns, and promoted it for what it was, which many people call the definitive android show, that it might do pretty well.

AA *Do you have anything you've always wanted to say to the fans of STAR TREK but have never said?*

GR Just the same thing as always: "Thank you."

WILLIAM SHATNER

He's an actor, he directs, he writes, breeds champion horses, keeps Doberman pinschers, has hunted big game with bow and arrow, and he flies. About the only thing he lacks is spare time. He can be deadly serious one moment, and laugh at himself or just about anything the next. He's William Shatner—to millions of people, also known as Captain James T. Kirk.

Actually, it's the other way around. Captain Kirk is William Shatner. They share the same degree of intensity and purpose, qualities that have pushed Shatner to the forefront of his profession, and made Captain Kirk a legend.

Shatner's presence and style are responsible for much of the dramatic intensity and delicate balance of seriousness and self-parody that is the core of STAR TREK.

I first interviewed William Shatner with my friends and fellow writers Steve and Erwin Vertlieb during the summer of 1969, when he was directing and starring in There's a Girl in My Soup *in Pennsylvania. At that time, when asked if he thought whether man was meant to fly, he responded, "If man was meant to fly he'd have wings . . ." His face had not the hint of a smile until almost 15 seconds later when the ends of his mouth curled upward, and he added, ". . . But we are flying, aren't we?"*

Shatner took time out from the development of STAR TREK V for the following interview.

AA *Before MGM signed you to a contract, you were previously offered one by another studio. Why did you turn it down?*

WS I don't know why I turned it down. It was all the money in the world, and I needed it at the time, but I don't know. It was some peculiar pride of not wanting to leave the stage, or something strange. I had no reason to do it.

AA *Do you have any regrets concerning any decisions you made earlier in your career?*

WS No. I don't regret anything at this point. That may change on the next phone call, but at the moment I don't regret anything.

AA *What are some of your recollections about working with Spencer Tracy?*

WS . . . Spencer Tracy was a man who did very much what I do on a set, and that is, he comes down and he does his job, and then he goes back to his dressing room. That's what he did on *Judgment at Nuremberg*, and the only real thing that I can remember about him was that he delivered a wonderfully worked out, intricate monologue that I was a party to, and later I said how impressed I was. This was said with all the nerve of a stage actor saying to a film actor how impressed I was that he memorized all that, thinking that film actors—because I was young at the time and I didn't know how they worked—would read it off something. And that suitably insulted him and he stalked off and didn't speak to me much thereafter. [laughter]

AA *Do you prefer to take the parts of heroes or villains, and do you feel that you've been typecast as a result of STAR TREK?*

WS Well, I don't know . . . I don't think in terms of heavies and heroes. A "heavy" is a hero, and a hero should be a "heavy." I mean, there should be a mix. To make a fully-fledged character isn't to be one-sided. The worst heavy should be shown with as valid a life as possible. Heroes are generally the leading men, and generally a story is written around the leading man or the leading woman. So for me to be typecast into playing the main part in a story isn't bad typecasting. But there weren't any other "spaceship" castings. I don't know how to answer that typecasting question, because I never heard people say, "Don't hire him," I only heard the people say, "Would you like to do this?" So I guess the typecasting thing has interfered, but I don't know how.

AA *How did you become involved with STAR TREK?*

WS Well, Roddenberry called me in New York and asked me to come to Los Angeles to see the pilot that they had already tried to sell—unsuccessfully. The idea had been good enough that they wanted to try again, so I came to Los Angeles and he and I viewed this hour-and-a-half film together. When I walked out I remember thinking it was a very imaginative and vital idea. I thought everybody took themselves a little too seriously. This was very profound people doing very profound things, whereas I would have imagined that a battleship in space would be the same as a battleship on the ocean, where professionals doing their job take it as professionals will: as workaday, and things have their rightful weight in life aboard the battleship, so that "full speed ahead" doesn't become a very profound, meaningful thing. That was my impression, and we spoke about that and the recasting of the thing that Gene intended to do. Then a script was written, and I made suggestions that Gene kindly said some time after had some import. So I was helpful in the piecing together of the part of STAR TREK in which I was involved. My general impressions were that it was a wonderful, vital idea that needed little change.

AA *How much of Captain Kirk comes from your own personality?*

WS On series television people come and go: usually a new writer and director every week. The only people who don't come and go are the producer, the cinematographer, and the actor. So with Gene riding herd on the way that we might have acted, and the cinematographer on the way we might have looked, the actor's responsibility was in the area of making the character as real as possible, asking for changes when things did not work. . . . I think there's a great deal of my own personality in the character, if only because in 79 shows, day after day, week after week, year after year, the fatigue factor is such that you can only try to be as honest about yourself as possible. Fatigue wipes away any subterfuge that you might be able to use as an actor in character roles, or trying to delineate something that might not be entirely you. By the second week you're so tired that it can only be you, so I think that in Kirk there's a great deal of me.

AA *Kirk and Spock both have characteristics that children have. Spock sometimes suggests a lost little boy, and Kirk often reflects a childlike energy level, a mischievous quality. Do you recognize such qualities in yourself?*

WS   Well, he and I are children. Having been actors all our lives, there is a great element of the child in both of us, and that comes out in our everyday life.

AA   *Were you happy with those portions of the STAR TREK television series that relied on your contributions?*

WS   . . . In the STAR TREK series? A series is filled with compromises. You start off with a grand idea, and I've done four series now, two lasting 13 weeks each, and the other two lasting three years and four-and-a-half years, so I'm pretty accustomed to what it feels like to do a series. A series starts off with a great idea and then time and fatigue affect everybody, so all everybody's trying to do is get the words out, to occupy 52½ minutes of film time. Anything better than that is a kudos to superhuman energy and intense desire to do better than just adequate . . . To do a halfway decent series is a Herculean task.

AA   *To what do you attribute your boundless energy and your continued ability to portray physically demanding roles, to retain your youth?*

WS   I don't know. I think perhaps it's genetic. I was built for the long run, not for the short dash, I guess. [laughter]

AA   *When was the first time you realized that STAR TREK had a very large fan following?*

WS   Well, I think [it was] some years after I had been doing other things and touring in plays that somebody came up to me and asked, "Have you seen your STAR TREK in a bar?" Apparently it was playing in a bar . . . and I said, "No," and that was the first I heard that reruns of STAR TREK were back. But it was coincidental, out of left field—a person having seen it in an out-of-the-way spot.

AA   *When did you get your first personal taste of being a media celebrity? Was it at a convention?*

WS   Yes, probably, and the conventions that I went to in those early years were filled with passionate fans who would assume the persona of their various heroes. Mostly they were people having fun. There is a fringe element out there that thinks that I *am* the captain of a spaceship, and they're difficult to deal with. They're very voluble, and they make their presence felt far in excess of their numbers, so I take that with a grain of salt knowing that the vast majority of fans are just having a good time. But that fringe element does make you think twice.

AA   *It must be strange being recognized while you're out with your family, going shopping, or just out for a stroll. Has being such an easily recognized celebrity had an effect on you?*

WS Yes, I've become very paranoid, and don't go out and do those ordinary things to any great extent. When I do I wear hats and glasses. I even wore a mask in New Orleans at the Mardi Gras. Since it's generally the custom to wear masks, I thought I could wear a mask and walk in the streets. Well, I wore this leather mask that covered my entire face, and people came up to me and asked, "Aren't you William Shatner?"

AA *And while your privacy has been so greatly reduced, you have to recall that this is basically the result of your practicing your craft so well.*

WS Oh, yeah, well that's what I keep trying to do, and I have to be reminded that it's a trade-off, the recognition factor and the virtues of being recognized.

AA *How does it feel to be part of a myth, known throughout the world?*

WS . . . I don't think of it as a myth—I'm trying to come up with a joke, but I won't do it—I think of it as an ongoing, very practical series of problems to solve. Right now it's a life-enhancing experience to be in this position to guide the next STAR TREK movie. It's my work, and it's new, and it's different and it's really exciting. To be able to say that after all these years in the business has got to be rather unusual.

AA *Do you read science fiction? And considering your schedule, do you have any time now to read at all?*

WS I used to be quite an avid science fiction reader. I haven't done much of it of late, and the reading I've done has been other things.

AA *Other than STAR TREK V, would you rather appear in and direct films that are not science fiction?*

WS . . . I don't work in that way. I'm going to do this horse picture because I've become crazy about horses. So I've invented a story and it has the horses as a background, and I'm hopeful that it will be done this summer. I'm waiting to hear about it now, as a matter of fact. And that's a kick. Now, I've just lost a film that I should have directed and acted in this summer, and the horse picture would have been done next summer. That picture was a kind of horror film, a wonderfully inventive horror film, which unfortunately fell through. But that looked like it would have been terrific to do. So any good story that comes along is what I want to do.

AA *Are you enthusiastic about directing STAR TREK V, or are you nervous about it?*

WS It's probably both . . . I've done a lot of directing, theater and some 12 hours of film. I don't feel inadequate on [the] technical aspects of making a film. On the contrary, I feel confident with the support group behind me, which includes Harve Bennett, and all the other people who have made the STAR TREK [movies], plus the cinematographer that we will choose. That will be helpful technically. [As for] my ability to tell a story and to dramatize it, to make it entertaining, I've been doing that all my life as an actor, as a director, and as a sometime writer. So what I'm really thinking—in both a film called *Bloodlines*, which I'm waiting to do this summer, and STAR TREK, which I'll do in the winter—what I'm really doing is biting my lip in anticipation. I can taste the joy of getting something down on film that is entertaining. I think making a good film shot is joyful. There's an ecstasy about doing something really good on film: the composition of a shot, the drama within the shot, the texture . . . It's palpable.

AA *STAR TREK IV featured a generous helping of humor, as did some of the best episodes of the STAR TREK television series. Do you plan to feature the element of humor in STAR TREK V?*

WS Yes. We discovered something in STAR TREK IV that we hadn't pinpointed in any of the other movies—and it just shows how the obvious can escape you—that there is a texture to the best STAR TREK hours that verges on tongue-in-cheek but isn't. There's a line that we all have to walk that is reality. It's as though the characters within the play have a great deal of joy about themselves, a joy of living. That energy, that "joie de vivre" about the characters seems to be tongue-in-cheek but isn't, because you play it with the reality [that] you would in a kitchen-sink drama written for today's life.

AA *What are your goals with STAR TREK V?*

WS . . . The basic idea is mine, and I worked on the story with Harve and David Lowery, who is writing the screenplay. I hope that the end result will reflect certain life experiences that I am going through, because as we take the characters through the aging process there are certain inevitable questions one asks oneself through each passage, each decade that we pass through, roughly. We ask ourselves questions which are universal that don't occur when you're younger . . . and so I hope that the end result will reflect some of these questions that I want the characters to ask. I say that because I think it's there now, but what the final film will show might be different. I hope it isn't.

AA *Have you had any feedback regarding your appearance on SATURDAY NIGHT LIVE, and your comedy routine regarding STAR TREK conventions and fans?*

WS   . . . Nothing really bad. On the contrary, I think most people have taken it in the same way it was meant to be, and that is just fun. . . . It was solely designed to make you laugh, and anyone who took it more seriously than that . . . It was a spoof.

AA   *Do you think the television of today is better than it was in the 1960s, when STAR TREK was originally on the air?*

WS   I don't watch much television, but those movies of the week, and things like that, are more sophisticated than anything that was on in the sixties, with some rare exceptions like STAR TREK.

AA   *What do you think accounts for the popularity of STAR TREK?*

WS   Well, nobody has ever enunciated it. It's what everybody perceives instinctively. It's what made STAR TREK appealing. When asked what it is about STAR TREK that made it popular, we all have a standard answer. I once had a big laugh with Leonard. I asked, "What do you say?," and he went down the list, and I said, "Well, that's exactly what I say." We talked about the themes and the people, but none of us ever said [it was] the *joie de vivre*, the "tap dancing," as Harve Bennett put it the other day. Nobody talks about the tap dancing. When I was young many years ago, Tyrone Guthrie, who was a great English director, said to me I had "happy feet." I was wearing white shoes in a play, and I knew what he meant. The timing in comedy has to do with the whole rhythm, and the rhythm comes out vocally, with your head . . . and in this case the rhythm came out on these white shoes, and I was "tap dancing." I think that was what Harve Bennett meant when he was talking about me tap dancing.

AA   *Is there anything you've ever wanted to say to the fans of STAR TREK, but have never gotten a chance to say?*

WS   Something I want to say to the fans? But I don't know who the "fans" are. I am asked how will the fans think about this, or what would the fans do if they found out about that, or how will the fans react . . . but I don't know who they are. The fans are a large conglomerate of people. They're a heterogeneous group of people. There's no single "fan." I mean, who are we talking about? Some fans like one thing, some another, and their individual tastes I can't ascertain. I never know how to answer that question, "What do you want to say to the fans?," or when asked, "What will the fans think about this?" I can't answer that question, either. The only thing I can say is I'm trying my best to entertain myself [with] STAR TREK, and hoping that that sense of

entertainment will be translated to the other people, whoever else is watching STAR TREK, because I care a great
deal about STAR TREK. I think STAR TREK is wonderful,
and I'm trying to keep it as entertaining as it has been.
That's my thought [for] anybody who likes STAR TREK.

LEONARD NIMOY

*While I was visiting Los Angeles conducting interviews for this
book, Leonard Nimoy was busy directing his latest feature, THREE
MEN AND A BABY, and we were unable to meet.*

*Luckily, Verna Harvey had conducted the following interview just
before the release of STAR TREK IV, which I'm very pleased to
include in the book. Ms. Harvey, an actress herself, was able to
obtain many excellent and informative insights into both Leonard
Nimoy and his STAR TREK persona—Mr. Spock.*

VH *It's been twenty years since STAR TREK first went on the air
and Spock emerged as the media's most famous alien. What
were your feelings about the role when Gene Roddenberry first
approached you with the idea?*

LN He described the character in very broad strokes because
he didn't have it all nailed down or written out. What immediately intrigued me was that here was a character who had
an internal conflict. This half-human, half-Vulcan being, struggling to maintain a Vulcan attitude, a Vulcan philosophical
posture and Vulcan logic, opposing what was fighting him
internally which was human emotion. There was a dynamic
there to work with from an acting point of view. It was more
than a one-dimensional character. I thought something could
come out of that and it sounded challenging.

VH *Did you ever feel you were taking a chance by accepting the
role of Spock?*

LN Some thought I was crazy and said "What are you going to
do when you're done with this? You're finished once it's
over." One friend even suggested that I play it in complete
disguise so nobody would know who was playing the role
and when it was over I could step out of it clean and I
wouldn't have to deal with being identified with that role if it
didn't work out, or whatever.

VH *What was your reaction to that?*

LN   I didn't believe it. I had no idea what the consequences might be. I was naive on the one hand but, on the other, I gave myself credit that I was making a commitment. I wasn't going to play it safe. It's true that it could have been a very silly kind of a character. I suppose to some, it is. Although, in terms of public acceptance it worked out fine. But there is no question that, to this day, people will not use me because of the connection.

VH   *Do you find that frustrating?*

LN   I can understand it. I bring a certain kind of baggage with me. I guess what I find interesting after all these years, in retrospect, is how little I thought of what it might mean to step into that character. I was stepping in without a safety net and I didn't realize it, simply because that was my commitment. If you go in to play a character like that, you don't do it safe. You do the strange makeup; the ears, the eyebrows and the haircut. You go in and do what has to be done.

VH   *The reaction to STAR TREK, from the beginning, was immediate. Were you ready for that?*

LN   No. I had no idea. No inkling at all. I didn't even bother to take my phone number out of the book. After the show went on the air people started to call me up. It took a while for me to realize that I was going to have to make some changes in my lifestyle. That was a great shock. I can't emphasize how great the shock was.

VH   *Did you ever feel yourself losing focus and being seduced by the fame and popularity?*

LN   It's strange. It's a whole different territory. It has nothing to do with talent. I went through a period of pushing popularity versus quality. I was really concerned about that because I could see where you could, very easily, be seduced by wanting to continue with the popularity and stop being concerned with the quality of the work. I did a lot of research into this and found a quote by Victor Hugo that was a lifesaver for me. He said, "Popularity is the very crumbs of greatness." Don't you love it? It became very precious to me. When I found that I thought, "I've got it. I've got it here in my hand and, with just these words, I have the guideline I need to know and where I must put my focus." The focus must be on the quality of the work. The popularity can come and go. Nothing you can do about that, it doesn't matter. But, to maintain popularity at the expense of the work . . . You're dead anyway.

VH   *That's so true. Cult figures are replaced daily and there's something pathetic about those obsessed with trying to perpetuate their popularity.*

LN   The danger is that you become a caricature of yourself. You try to repeat yourself and you're looking in a mirror all of the time. What you're doing is studying those things that you think are the elements that have made you popular and trying to see that you perpetuate them. Then you become cast in your own concrete. It's a pretty empty road and if you haven't maintained substance, then you're a rather sad figure.

VH   *For three years, you played a highly intelligent being with few, if any, emotional responses and your judgment based totally on logic and reason. How did that affect you personally?*

LN   Well, I think it was helpful emotionally, but it was a double-edged sword. It was helpful in making me see things more precisely and dispassionately; to get an objective view of the situation. It taught me that. What I didn't realize was the pressure cooker it put me into because I was, in character, suppressing my emotions. It would start early in the morning and end late at night.

VH   *How did the behavior manifest itself?*

LN   Well, as soon as I sat down in the makeup chair, Freddie Phillips, who made me up for three years, five days a week, said he could see the change take place. Not just the physical change. The sense of me changed. I started to become more withdrawn, cooler, distant and more objective in that hour and a half.

VH   *Were you conscious of that change?*

LN   Once I'd got it all on, it was the strangest thing. I saw it happening in the mirror. It was as though, if I fooled around or laughed a lot, my face would crack. As though I would damage myself in some way; destroy the character and hurt myself. So, I would just sit around and the rest of the cast would be fooling around, telling jokes or whatever and I would just sit there, impassive. I would be enjoying myself but I wouldn't express it. I guess I was afraid that someone might catch me, with a camera, doing something that Spock wouldn't do.

VH   *I remember, reading in your book, "I Am Not Spock," you wrote of an incident when the cast were messing about and you reacted in a certain way and one of them said, "Oh, he's in his Spock bag again." Did it ever hurt, at times, to be an "alien" among your workmates?*

LN   Yes, it did. But, I felt good about it because the work was benefiting from it. When I stepped into a scene I was in character and I didn't have to be concerned with getting my head straight. I was Spock all day long. I really was.

VH   *How about stepping out, at the end of the day?*

LN That was difficult. I had a tough time with that. What I realized was that I was repressing a lot. Not allowing myself the freedom to laugh, shout and let off some energy. It made for some very painful times. When I saw that, I began to work on finding time to laugh and cry and I got a better fix on what it was all about. I realized that I wasn't unhappy. I was really very excited about what was happening and I was feeling proud of the good work I was doing.

VH *But, what you were unhappy about was the fact that it was affecting those around you and that they were having trouble dealing with the way you were.*

LN Yes. There were people having a hard time with that and it was reflecting back on me. I thought, "Why are these people unhappy with me? I'm doing what I came here to do." That was difficult.

VH *Isaac Asimov described Spock as a security blanket with sexual overtones. What do you think he meant by that?*

LN Well, I think he meant that the character was a fatherly, wisdom figure. That he would be nice to have around in a troublesome situation. That's the security aspect of it. The sexual aspect of it was more complicated. I was told, for example, that there was something exotic, sexually, for ladies. Even to the extent of fantasizing about the genitalia of this character! Something exciting because of the devilish eyes and ears. A character who could not express emotions and, therefore, could not express love. That could represent a challenge to a lady who believes she may be the one able to teach him about love. Not overt sexuality. More subtle, but there, nonetheless.

VH *Had you considered Spock's sexuality before the magazines picked up on it?*

LN No. Not at all. The first indication was when a lovely actress visited the set with my agent. I was in costume with all the makeup on when we were introduced. She said, "Oh God, can I touch your ears?" It's a silly thing to say, I know, but she was serious. She really wanted to touch them. That was the first indication I had that women might be attracted to this character. [Laughs]

VH *That's great though. The very antithesis of the macho, male pinup!*

LN I wrote to Asimov, not long after his article, and said something to the effect that when I first came to Hollywood, Marlon Brando had won the hearts of the American film-going audience by playing a monosyllabic, brutish animal. If what he was saying was true about an intelligent, unemotional character being the new sex symbol, then great, I'm delighted!

I thanked him for the compliment. I was really pleased for that reason, among others, to be considered sexually attractive. [Laughs]

VH *It makes you wonder if that isn't, perhaps, what more people want but they accept the obvious because it's easier to market.*

LN There was a cover story I read recently which touches on this question. Talking about what really makes for sexually interesting men. For example, there are some men who are so physical and tough, it's a joke. [Laughs] I'm sure it's true. It's cheaper and easier to sell a hunk and have all the women gasping, "Oh God, he's so attractive."

VH *How come, that with all the positive response to STAR TREK, that the network wanted to take it off after only two seasons?*

LN Well, you have to understand, and this is a shocking thing to a lot of people, we were never a really big hit. We never had a really big audience. What we had was a remarkably vocal audience. They were intense. Obsessed. Obsessed with the show and with Spock. In terms of numbers, I suppose there were a few million, but not enough to make it a big TV hit. They put it in for one more season, in a bad time slot, and that was it.

VH *Did you feel a loss when the show was canceled?*

LN I had mixed emotions. I felt tired and drained. It had become a battle to maintain the quality of the show. We were not having a great success with the episodes in that third season. I felt a great sense of entrapment because I was under contract if they wanted to do more. I wasn't looking forward to it through fear of losing quality. I was making money but I felt I wasn't involved in anything prideful anymore. You hate to see anything good die but, on the other hand, you hate to see anything good piddle its way into mediocrity or worse.

VH *Was accepting the role of Paris in MISSION: IMPOSSIBLE calculated to remove yourself from the association with Spock?*

LN To a certain extent, it was. I thought it was an opportunity to do a wide variety of characters so that I would, perhaps, become better known as a character actor rather than a Spock actor. It didn't really work out that way, in fact, but that was one of the reasons for doing that show.

VH *Did you ever have visions of becoming a movie star?*

LN I never saw myself as a potential leading man. Never. I always saw myself as a character actor.

VH *Why was that?*

LN I looked all wrong for Hollywood. Tab Hunter was the big rage when I arrived. The blond, beautiful guy. That was what they wanted. Ethnic types were not in demand. I just thought, "I'm here to act. They must need some character actors."

VH   *How did you get into acting to begin with?*

LN   I became involved with a community theater near my home in Boston. That was when I was about eight years old. I was hanging around there one day and someone asked me if I could sing. [Laughs] They cast me as Hansel in "Hansel and Gretel." The funniest thing about it was that on the day of the first performance, someone asked me if my parents were coming to see the show and I hadn't thought to tell them I was doing this. It was the strangest lack of connection.

VH   *So, your interest didn't come from home. Who encouraged you?*

LN   Some years later, still at the community theater, there was this budding director, Boris Sagal. A very talented man. Formidable, energetic. Charged with ideas. He cast me as a juvenile in a play called, "Awake and Sing." This was adult theater. Heavyweight stuff. I'd seen very little of that, but I was very interested. Very curious.

VH   *How did that work out?*

LN   It was dynamite. I had no idea what I was getting into. The play was about a Jewish family in the Bronx. The social level was pretty much the same as my own. Strong mother figure. Father who kind of wanted to get along with as little trouble as possible. In the play there was a daughter and a son. In my own family there were two sons. There was the grandfather. I had one who lived with us in the same apartment. He was my mother's father and the first to come over from Russia and settle in Boston. He worked and sent money to bring the rest of the family over.

VH   *The pioneer.*

LN   Yes, and the thinker. I always had the sense that he was the one interested in ideas. Interested in social structure and politics. He was the one who would find some way of relieving the pressure whenever he felt the controlling hand on me was too strong.

VH   *Was home very restrictive for you?*

LN   Yes, it was. A very controlling atmosphere. So, the play was of a similar family structure to my own. The young boy being worked over by the mother, who was desperate to get the family some stability. In the play, the grandfather commits suicide but makes it look like an accident. We discover that he's left the insurance policy to the young boy, his grandson. The dream being that the kid is the future. Finance the kid with ideas. You don't finance the bourgeois attitude. You finance the thinker, the dreamer.

VH *Did you invite your parents this time?*

LN Yeah. They came to see it. That was interesting. I remember the night well. When I got home—silence. Nothing. Finally, when it was obvious they were not going to say anything about the play, I asked them what they thought. My mother said, "The lady who played the mother, she was wonderful." Total identification with this lady, struggling to lift the family out of poverty. That was the only comment. They wouldn't make any comment on my performance. They never would. The emphasis was always on "Get approval from others. To get approval from us is easy. You don't have to accomplish anything." Therefore, approval was always withheld as though it were meaningless. It was a tough, tough game.

VH *Approval must have been very important to you.*

LN Oh yes. I guess that was my first challenge. To get approval. To get stroked. There was a desperate need to be liked. At school, if a teacher came down on me for something, it broke my heart. I would get so choked up, I couldn't talk. One of the things I remember discovering that was so wonderful about acting, was that these situations couldn't happen to you. You had the control of knowing the dialogue had been designed, so you were never at the mercy of whether or not you were going to be able to express yourself in a terrible moment. You could prepare for it.

VH *A safe environment?*

LN Exactly. A safely controlled environment where you knew exactly what was going to happen to you. As you gain experience and the opportunities to make choices, if you don't like what happens to you, you don't have to take the job. [laughs]

VH *With so much pressure, it must have taken a lot of strength and determination from you to stand your ground. Where do you think that came from?*

LN It may be that you really have this need, in a more positive way, to do something and use the negative energy that's being thrown at you and turn it around.

VH *Make it useful to yourself?*

LN Right. I was screwed up. Lost. The only place, the only thing that seemed to be giving me any sense of satisfaction, were these plays. I should have been living in the theater. I felt so totally right there. So totally alive, excited, intrigued and confident. The kind of stupid confidence when you don't realize how much you have to learn. I felt totally confident. This was what I was supposed to be doing with my life.

VH *There must have been a lot of opposition from home?*

LN There was a lot of pain. A lot of tears. A lot of arguments. I think they thought it was a whim of some kind. As time passed and it became more real, the situation grew more intense.

VH *What did they have in mind for you?*

LN Any profession. Go to college. Get a degree. Acting is not a profession. Acting is a whim. It's a child's game. It's foolishness. It's for drifters. It's for unstable people. It may be true. [laughs]

VH *How do you think the social status of actors has changed since then?*

LN Well. I think the reality of it is that it's changed a lot. I'm not sure that the public perception has changed that much. If you were to go into the Midwest someplace and ask two or three generations what they thought about actors and actresses, their perception would probably be that they're strange people; drifters, alcoholics, promiscuous or whatever. Probably, they go on what they've read. The divorces. The drugs and all of that. I think the fact of the matter is, that actors and actors' unions and organizations have all moved very much into the center of average American life, which is where they want it.

VH *Not long after you arrived in Hollywood, a new breed of actor, including Brando and Dean, was emerging. Were you affected by this new movement?*

LN Well, as a matter of fact, when I arrived, these guys were on the East Coast. Their castings came out of New York. Dean came out with Kazan. I had come 3,000 miles from where it was happening. What was happening in Hollywood was the end of an era. What was happening in New York was the beginning of what would come to L.A. A whole new kind of filmmaking and a whole different approach to acting in films.

VH *Did you want to be part of that?*

LN I felt disconnected. I didn't know how to get in touch with it. I went into the army after I'd been here only two or three years—just as I was beginning to see the possibility of building an acting career here and making a living. It was while I was in the army, in Atlanta, that I began to hear about and see the results of the new movement.

VH *When you returned to Hollywood, you went into an actors' workshop to study further. Why was that?*

LN I could see, watching the work of Brando, Clift and Dean, that there was something they were doing, some kind of life they were creating in their performances that mine didn't

have. Mine were dead on and predictable. There was
thing dangerous and lurking; there was always some s
in their work. Something that intrigued you and sucked
into the scene. It was around '58 then and I began to hear
about Jeff Corey, who was creating heat in L.A. as a coach. I
studied with him and that's when everything kind of exploded for me. That's when everything changed. Very, very
fast.

VH *Was that training valuable in maintaining feedback during
periods between engagements, when negativity and the fear of
not working again can begin to creep in?*

LN Yeah. In a word, it validated everything. It gave me validity.
Prior to that, I was just another guy on the street looking
for an acting job. Once I began that work, I could see where
I stood with my peers and I began to develop my dramatic
imagination. To learn to take chances and create nuances
and subtleties in my performance. I was no longer worried
about getting work. I rose above that, in a way. I knew I
would work and that I could make a living. Whether or not
that would explode or not remained to be seen but, at least,
I was in the crapshoot. The rest was a matter of luck and
chance.

VH *It sounds like that was a very liberating time for you in a
personal way too.*

LN Jeff woke me up, very, very quickly. I began to understand
what my internal life could be all about.

VH *Later, you opened your own studio. Do you think your experience as a teacher has contributed to your ability to communi-
cate as a director?*

LN Oh yes, a lot. It gave me a lot of confidence in that I could
watch two people doing a scene and, in very quick, two-
handed strokes, help them to bring it to life. To this day, I
still feel that some of the most exciting work I have ever
seen or done was in those classrooms. The reasons for that
are many. For one thing, the atmosphere was designed to
create. A place where you were free to take chances. You
might fall on your ass, but so what? On the other hand, you
might really soar to some heights that you might not find in
an atmosphere where it was not safe to fail.

VH *Do you enjoy taking chances, working without a safety net?*

LN It can be a thrilling experience if you can pull it off and get
away with it. It can be dangerous, sometimes emotionally
and sometimes for your career. You can be out there,
making an ass of yourself or you may be doing something
brilliant and you're praying that the director has enough
taste to say this is either working or not. If he doesn't, then

you're out there on your own. I did it on "Deathwatch" because I trusted the director, Vic Morrow, implicitly. I used to do it a lot on MISSION: IMPOSSIBLE. Funnily enough, nobody ever saw it or cared that I was doing it. I did some very strange things on that show. [Laughs] I did it, to a certain extent, on "A Woman Called Golda" with Ingrid Bergman. There were things I was doing there that could have looked so tacky and bad. I suppose I've done it more on stage than in any other situations.

VH *Things really started to move for you after MISSION: IMPOSSIBLE.*

LN Quitting that show was kind of a dangerous thing to do but I felt confident. But '71 was the first year out after six years of TV series and it turned out to be a perfect year with a mix of all the things I wanted to do, including the movie "Catlow" with Yul Brynner, followed by a national tour of "Fiddler On the Roof." That was a glorious tour. We did great business wherever we went. After that, a show for NBC and a production of "Man In a Glass Booth."

VH *You started directing in '72?*

LN That's right. I directed a show for "Night Gallery." It was about that time that STAR TREK was sneaking up on me.

VH *Had it gone into syndication by then?*

LN Yes, in '70 or '71. But I really started to feel the momentum of it in '72.

VH *Why do you think that was happening?*

LN I'm not sure. I can tell you this. In '69 Neil Armstrong stepped out on the Moon and that was the first time we had a sense of an intelligent life-form, one of ours, standing on another planet.

VH *Do you think that changed the focus of science fiction in the public mind?*

LN It gave it a new kind of respectability in a way and we were the only show that had really been based on science fact. Some of it was really bad science, but everything we did we tried to do with a scientific credibility as opposed to fantasy. We were kind of the NASA connection; the NASA fantasy and the show that NASA watched. The Smithsonian Institute put a model of the Enterprise in the Air and Space Museum in Washington, D.C. We had a certain kind of credibility. When people started watching the show, they discovered they liked it and became addicted.

VH *The birth of the Trekkies!*

LN It was bizarre. I had more and more requests for interviews and appearances wherever I went. All people wanted to talk about was STAR TREK. Conventions sprang up. It really grew out of a grass-roots thing but thousands showed up and they couldn't accommodate the crowds. They kept getting bigger and bigger. It was extraordinary. Eventually, the promoters got into it and it became a sad, rip-off situation. You could feel the plastic of it start to set in and I stopped going, for the most part, because they were just too tacky.

VH *Did you think that the increase in public interest might lead to a revival of the STAR TREK series?*

LN No, I really didn't. I thought it was all over but that the phenomena wouldn't go away. It was frustrating for me because the work was over but, no matter what I tried to do away from it all, the focus was always on it. I was doing stuff like "One Flew Over the Cuckoo's Nest" and all the press wanted to talk about was STAR TREK. It drove me nuts! That's when I got this terrible reputation for hating STAR TREK and that, if it wasn't for me, there would be more STAR TREK. It got crazy and it just went on and on.

VH *Was the title of your book, "I Am Not Spock," a response to that?*

LN I was reaping the seeds I had sown with the book, which was about my STAR TREK experience. A series of answers based on questions that I'd been asked, over the years, about Spock and all the other roles I'd played. I did a whole piece on alienation. About the fact that I had always drifted toward playing alienated characters, always enjoyed it, even as a kid, starting with Ralph in "Awake and Sing."

VH *Do you relate to the alien?*

LN Well, I did. I can't say that I do anymore. I'm too successful. [Laughs] I was not really well integrated into society early on. I was the one who would sit at a party and not talk to anyone. If anyone approached me, I would be polite but I wouldn't go out of my way to be gregarious. I just wasn't good at it.

VH *So, where did the title of the book come from?*

LN There was a chapter in the book with that title. It dealt with some of my concerns about being locked in and perceived only as that character. I tried to do a sensitive, intelligent study of actor-character relationships. When they were looking for a title for the book, I suggested it because it was a chapter title. I thought the idea made sense and might be provocative. Well, it was more than provocative—it was controversial! But in a negative and not a good way.

VH *What was the public's reaction to the book?*

LN Well, It wasn't immediate. It wasn't like it exploded in my face. What it did was contribute to the hostility that already existed toward me. The main problem was that there was no new STAR TREK so, there was no test. Do you understand what I mean by that? There was no test of my being against STAR TREK; there was only speculation and it was very frustrating. I was trying to attract attention to what I was doing rather than what I wasn't doing. All that attention was going to what I wasn't doing, which was STAR TREK.

VH *How were you able to deal with that following so much adoration in the past?*

LN It was tough. Every once in a while, I'd flip out. I was doing "Equus" in New York in '77. I went in for a matinee and there was some fan mail in the dressing room. I opened one of the letters. It was one of those "We made you; we'll break you" kind. It happened that there was a STAR TREK convention that night which I hadn't planned on attending. I decided to go and when I arrived there they put me in a packed ballroom. I told them my story and read them the letter I had received. I told them how it felt and how the whole thing had turned around. That I was under attack without having done anything as though it were my fault. It began to clear the air for the first time in five years! When I walked in, there was a semi-hostile crowd, believe me.

VH *In what ways did you see things turn around after that?*

LN That night, ticket sales for "Equus" jumped enormously over what the pattern had been. A lot of people at the convention, who'd never intended to come and see me, decided to show up and see what I was doing. I had been getting a theater audience but now STAR TREK fans were showing up. Sure, there were some hard-core fans who would never turn their backs on me. Never. But there were a lot who couldn't have cared less about the fact that I was on a stage only ten or twelve blocks away. That day I felt a turn.

VH *It wasn't too long before they did get what they'd been waiting for: a STAR TREK movie. How did that work out for you?*

LN I had a difficult time finding my way into it. I didn't understand what my function was in the movie. I was confused. Finally, near the end of filming, we got the last few pages that we'd been waiting weeks and weeks for. We hadn't known how the picture ended! Bill Shatner and I got together and discussed ideas that would involve us in some way but the three or four moments we had created were cut out. I felt that, had they been included, it would help the audience. It would help to humanize that thing up there. To help the audience care about it.

VH *But those who were making the final decisions had a different approach?*

LN   Well, I can't fault them. They had a concept. I think the concept was a kind of "2001" approach. Very cool. Very scientific. Steely gray. A very metallic film. That's what they wanted and, I suppose, they had the right to do it. Bob Wise, who directed the picture, was very honest about himself and said he wasn't sure what made STAR TREK work. He made a fine, meticulous film but, I think, he kind of turned over his hopes for the film to other people who, he thought, knew what STAR TREK should be. Anyway, the picture went out and everybody said "Well, OK. Here's your STAR TREK movie." A couple of years later, they put it out for a commercial TV run and they needed to add some extra footage and put in the additional shots that I had suggested. I started to see, in the newspapers and magazines, that people were responding and saying that this version was better than the one shown in the theaters. That they had a better understanding of what was going on.

VH   *It sounds like, for you, that it was an obligation fulfilled?*

LN   The whole ebb and flow of this thing, the yin and yang of it, is that there are projects that I really wanted very much to do and those I felt I should do, obligations. I felt that, with STAR TREK—THE MOVIE, it was an obligation fulfilled. I guess it was just after that, that I started on "Vincent."

VH   *Did the concept of "Vincent" come out of the fact that you were looking for, and needed, something that was for you?*

LN   Yes, I certainly felt the need to develop a project of my own. I was looking for something.

VH   *How did this project come about?*

LN   It came about in a surprising way. I had been making some personal appearances at colleges and after one of them I got talking with a young guy who was working on some of Van Gogh's letters. Playing Theo and talking about his brother, Vincent, and reading these letters. I liked the idea of Theo talking about his brother because I felt it could be totally believable. Nobody knew what Theo looked like. If I walked on stage and said, "I'm Vincent Van Gogh," nobody would believe me. They all know Van Gogh looks like Kirk Douglas. [Laughs] It was a lot of work and I put in a lot of hours, but it was great. When I started it, I had intended to do it exactly as I did those college dates—with a briefcase and the black suit that Theo would wear. However, it grew and developed into a mounted production put out by The Guthrie Theatre. It was wonderful.

VH   *What was the reaction?*

LN   The audience was stunned, I could sense it. A lady stopped me in the street one day. She was speechless, almost in tears, and said, "I'm amazed." She could hardly talk about it. People say, "Thank you for doing that." It's very gratifying.

VH *You must have felt very good after that. How did you follow it?*

LN I followed it. That's been the most difficult thing for me to do in my career. Doing something like that and feeling so powerful. To hold people like that—you feel so large. Then there are the things that are obligatory. I don't belittle it, because playing Spock is not an ignoble thing. He's a very decent character.

VH *But it's the difference between being the interpreter and actually being involved in the creation of a project?*

LN Well. that's why coming to direct these things is more satisfying.

VH *Why did you decide to work on STAR TREK II, having been so disappointed with the first one?*

LN Well, I really was adamant that I would not work on STAR TREK II because I had been so frustrated with the other and I was feeling very negative about the whole thing. Then the producer, Harve Bennett, called me up and said, "How would you like a great death scene?" I laughed. He caught me completely by surprise with that one. The more I thought about it, the more I thought, "Well, maybe, that's the honest thing to do. Finish it properly rather than turn your back on it." So, eventually we agreed that Spock would die. There was a lot of controversy over whose idea it was and why. It was even said that it was the only way I would do it and that it was in my contract that Spock would die! It got to be a messy situation. Anyway, I liked the script and the director, Nick Meyer, a lot.

VH *Did you truly believe that this was going to be the end of Spock? You had no inkling that he might be resurrected?*

LN I really believed we were finished with this.

VH *How were you on the day you had to shoot that scene?*

LN I really hated it. It was a terrible day. I was very upset and emotional. I knew the scene would play well. I wasn't worried about it and I knew Bill Shatner and I could handle it. But dealing with the idea that this really was the last time I would be involved with this character after, at that point, sixteen or seventeen years was very difficult. I felt a great sense of divorce. It had been a long, complicated ride but there had been a lot of good times. A lot of good things to think of. I thought, "This is really historic, in a sense. In terms of pop culture and TV audiences." It was a pretty loaded situation.

VH *How did you feel after it was all over?*

LN Very depressed. Then I began to think, "Well, let's see what happens here. Maybe something will come of this." I guess I was trying to explore another level. Go through the process rather than make believe there's nothing to deal with anymore. I began to think that something good would come out the other side.

VH   *Close a door and another will open.*

LN   That's right. Then, when I saw the movie, I thought, "That's very interesting. Where are they going with that?" [laughs] The ending seemed to say something was going to happen. It did not necessarily mean that I, as Spock, was going to come back. Anything could come out of that tomb. [laughs] This is Science Fiction! I had no idea what would come of it. I just knew they were going to call me. I thought STAR TREK II worked well and was much closer to what STAR TREK was all about than the first one.

VH   *And, of course, they did call you.*

LN   They called me and asked me if I would like to be involved, in any way, with STAR TREK III. I said, "You're damned right, I want to direct that picture!"

VH   *Between those pictures, you worked on "A Woman Called Golda," for which you were nominated for an Emmy. You were playing opposite Ingrid Bergman, who was very ill by that time. How was that?*

LN   Working with Bergman was great. She was wonderful. When we started filming, I didn't know just how sick she was. There was actually talk of whether or not she would finish the picture. She had a very badly swollen arm and she wore long-sleeved dresses with frilled cuffs to help hide her swollen hand. She was in a lot of pain but she worked great. I was told, later, that Bergman had said to the producer, "Thank you for surrounding me with wonderful actors like Leonard Nimoy."

VH   *A lady of great strength and courage. The way she was treated over the Rossellini affair was so shabby and yet she always maintained her dignity.*

LN   Chaplin was the same thing. They turned on him—vicious! Then years later, when it's all over, they have him back, give him an award and everybody stands and cheers. They were about to do that when Orson Welles died.

VH   *Comes out of guilt.*

LN   No question about it: "I think we've shit on him long enough now. Maybe it's time to let him know that we think he's good." There was something in the *Los Angeles Times* when Welles died. John Houseman was called and, evidently, someone said to him that the feeling was that Welles never fulfilled his potential! Houseman said, "That's bullshit. Sheer bullshit." It's a myth he didn't fulfill his genius. It's been said, and I think it's true, that this industry didn't take proper advantage of his genius. But to put it on him, as though he'd screwed up somehow . . . It's bullshit! He laid down some fantastic work. What a lot of people did was lay down some fantastic obstacles for him.

VH *You've just completed STAR TREK IV. I understand you were also involved in the concept and development as well as directing and acting in the film?*

LN Yes, very much so. The central aspect of what the movie is really about, the plot, came out of a conversation that I was having with a scientist friend of mine. It was agreed, very early on, that we wanted to do a time-travel story going backward. A trip back from the 23rd century, close to contemporary times. The reason for making this trip is out of a major concern about the things that we are losing from this planet today—intentionally, consciously or otherwise. That, in the 23rd century, someone will wake up and say, "Gee, I wish we still had one of those because we could use it now."

VH *You've been doing a lot of research into recent scientific breakthroughs. What kind of information have you been picking up?*

LN Well, I have had a lot of good conversations with scientists. Some of the things I have learned from them have been technical, some philosophical. I think the most pertinent to what is happening in this film is that there are scientists who are deeply concerned, because of a prevalent attitude, that we don't have to worry about what we do on this planet. The attitude is that whatever problems we create, science will fix. They are afraid that something will go terribly wrong and someone will turn around and say, "Fix it," and they will have to say, "We can't. It's gone too far and it's something we can't control." That's one thing. Another aspect that, I think, we've gotten into the picture is showing that we are not the only living beings on this planet. If what we've touched on succeeds in what, I hope, is a fun feast to watch, an entertaining film, that would be a lot.

VH *There's a lot of criticism on the amount of money that goes into space exploration. What are your feelings on that?*

LN Well, I believe very much in the value of space exploration for scientific purposes. However, I'm also well aware that much of the motivation for funding space exploration comes from military motivation. Something you don't hear too much about is that NASA scientists are very depressed and unhappy about the idea that space is being militarized and that there is such a thing as the Star Wars defense program. The dream is to explore space for the benefit of everybody. To unify this planet through the exploration of space. The dream is not to militarize space.

VH *Do you believe that it would be possible to relieve the tensions on Earth by working together in space?*

LN I don't know. That's the dream. I sincerely believe there are people in the Russian and American hierarchy who would really like to do that. But the politics of it are not terribly supportive of that. It's a militaristic atmosphere. If we can avoid war, which I certainly hope we can, all of this military input becomes useful because it does drive science forward as it did with the aircraft in World Wars I and II. Unfortunately, in those cases, it came out of actual wars. Right now, it is coming out of the fear of war. What really bothers me are the scientists who talk about how we can survive a war of that kind. It's irresponsible and stupid. Preparing people, mentally, with the idea that if we had a nuclear war it would not be so devastating and that enough people would survive. That's outrageous. That's sick. It doesn't begin to take into account the scientific reality of the devastation that would take place.

VH *What does science fiction mean to you?*

LN There are, to me, two major scientific territories. There are a great amount of subgroups as well, but the two major territories have to do with human values and hardware values. I have never really been interested in the nuts and bolts of science fiction. I think some people do it brilliantly and there's obviously an audience for it. I've always been interested in it as a way of expressing ideas that are very human. When it touches on the human experience, condition or whatever.

VH *Do you feel that your participation in the series "In Search Of . . . ." perpetuated your image as someone involved with science and discovery? Is that how you see yourself?*

LN That show was far more successful than I ever thought it would be but it does not necessarily represent my thinking in every respect. A lot of it was done tongue-in-cheek and has to be taken as such. What it did reflect was my curiosity. I like to ask questions. I may not be satisfied with the answers but I see it as an opportunity to learn more.

VH *In recent public appearances, when talking about STAR TREK, you've compared your involvement with it to a love affair. At what stage of the relationship do you feel you're at now?*

LN With any new project and, in a sense, this is a new project, a new STAR TREK project, you take it as an entity in itself. It goes through it's own emotional twists and turns. You start out with fantastic anticipation, great excitement and there are points where you have to renew your energy and start again. Then you reach a point of exhaustion and you can't wait to be finished with it. In the end, hopefully, you feel a great sense of satisfaction. So, right now, there is this kind of process with this particular film, so far as the whole "Star Trek" experience is concerned. We were back on a kind of honeymoon affair during STAR TREK III, which was the return—the beginning of a new relationship, in a sense. STAR TREK II was the end of the relationship, of that particular aspect of it. STAR TREK III was the beginning of the new aspect of it. A very good, clean one. A mature one that has some wisdom about it. One that has a broader point of view than some of the turbulence it has known.

VH *And STAR TREK IV?*

LN I think, what's laying here is potentially worthwhile. It's unique, quite different from the others. STAR TREK I was in a category by itself; "II" kind of stepped back on to STAR TREK track; and "III," farther along that track. I think it proper that it should have. The nature and tone of this is a lot different from the previous ones. It's gone very well.

VH *Any thoughts about what you'd like to be doing in the future?*

LN Well, I tell you. If I could find a way, for example, to spend the next five or ten years of my life, knowing that at the end of that time I would have a product that is as important to our life and times as a man called Lansman did when he made a nine-hour documentary on the Holocaust called "Shoa," I'd be the happiest man in the world. I would take a severe and drastic cut in income for the next ten years to find that kind of commitment to a body of work. I doubt if I'll find it. I think Lansman's film will become an important, historical document. This is the first time that someone really found a way to crack into the unbelievable reality of that event. I envy him that he was of a generation and of a family of a geographical, philosophical and historical bent to be put in touch with that question. To get a camera and some money and go out and shoot the stuff he did. I admire him, but I envy him as well. I felt some of that passion when I did "Vincent" but, let's face it, "Vincent" is not anywhere near an important historical document as "Shoa" is. They're just not in the same class. So, I understand what the passion could be and that passion is sublime as well. It's wonderful when it happens. It's great.

DEFOREST KELLEY

I conducted my first interview with DeForest Kelley in 1982 on the Paramount lot. As we walked from the commissary to the STAR TREK offices, he stopped on a street that was cut off from the busy part of the studio. Dressed in western jeans, boots, his shirt open at the neck, De looked timeless, eternal. "There are ghosts here," he observed, looking up the empty road, remembering old days and old friends.

De appeared in countless westerns here as a heartless gunfighter or a tinhorn gambler; in crime dramas as a psychotic murderer, or a witness who didn't want to get involved. He became known for his portrayal of these unsavory characters, yet it was his role as an old country doctor that finally brought him recognition commensurate with his talent. As Dr. Leonard McCoy, De is a warm, caring individual, someone who can be trusted completely. "Bones" is the doctor we'd all like to have . . . and a very real reflection of the actor's personality as well.

AA *I'd like to go back for a moment to when you were offered the lead in a movie at Paramount.*

DK I was brought here for one film in 1942, '43 or '44. I was a young kid doing theater work in Long Beach, and Paramount became interested in me for a film called *This Gun for Hire* that they were going to do. It turned out I didn't do it, of course. Alan Ladd did it and became a big star.

AA *Weren't you more or less slated for it?*

DK Oh, yeah, yeah! I did about 13 auditions up there, and they finally called me into the office and I asked them what it was, and they said, "It's a lead picture," and I said, "What is it?," and they answered, "Well, it's with a new actress we have here"—who was unheard of then—"Veronica Lake; [it's] called *This Gun for Hire*. I went back to Long Beach, where I'd been nothing more than a beach bum doing theater work and having a good time. I threw a big party for my buddies, got a call one day, and I went back to the studio to see Bill Meiklejohn, [a Paramount executive casting the film]. I looked on his desk—he'd gone out of the room for a minute—and there was a pad there and it had two names on it: DeForest Kelley and Alan Ladd, and there was a black line through my name.

AA   *Ouch!*

DK   So I knew when he came back what he was going to say. He told me, "I just want you to know that we're still interested in you. When you come out of the service, we'll do something with you." And when I went in the service, I was sent out here again to do a navy training film for producer Jack Chertok and director Will Jason. Jason asked me, "What are you going to do when you get out of the army, kid?" "I don't know," I said. "Why?" He said, "You could make pictures. Let me show this film to some people." So they showed it to Columbia and they offered me a contract and I said I had to talk to Bill Meiklejohn at Paramount. I didn't have an agent and I called Bill Meiklejohn. I went over to see him, and he said, "What's this all about?" I said, "Well, I did this film and Columbia told me that if you didn't sign me they were [going to sign me]. So he said, "I'll look at this film and I'll let you know." I had to leave a day or two after that to go to Denver to be separated from the army and while I was in Denver I got a letter from Paramount offering me a contract. So I signed with them.

AA   *And your first film was* Fear in the Night? *I guess that's when the typecasting started, because you played a . . .*

DK   . . . Neurotic, high-strung young guy . . .

AA   *Your subsequent feature film and television roles usually had you cast as heavies. I've come up with most of the titles of your TV episodes, except for the WANTED: DEAD OR ALIVEs. I even have five YOU ARE THERE titles.*

DK   Yeah, at least, and it went back even farther than that. I'm trying to think of other series that I did.

AA   *Well, how about STUDIO ONE in 1948?*

DK   Yes, yes, I did that.

AA   *And THE GALLERY OF MADAME LU-TSONG?*

DK   Yeah. That was with Anna May Wong, out of New York.

AA   *Right, right. I think that was the DuMont Television Network.*

DK   Yes, it was. I did a number of shows there for them. There was a detective thing Lloyd Nolan was doing in New York. I did his show and then I did *The Web* with Sidney Lumet, starring James Daly. [chuckling] They're both quite antique.

AA   *Well, there was a different set of technological requirements.*

DK   Yes . . . I left Hollywood because I could see that "live" television thing coming and I went to New York to get that kind of experience. I did a combination of film and live work on a stage, where, if something went wrong, it went *Wrong*. I did another one out of New York for a producer—I think his name was Frank Robinson—called THE BIG STORY.

They did that live and on film and they sent me to Tampa, Florida, in December, for the film portion of it. I remember how cold I'd been when I left New York, and when I arrived in Tampa the sun was so warm that before I got into the hotel I sat down on a bench outside and just soaked up that sunshine. I'll never forget that feeling, that warmth going through my body . . .

AA   . . . *And you've lived in California ever since?*

DK   No, I went back to New York after that. I was on a radio serial for a while called "The Doctor's Wife," and then I did some radio here on the West Coast when I came back.

AA   *I have a tape of a radio episode you did in which you played a ventriloquist and the dummy came to life . . .*

DK   . . . "The Whistler," a very famous radio mystery show done here on the coast.

AA   *The first LONE RANGER you did was called "The Legion of Old Timers," and it was the first one in production order after that series' pilot. Then you did another one in 1950, and another in which you played a doctor in 1952.*

DK   Oh, yeah.

AA   *I remember a MIKE HAMMER you did . . .*

DK   Oh, *God*, that's a long time ago.

AA   . . . *called "Bride and Doom," from 1961. You did a great psychotic act at the end, giving your confession from a wheelchair.*

DK   That wheelchair thing . . . we were in that room and the director [William Witney] said that he'd hate for it to be so stilted. He said, "Let's work out a deal for De to maneuver in a wheelchair." He asked me, "Have you ever used a wheelchair?" I said, "No." So he gave me about 15 minutes to learn to operate that thing. As I recall, there's quite a long scene that went on and it was rather continuous. It came off at that time with a great deal of celebration. That was the first time I had worked for Bill Witney. In fact, the first thing I did after STAR TREK was the heavy in the pilot of THE COWBOYS [1974] at Columbia, and Bill Witney directed it.

AA   *In 1961 you did an ALCOA GOODYEAR THEATRE, also known as AWARD THEATRE, called "333 Montgomery," in which you played attorney Jake Ehrlich. Was that the first time you had worked with Gene Roddenberry?*

DK   It was, and Arts and Entertainment is going to screen that on THE GOLDEN AGE OF TELEVISION. I had previously done a cavalry story shot in Utah, the title of which was something like "The Marquis of Queensbury Rules," and Roddenberry had written that script but I did not know him at that time. My next experience with him was with "333" and that came about as a result of a feature motion picture I had done at RKO for Bill Dozier called *Tension At Table Rock*. I had also done some western pilots for Robert Sparks and Bill Dozier at Columbia and the pilots sold, so they became interested in me and they sent me up for "333" and Jake Ehrlich, the lawyer, selected me.

AA *Do you have any idea why "333 Montgomery" didn't become a series?*

DK The pilot material was too strong, and the network didn't like the idea at all [that] my character, Jake Ehrlich, had defended a guilty man that the audience knew had committed this crime, but he got him off with a prison sentence. And in the end, he said something—I've forgotten—something like, I don't like you but I just did what I had to do, or something like that . . .

AA *So you believe they chose the wrong story for the "333" pilot?*

DK Yes, yes, and then several years later down the line came the hit series with E.G. Marshall, [THE DEFENDERS, which ran from 1961-1965, and featured E.G. Marshall in a similar role.] so the time was also wrong.

AA *What were the names of the pilots you did for Robert Sparks and William Dozier?*

DK I believe that one of them was RAWHIDE. Another was called TWO FACES WEST.

AA *The TWO FACES WEST pilot was called "Image of a Man," and was telecast in January, 1961.*

DK Yes, '61. I think I played a guy named "Amos True." No, that was in *Gunfight at Comanche Creek*.

AA *Oh, were you despicable in that.*

DK Yes, I was a very unlovely guy in that . . . there was a scene that was cut that made him somewhat more unlovely. As I rode into town with my partner, Gene Evans, a dog was barking at the heels of my horse and I pulled out a six-shooter and shot him and just rode up to the saloon, entered, and ordered a drink . . .

AA *What do you enjoy most—playing heavies or heroes?*

DK Heavies. I say that off the top of my head because I've played heavies, and some pretty straight guys along the line, and the heavy is usually the most interesting . . . You knew you were going to get knocked off. The trick was to try to stay alive as long as you could.

AA *Joe D'Agosta told me that Gene Roddenberry wanted you for the doctor in the first STAR TREK pilot, but that a decision had been made to go with an older man, an old country doctor type, and that's why they got John Hoyt.*

DK   Gene [Roddenberry] had never discussed STAR TREK with
me at the time except in the commissary one day before he
started [production of "The Cage"] and he said, "De, I've
got two properties . . ." I think he said for CBS at the time,
and that one of them was a science fiction thing called STAR
TREK, and the other was HIGH NOON.[1] Of course, I had
been in a great number of westerns. He said, "Now, in the
science fiction story there's a very interesting character.
[This may be a very early reference to THE LONG HUNT
OF APRIL SAVAGE.]
He's an alien and he has pointed ears, and we're going to do
him green." I said, "I'll wait for HIGH NOON."

AA   *Do you mean he approached you for the part of Spock?!*

DK   That's right. We were sitting in the old RKO commissary.
(It was really Desilu—he had an office there.) That was the
conversation . . . I'll have to remind Gene of that. I told that
story once or twice and I don't know that Gene even knows
that he said it, but he did. He said, "Okay, if that's the way
you feel, that's the way it is," and it was always my impression that one reason the network didn't want me as the
doctor was that I had portrayed so many heavies that they
didn't feel I was really right for him.

AA   *Mr. D'Agosta's recollection was that he couldn't visualize
you with a bedside manner.*

DK   It could be. Somebody has told me down the line that the
network had me classified as [a heavy]. That, after all, was
all I had done for ten or fifteen years: bad guys. Then Gene
said to me that he had another pilot that he was going to put
me in. It turned out to be POLICE STORY. When they
screened that for the opinion of an audience I got lucky and I
got a very good reaction on it. In that I portray a criminolo-
gist with Steve Ihnat. I called Gene to thank him for having
put me in two pilots. . . . He said, "Don't hang up. The
network has decided now they'd like to have you for the
doctor." That's the way I found out about it.

AA   *Do you know if they ever gave any thought to Steve Ihnat?*

DK   For STAR TREK? I don't know that, but Gene had a high
regard for Steve, and Steve was an excellent actor. He was
a fine actor. We had great hopes for POLICE STORY with
Gene's background . . . one of those weird things. That
show should have gone . . . I don't know for the life of me
what killed POLICE STORY. For that time, it was a good
pilot, too. It was Steve Ihnat, myself, Rafer Johnson, and
Grace Lee Whitney. When all this came together, I was
holding two contracts; with one I would have been working

in STAR TREK and POLICE STORY at the same time if it had sold.

AA *That would have been almost unprecedented.*

DK It *was* at that time. No one had done it at all.

AA *When you joined the STAR TREK cast, what was defined about the doctor? Was he supposed to be a cynic, an observer?*

DK Yes, he was, and Gene had laid out a character analysis for him which fits what you see, with the exception that he was such a different character that he did not conform to ship's dress completely. They originally had him wear some kind of a sweater as opposed to the uniform itself; a very unconventional type of character described as "a future-day H.L. Mencken." So, I tried to base what I could on something like that and then found out how I was going to react to other players I was now involved with, and with the characters themselves, and we began to feel a certain communication with each other. When something begins to work, you recognize it. You build on it.

AA *You had worked with Leonard Nimoy before in an episode of THE VIRGINIAN.*

DK [Chuckles] He later reminded me of that . . . A drunken doctor and I let him die. I was in Gene's office a long time before, when they were casting STAR TREK, and I had no idea of being any part of it at the time. I think I was in there for POLICE STORY, and I remember seeing Leonard sitting in the director's office as I walked out. He looked at me and I looked at him and we really didn't even acknowledge each other. At the time I didn't know who he was.

AA *Had you ever worked with William Shatner before?*

DK No, I hadn't. I had admired Bill's work out of New York. I had seen him on television and I was very impressed with the first thing I ever saw him in, as the young assistant of Paul Muni. It was a live television show out of New York, and I had seen him in a couple of other things. Carolyn and I both thought he had great potential at that time and when I saw that he was going to be in this show, I was very pleased. . . .

AA *What's your earliest recollection regarding the filming of "The Corbomite Maneuver?"*

DK . . . I opened the show. I was in the very first scene filmed with Bill. Gene Roddenberry came down to the set, called the crew to attention, gathered everybody around and made a speech on what we were embarking on, the dedication that had gone into the show, and that he wished it to continue with everyone who was involved in the show: himself, and everybody from the stars to the man who sweeps the floor. He had this thing all laid out in the medical lab, giving Bill a physical examination. I said something about, "I'm a doctor, not a moon shuttle conductor. . . ," and that was the first scene shot in the series.

AA *They also had another recurring line they were giving to McCoy at the time: "I never said that."*

DK Yes, they were not too consistent. They didn't follow through with it, but that was popping up here and there.

AA *Had you ever worked with Joseph Sargent before?*

DK No, that was my first time and I thought he was delightful. He was just excellent, and I had a feeling that he was going to go on to do other things, bigger things, and he has done very well.

AA *That must have been a difficult episode to direct. There was basically no foundation for any of the characters.*

DK Precisely. That was the very beginning of it and they were very fortunate to have selected him, I think, to direct that segment . . . Nobody really knew at that point exactly where we were going. Is that the episode in which I come on the bridge and tell Bill off about something?

AA *Yes.*

DK At that time Roddenberry said that he wanted to establish the fact that McCoy was the one man on the ship [who] could override [Kirk] if he felt the situation warranted it.

AA *Did Gene ever discuss the importance of McCoy in the format with you?*

DK Yes, he discussed the relationship I was to have with Kirk, more so than with Spock, that I was his confidant and I was the man he could come to when he had something on his mind, or was in trouble; that sort of thing, that he could tell me anything . . . that kind of a relationship . . . real good friends, you know, respectful of each other. I hope I'm not turning something around, but it seems to me that Leonard and I discovered ourselves with a certain scene somewhere down the line, where he reacted [to] me and I gave it right back to him, and the director, whoever it was, covered us both very thoroughly. If you'll notice, on a lot of these shows they don't do that because it takes too much time. They would do a shot of Leonard and I'd be off camera . . . then they would get my reaction and go back to him and then back to me, sometimes back to Leonard . . . I don't know just where, Allan, but we found it. Of course, the lines were there, and when it was spotted in the dailies, they just started to write for it.

AA *Did you, at any time, sit down with Leonard and plan what you were going to do?*

DK Yes, we did. We discussed that quite a bit.

AA *It's interesting that because of the chemistry that developed between you and Leonard, you two became identified with each other.*

DK Yes, yes. Very much so. My mail reflects Leonard, and I'm mentioned in *his* mail; it's just a duo thing.

AA *There have been some STAR TREK episodes structured around Kirk's command decisions and some structured around the qualities of Spock's human and Vulcan sides, but none of those stories can be said to be seen exclusively through the eyes of either one. But I can think of a lot of STAR TREKs that seem to be seen through the eyes of McCoy as adviser to both.*

DK I think McCoy represents the perspective of the audience, that if you were along on the voyage you'd think, "These people are crazy! How in the hell do they expect to do that?" The viewers are looking at these very real people in very bizarre situations and they want to identify with somebody and McCoy's the nearest guy they could identify with.

AA *Spock and Kirk both have their priorities but McCoy's only priority is being human.*

DK That's right. Exactly. It makes a very interesting situation. . . . You know, there was a time when we were not to do a feature. We were to go on television and do maybe so many 90-minute STAR TREKs a year, which I thought would have been a dynamite situation because that way we could really have developed these people, showcased them to a tremendous audience . . . But the pictures started making money.

AA *Over the years, you, Mr. Shatner and Mr. Nimoy have either put a lot of yourselves into your characters, or have absorbed some of your characters' qualities yourselves.*

DK Well, I don't know, maybe we each have soaked up so much of these characterizations. . . . If you know Leonard and Bill as well as I do—and I don't mean on a social basis because we don't see each other that often—but when the three of us do get together, there's some kind of a very warm feeling . . . with great laughter and a kindredness that you simply cannot shake. I feel a great deal of Kirk in Bill. Bill is a very active guy, very energetic, imaginative. He also still possesses a childlike quality in many ways, which is wonderful; it produces that energy and that moving forward type of guy. Leonard is more laid back, analytical, with a brilliant mind, very knowledgeable. There is a great deal of these characters in us, but I believe it was there before and it was either a miracle casting job on Roddenberry's part, or the happiest accident that ever happened. . . . I think that's what's going to be difficult with the new series, to find that kind of chemistry. I certainly wish him the greatest success, but it is difficult sometimes to have it fall together magically.

AA *Of all the directors with whom you've worked on the series, do you have any favorites?*

DK . . . Joe Pevney did a lot of 'em with us and he was a great favorite of all of us. . . . Marc Daniels did some good shows . . . a very knowledgeable director; sometimes I think I did some of my best work for him.

AA *He's still active, by the way.*

DK Yes, I know he is. He's a remarkable man. He's very young at heart . . . It's terrific.

AA *His career also goes back to very early television.*

DK Oh, yes. He was in live television. I did not know him in New York. I had not worked with him, but . . . he helped bring a great deal of discipline to us, by the way. He had that New York background. I don't know if Leonard had that at the time, but Bill had had it and I had had it, where you sit down at a table and work on the scenes that are upcoming, and we established that for STAR TREK. They had a big, long table, and instead of our going to our dressing rooms or sitting down in a chair and reading *The Hollywood Reporter*, we went to the table and started to discuss and prepare the scene that was coming up.

AA *Was there ever a situation that you wanted to see in the series but was never done?*

DK I never felt that the right show was really ever done with McCoy. They touched on romance in "For the World is Hollow and I have Touched the Sky." . . . I would have liked to have a seen a woman come aboard, creating some sort of mystery regarding McCoy's involvement with her in some manner that could have been an interesting show, that could have done something with his personal side.

AA *That almost happened in "The Man Trap," one of the earliest episodes, but it turned into a monster story.*

DK Exactly, 'cause that wasn't *it* . . . There was also talk of bringing aboard McCoy's daughter, Joanna . . . that maybe McCoy would get the idea that Kirk was going for her. It would have been that kind of a situation, which would have made for a hell of an interesting story. But we were going to do a number of things had we gone on, that we never got to do.

AA *What did you think of STAR TREK—THE MOTION PICTURE?*

DK I saw it more or less relaxed here sometime ago when they reran it. I enjoyed it more even though it was not at all what I had had in mind. I don't know, maybe fate is kinder to us, sometimes, because STAR TREK IV was more what I had in mind for STAR TREK I. I don't mean, necessarily, with the whales, but I had suggested a time travel story . . . not "City on the Edge of Forever," but something with that feeling with a minimum of special effects, because STAR WARS was out and so heavy with that. The second one was a little better, the third one did very well, and the fourth one got even better. . . . We were up against a very difficult situation, Allan. In a series, where we had a shot at 79 shows, there's something in there that maybe everyone would like, and when you go for a motion picture, it's a very tough job because you're trying to satisfy everybody with one shot. I think it took a lot of courage from Paramount to decide to go with STAR TREK—THE MOTION PICTURE and the other features.

AA *Have you made any suggestions to the producers and directors of the STAR TREK motion pictures?*

DK I don't think anyone is really interested in what I have to say. On rare occasions, if I feel strongly about a particular scene or something that I want to say, then the director will certainly, to coin a phrase, "lend me his ear." But as far as anyone calling me into a meeting to contribute what I might have to say, no.

AA *Harve Bennett told me that when you saw the first draft script for STAR TREK II, you had some ideas to help make the story reflect the original continuity.*

DK Well, Harve Bennett is a very exceptional man. We met for lunch and when the script was sent to me, I turned it down. He wanted to know why and asked me to come over and have lunch. Our lunch turned into a two-and-a-half-hour discussion during which I told him what I thought was wrong with the script. I didn't expect him to take that advice. Now, whether it was me or his having had previous conversations with other people, I don't know, but he [rewrote] the script and it made all the difference in the world.

AA *Well, according to what he told me, it was mostly what you had told him.*

DK Very generous of him to say so and again, it just reaffirms what I've said about him. He's very talented.

AA *Has your life changed since STAR TREK IV was released?*

DK Yes. The recognition is even greater because it picked up a crossover audience and people who are approaching me strictly from the standpoint of having gone to see a motion picture that they thoroughly enjoyed, never having seen STAR TREK. So, it's really quite unbelievable how it's affected at least me in that respect. It is taking away what [little] privacy I have left to go anywhere publicly; it's rather unbelievable, you know, the power. I am always happy to receive letters from young people who have gone into medicine as a result of McCoy, and I think the publicity I'm proudest of was in *The American Medical Journal*. My doctor asked me if I had ever read that paper. I said, "No," and he showed it to me. "Take a look at that," he said. "In my fifty years as a physician, I've never seen a layout like that on an actor in that publication . . ." And boy, did I get mail from doctors after that!

AA *I recall hearing that you spent some time in a hospital visiting a terminally ill young boy who thought very highly about Dr. McCoy.*

DK I found that experience such a heavy situation . . . I had never done that before, and I ended up staying there three days. . . . I began to get heavily involved, and it had quite an effect on me. Evidently, I'm not the type who could go through that on a regular basis, and, of course, that was a unique situation; the boy wanted to meet me.

AA *You were his hero. Did that help to make it clear to you the great regard people have for you?*

DK Yes, it was a shaker. It was the first time it really hit me like that. You lose sight of it because life has to [go] on, you know. We all have to march on through this life, through personal problems or what-have-you, but that one stopped me and I took stock . . . you know, it's pretty shaking to think you have that kind of an influence. It's hard to put it into words, I don't know quite how to explain it—I was told, "Yeah, he wants to see you." You know, Christ! Who wouldn't go under those circumstances. It wasn't just me, I would think that any actor would, but it certainly does impress upon you how important you are in the eyes of certain people.

AA *How do you feel when you realize that you are a part of something so enduring in popularity?*

DK I think again how fortunate I am, and I come back to thinking that not many people in this industry will have that opportunity because in many ways there's nothing deader than a dead actor. Once they're off-market, with rare exceptions, such as screening the Bogart films, and that sort of thing, there's not much left to be said about them after a number of years. I don't know what it's likely to be after we're gone, but I approach each film as if it's the last one.

AA *I believe that in the history of television, STAR TREK is the first instance of something that has achieved the status of an international myth.*

DK Oh yes. There's no doubt about it. Carolyn and I have, on occasion, stopped and realized that the remnants of this thing will be here long after we're gone, that it really has become, in a way, part of our culture with a lot of young people and older people.

AA   *If you had it to do all over again, would you sign on as Dr. McCoy?*

DK   Onstage in St. Louis, at a convention, somebody asked that question. I really stopped and gave it a lot of thought 'cause that's a heavy question and I said, "Yes, I would." Yeah, I would do it again because I think it's been a phenomenal experience and I don't think it's an experience that every actor is able to have. It's a damned unusual show to have been a part of. You know, everything is a mixed blessing, you can't have everything, but, my God, it certainly has provided us with some eye-openers.

AA   *Is there anything you want to say to the fans of STAR TREK that you've never gotten an opportunity to say before?*

DK   No, I feel that I have said it to them . . . They're the most devoted group of people that I've ever known in my life and contrary to what a lot of people think, they don't all have antennae coming out of their heads.

AA   *Your life crosses the centuries: you're the son of a twentieth-century Baptist minister who wanted to be a doctor, and in a sense became a doctor of the future.*

DK   Yes, that's pointed out in that *American Medical Journal* article. I'd wanted to be a physician and couldn't—and yet became the most well-known doctor in the galaxy.

JAMES DOOHAN

Think of James Doohan, and you think immediately of the phrase "Beam me up, Scotty." In real life, however, Jimmy has both feet planted firmly on the ground. He's one of the most straightforward people you could ever meet, a family man and career actor with a realistic attitude toward life.

James Doohan, though, has something in common with his world-famous alter ego: the same spark is in his eyes. One gets the impression that this man really could work miracles, both technical and otherwise.

When Jimmy stands among the fans at a STAR TREK conven-tion, a group of people will usually remain near him after most of the others have left. Even those individuals who usually have trouble communicating will join the ensuing discussion, all smiles and admiration.

Jimmy shares Scotty's fascination with technical journals, and is often invited to tour scientific laboratories or address groups of scientists and engineers. He does not, however, prefer the same type of transportation that Scotty does. Doohan would much rather take the train and watch the scenery, and is familiar with the most scenic railway routes in the United States and Canada.

AA *When did you discover that you were so good at doing dialects?*

JD When I was about six or seven years of age, but I never thought about it. I can remember my father saying, "How does he know a Cockney accent?" The truth is, I never even thought about it, I just did it.

AA *Did you find you just heard it once and then you were able to duplicate it?*

JD It takes me half a second. I have a "photographic" ear; one of my brothers has a photographic mind.

AA *What profession is he in?*

JD He's a retired army general, a speed-reader. He knows what's on the page, and he reads like this [indicates quick motions across the page]. . . . It takes him about an hour and a half to go through a novel, just zipping through it.

AA *How did you decide to become an actor?*

JD I had no desire to get into show business, none at all. I happened to listen to a radio show one night when I was nearly ready to go to the university, and I said, "Hell, I could do better than that." Four days later I was at drama school in Toronto, and six months later I had won the top scholarship, which was to The Neighborhood Playhouse in New York City, and when I finished there they asked me to stay on and teach, which I did for about three years. I didn't like teaching. I hated it.

AA *You wanted to be out acting, instead of teaching?*

JD Yes . . . I just didn't like the academic part. I took the job in the first place because I didn't think I knew enough about the business, because . . . What the hell. What else did I know? My father once asked my brother Bill, "What's [Jimmy] getting into the acting business for?", and Bill said to him, "Don't worry about him, he knows what he's doing," which of course I didn't. . . . At the end of my first year I was asked to teach when I finished my second year and I said yes almost instantly. Jo Van Fleet was Sandy Meisner's assistant at the time. When she left because her term was up she had quit acting altogether. This was before *East of Eden*, and she did such a terrific character there. I had never seen her act.

AA   *Did Walter Koenig also go to The Neighborhood Playhouse?*

JD   Yes, I think he was there in 1958. Leslie Nielsen won the scholarship after I did, and of course I taught during his last year. When I was doing some show in 1961 at 20th Century-Fox, Joanne Woodward had won the Academy Award for *The Three Faces of Eve*. She walked on the set, gave me a big kiss, then turned to everybody and said, "This man taught me everything I know." She was a good student, but I didn't know she was going to be as good an actress as she turned out to be.

AA   *You did something called SPACE COMMAND on Canadian TV?*

JD   Yes. I've done three space shows. JASON OF STAR COMMAND was the third one I did. I did one year and they didn't really give me anything to do, so I said, "Goodbye."

AA   *What was SPACE COMMAND about?*

JD   Damned if I know [laughter]. I don't remember any fantastic lines that I said . . . [It was] live television. I was at a convention in Atlantic City, and during the question and answer period someone asked, "Did you ever do a TALES OF TOMORROW on live television?" I said, "No," and he added, "With Lee J. Cobb," and I said "Yes." I immediately recognized that I had. I had done two of them . . . I think that was probably the precursor to TWILIGHT ZONE . . . I did at least five TWILIGHT ZONEs, and people only see one.

AA   *I remember the hour episode, "Valley of the Shadows."*

JD   I don't remember doing that.

AA   *James Goldstone remembers bringing you into STAR TREK.*

JD   Oh, yes, he brought me in, definitely . . . I worked for Jim afterward in about 10 to 12 [other] shows between then and the selling of the pilot. All he wanted to hear were different accents, and that's what he heard. He called my agent and said, "I want Jimmy down here," and when I got to the set he asked, "Well, what sort of an accent shall we do today?" That was kind of fun.

AA   *Do you remember your first contact with Gene Roddenberry?*

JD   Yes, it was right on the day when I read for them. I hadn't met anybody before that, because my agent didn't have me up for it. [After] Goldstone called me, I called my agent and told him that I was going to do it. D'Agosta was there, and another fellow who was Gene's assistant.

AA   *Morris Chapnick?*

JD   Yes, Morris Chapnick, and Bob Justman . . . I think there were about four of them. I did a bunch of accents for them: they handed me the pages of the script, I did the accents, and they asked, "Which do you like?" So I told them. I said I preferred the Scottish, because I think it's traditional that Scotsmen are famous as engineers. They said, "Well, we rather like that, too," so I immediately just came right out and named him Montgomery Scott, after my maternal grandfather. My middle name is Montgomery. I'm named after him, and I have two sons with Montgomery in their names.

AA *I wonder how many people think you've named your sons after your character?*

JD Oh, yes. True, a lot of them do . . .

AA *Were you happy with the scope of the role?*

JD Not really, but that was the first series in which I had a part that was of some substance. I had worked in Toronto for eight years, and was Canada's busiest actor, according to everybody who was up there. The only other series I had been on after I left Toronto was PEYTON PLACE . . . A lot of the scripts that came in were centered around us at first, but then [they were changed].

AA *About the best episode for Scotty was "Wolf in the Fold." Eventually, so much of the other characters came out.*

JD But that took a while. It was mostly Leonard and Bill in the first season. In the second half of the second year, and the first half of the third year, DeForest started to get something . . . To me, it all depends on money. They figured if they had to give star billing to somebody, they had to pay them.

AA *George Takei told me that when you first arrived to do "Where No Man Has Gone Before" you were both assigned to the same dressing room.*

JD Yes. That was the first time we'd met. If both George and I worked on a Friday and we were free, we would go to the cast or crew party on Friday night, and then to Tokyo Gai-Kan, which was about the only sushi place in town at the time. And now, 21 years later, they're all over the town, they've become a whole new way of eating. I loved it. I sat there drinking Scotch and eating sushi, and then for a long time I didn't get any sushi because we weren't doing the show. We did the second pilot in May, 1965, and they didn't sell it until the end of February or the beginning of March. I just went on with my life, waiting for things to happen.

AA *Did you expect it to sell?*

JD I had no idea, no idea at all. Shortly after I came to Hollywood, I was up for the part of THE DOUBLE LIFE OF HENRY PHYFFE. I walked into that producer's office to read for the pilot. I had the script for about 20 minutes, and I read five lines, thinking, "Oh boy, this is great. This is right down my alley," because I had played a character like it on the stage, in Berman's *The Second Man*. I had played a physicist with a one-track mind. After I had read for him, the producer said, "When you walked in, I just knew you weren't right for the part. You read for it, and all of a sudden I know you *are* right for the part." He called my agent and said, "I would like to hang on to him for at least six weeks." I got paid for nothing, for the reading, for six weeks.

AA *That's very unusual.*

JD You're damned right. Then Marty Ingalls got the part for the pilot. I heard about the casting and I thought, "They're going for comedy, they're not going for the characters." ABC didn't want Marty Ingalls, they wanted Red Buttons. They may have had a contract thing with Red, but Red was not right for it. He just wasn't doing the character. I felt terrible. There I was: I knew I was just right for the part. I'll bet you the damn thing would have run five or six years.

AA *Do you remember anything specific that happened during the production of STAR TREK, pleasant or unpleasant?*

JD You forget unpleasant things. I can remember a young lady wanting to find out what a Scotsman wore under his kilt. She found out. Oh, God, it's so long ago.

AA *This was on a set?*

JD Yes, on the set . . .

AA *Do you have any favorite directors of those who worked on the show?*

JD Yes, Joe Pevney and Marc Daniels. But actually, I think our best director is Leonard [Nimoy]. He knows it so well, and is able to just say a few words, and we know exactly what he's after, except that in the third movie he talked an awful lot, but in Number Four it's as if he had said to himself, "Well, I'm not going to open my mouth."

AA *Then you detected a change in his attitude when he was directing?*

JD Yes. It was really subtle. I think he talked to himself on the set and said, "Hey, I think I talked an awful lot when I did Number Three, and I think I don't have to do that." It's confidence also. Let's hope that when Bill directs, we have the same sort of thing . . .

AA *Did you ever have anything to do with any other science fiction TV series as a recurring performer, other than SPACE COMMAND and JASON OF STAR COMMAND and STAR TREK?*

JD I did two VOYAGE TO THE BOTTOM OF THE SEA episodes and the day that I signed the exclusive contract to do the pilot of STAR TREK, I was asked to sign a contract with VOYAGE TO THE BOTTOM OF THE SEA as the chief engineer of the sub. . . . I signed the STAR TREK contract on Tuesday, and on Thursday I was asked to do "VOYAGE" with no accent. Who knows? In the long run it might have been better for me, except that STAR TREK, parts-wise, was much better.

AA *You'd have become terribly frustrated later on, when the scripts made less sense.*

JD Well, that's true. But at least I wouldn't have been typecast. The thing that typecasts me is the accent. . . .

AA *Had you every played a Scotsman before Scotty?*

JD Only once, on a HAZEL ["Hazel's Highland Fling"]. Even on all the radio I did, I never did Scottish. I love that dialect . . . I love all dialects. I remember Sandy Meisner of the Neighborhood Playhouse. I was playing an 87-year-old Jewish tailor, and he was sitting there laughing at this Irishman doing a Yiddish accent. It was more fun than a picnic. I've done every accent I can think of. . . . I did a commercial Lancashire accent and there was a guy on the same show from Lancashire. . . . He came up and asked me, "Where are you from, in Lancashire?" I told him, and he looked at me and said, "You do it well," and I said, "I usually do." I'm darn proud that I can do these things, and I know that I do them well, because it's a blessing that I have. I have an ear that can hear them. . . .

AA *But has that talent, coupled with the fame you have as "Scotty," typecast you in roles that require dialects?*

JD Oh, yes . . . and the first time I ran into typecasting was the summer of '72, when I came back from Spain after doing *Man in the Wilderness.* I'd walk into a producer's office, and his secretary would say, "Oh hi, Scotty," then I'd walk into his office and he'd say, "Well, Mr. Scott," so I knew I was being typecast, not only with dialects, but specifically the Scottish dialect. . . . The only job that I have done that is non-accent and non-space in 18 years is the one episode I did of HOTEL. I just played a small part in it, but I'd do any part as long as there's no accent. I got that because Aaron Spelling is a big Scotty fan. I did a MAGNUM P.I., and they wanted a Scottish accent.

AA *Did you ever go through a time when you didn't want to be associated with STAR TREK because of the typecasting?*

JD No, not really, because I had a sneaking suspicion that the typecasting was going to occur anyway and that I might as well not worry about it. A good friend of mine told me, "Jimmy, you're going to be Scotty for the rest of your life. Don't worry about it."

AA   *Has your family expressed any reaction to your status as a celebrity as a result of STAR TREK's popularity?*

JD   About ten years ago the wife of my oldest brother Tom said to me, "Oh, my goodness, Jimmy, you're known all over the world, aren't you?" I answered, "Yes, Joan, I guess I am." She said, "My, oh, my," and that was that. But as STAR TREK gets bigger and bigger they really accept it.

AA   *Did you read any science fiction before you did STAR TREK?*

JD   Oh, yes, and I've read very little since. There are not many people writing pure science, for me. Just this morning, I received a call from the director of the China Lake Naval Station, which has got the greatest number of research labs in a line. It's unbelievable. I've been through them once . . . [The director] was talking about the new superconductors. There's really so much going on, even in the field of weapons. He said, "You've got to come and see the new superconductors we have here," and I said, "Do you realize that will probably be the start of one of the biggest revolutions in science that we will ever have?" I said I think it's bigger than the microchip. It's amazing what they can do, because in New York when daylight comes [the power] will gradually be shunted over to the West Coast, and the West Coast will shunt it back at the start of nighttime. I don't know if you read the article in the *National Geographic* magazine three or four years ago, about the enormous hydroelectric power plants in Quebec, 20 billion dollars, and that [power] is going to be so easy to transport down . . .

AA   *Do you find that people treat you like a scientist because you've played one, and because of the knowledge you have from reading and conversing about science?*

JD   In a way . . . I can remember a certain research place that I went to. I won't go into the details, but they were working on an ion propulsion engine. They had it in a vacuum tube and I was watching it for a while, having it explained to me . . . I said to them something along the lines of, "Have you taken into account the pollution inside the vacuum chamber, the burned stuff flying around in there?", and they looked at me. They hadn't taken that into account at all, and they told me, "God, you just gave us six months more work." I said, "I'm glad I did," and they said, "Yes." That was kind of funny. People in these places are a little amazed at what I know, but that's because I read these things, and I have done so since long before STAR TREK ever started. I remember I was fascinated with ocean liners; I used to know the length and breadth of them, how many knots they could do, and that sort of thing. For instance, I know the first *Queen Mary* was 1,083 feet long, and the *Queen Elizabeth* came along, and it was 1,089 feet long. Bigger, but not by much, and maybe another 500 or 600 tons.

AA *What do you think of STAR TREK—THE MOTION PICTURE?*

JD I liked it. A lot of people didn't like the first part of the film with me showing the Enterprise to Bill, but I loved that. There were people saying, "Well, get on with it." The only part of it I didn't like, was getting to V'ger . . . You can't do a space show without special effects, but, my God, keep it down to a minimum, only when they're necessary.

AA *What are your hopes regarding STAR TREK V?*

JD The only thing I want is a really good story; that's all I really care about. And I hope that we don't get into a, "Gee, we've gotta beat STAR TREK IV" syndrome. . . .

AA *Why do you think STAR TREK is so successful?*

JD I don't think anybody really knows. The most common thing you hear is that it gave hope for the future, and it did that 'way back in the time when there was just about no hope at all. Now I think there's an awful lot of hope . . . I have all the faith in the world that nothing terribly drastic is going to happen although what might happen is something like AIDS, a plague sweeping the Earth, decimating the population . . .

AA *What is it like to be associated with something that's become a part of the world, so popular?*

JD In the way that's being accepted, it's truly a marvelous kind of association, really. I think it's a great thing to be part of, and anyway there's a tremendous amount of love associated with it. That's why, to me, when the fans want an autograph, they get an autograph. I cannot understand the excuses of the people who do not want to give an autograph. To me there's just no love there, none at all. When they want an autograph they get one. That's the way I look at it, because the whole thing is a big love affair anyway. When I start autographing, I usually go until the last pen runs dry.

AA *I've seen you do it.*

JD I do it. To me it's a labor, but it's a labor of love and I don't mind doing it . . . "You love it, I love it." That's the way I look at it. I started out signing autographs in New York in 1973 at the Commodore Hotel, and the other actors did not like that. Pretty soon they had to go along with it.

AA *Do you have anything you want to say to the fans of STAR TREK?*

JD Just . . . "Live Long and Prosper," and may all of you love for the rest of your life.

GEORGE TAKEI

Picture, if you will, a specially created alternate ending for "The Immunity Syndrome." The giant, one-celled life form is draining the energy of the Enterprise and her crew, until . . .

KIRK: *Gentlemen, we've less than 30 minutes left in which to do something.*

McCOY: *But, Jim, what can we do? There's no source of energy aboard the Enterprise that we can tap into.*

SPOCK: *Oh, yes there is, Doctor. You have overlooked the obvious.*

McCOY: *Of course! Jim, why didn't I think of it before? Sulu's our answer!*

KIRK: *Bones, you're . . . right! All we have to do is hook Sulu up to the ship's dilithium crystals. He has more than enough energy to do the job!*

Of course, this situation is slightly exaggerated, but I can remember being a guest at two STAR TREK conventions at which all the guests, including George Takei, attended parties until late in the evening. Each morning afterward I was awakened very early by the sound of laughter and a pair of sneaker-clad feet. Wobbling over to the door, I opened it slightly to see who was outside. On both occasions I found myself looking into the broadly smiling face of George Takei, bouncing up and down as he ran in place, asking, "Hi, how are you? Want to go jogging?"

George also directs his boundless energy into areas other than acting and STAR TREK. Among other things, he is interested in politics and is an active member of the Japanese-American community in his home city of Los Angeles.

AA   *What effect did your family's relocation to a camp in Arkansas during World War II have on you?*

GT   I was very young at the time, but I do have certain images connected with that experience. All the adults, both men and women, were issued regulation U.S. Navy peacoats, and I remember that on cold nights there would be fires going in large metal canisters. I recall the picture of these fires, and the dark shapes of the people crowded around them, trying to keep warm in the outdoors with the snow on the ground. Despite the cold and the starkness,

I remember thinking as a child how beautiful a picture that was.

AA *Did it seem like some sort of vacation to you, in the Arkansas landscape?*

GT That's what my family told me it was, how they explained it to me at that time. It was only later that they gradually told me what had really happened to us, of their anguish and outrage, and why.

AA *Did learning the truth about that experience have anything to do with your interest in politics during your later life?*

GT My father taught me about political awareness. He always saw to it that I was running for some office in school, or learning about things of that nature. He wanted us to participate in order to keep things from happening *to* us, as well as making good things happen. Both my brother and I were student body presidents, and, in fact, I guess my father kind of fancied himself a "Joe Kennedy," because he did pour some money into our campaigns [laughter] for student body officers, and he would urge me—I was the older one—to use my connections and contacts to get my brother elected. . . .

AA *Did your father live to see STAR TREK act as a force for unifying people?*

GT Yes, indeed he did. He was very active in my political campaign, when I ran for City Council, and he was also distressed by some of the discoveries that we made about the nature of a political campaign, how it brings out the ugliness in some people. And he was also there when I got my appointment from the mayor to the Southern California Rapid Transit District Board of Directors, and he was very, very proud. He insisted on being in the picture with me and the mayor. I was also glad that I was able to give that to my father, the opportunity for him to participate in that sort of thing. It's his doing, and he really deserved to be there. I'm very proud of my father, and I really am a product of my father's guidance and wisdom and resources. He passed on in 1979. My father was himself very active: he was one of the early leaders of the revitalization of Little Tokyo, the Japanese district in downtown Los Angeles, and he was on the board of the Senior Citizens Housing Project, Little Tokyo Towers down there. There's a memorial to him in the garden of Little Tokyo Towers.

AA *You studied architecture at U.C. at Berkeley . . .*

GT . . . for two years. Then I switched to U.C.L.A. I changed my major to theater arts there.

AA *Was that where you had your first exposure to acting?*

GT No. I had acted in high school and junior high school as well. My mother says I made my theatrical debut in the maternity ward. I've been acting since I was a kid. The back yard became the back lot, and I was putting on plays in the back yard. So, college was not my first exposure to acting.

AA *I know that* PLAYHOUSE 90 *was your professional acting debut.*

GT Yes, it was. It was written by Joseph Stefano, and the producer was Herb Brodkin.

AA *And* ALCOA PREMIERE?

GT George Schaeffer directed that. It was one of the early Viet Nam stories. I remember being impressed by the set, because they had recreated a huge bamboo grove inside a sound stage.

AA *Tell me about* THE HOUSE ON K STREET.

GT It was a pilot that I did with Dean Jagger. It took place in Washington, D.C., and the episode title was "Hammer Fist." The House on K Street was a top secret scientific detective installation located in a Washington town house. Dean Jagger was a science sleuth, and I was his brilliant assistant. That goes back to 1959. It was a pilot that never sold.

AA *How did your appearance in* Red Line 7000 *come about?*

GT The character was originally B.J. Simpson. The producer, Howard Hawks, decided that it didn't have to be played by an obvious "Simpson" type, so he cast me and changed the name.

AA *How do you feel about being cast to play Chinese characters? Do you feel that Hollywood simply lumps all Asians into one category?*

GT I'm an actor, and my job is to portray all sorts of different individuals. Sir Laurence Olivier's Othello was magnificent, and he's not black. As an actor, I don't have to be of a certain race to portray a member of that race, any more than I would have to be a certain *type* of human being in order to portray that type. For instance, one doesn't have to commit murder in order to *portray* a murderer. One does not have to be one's character or have his physical or emotional attributes in reality, in order to portray that character.

AA *How do you feel about non-Asian performers portraying Asians? Do you usually find that non-Asian performers portray Asians as stereotypical characters or caricatures rather than individuals?*

GT Exactly! I must admit that I have never seen a portrayal of an Asian by a non-Asian actor that I have liked. I was in *A Majority of One*, and as great an actor as Sir Alec Guiness is, I felt that he did not do his homework for his role in that film. And Marlon Brando did not convince me that he was Sakini in *The Teahouse of the August Moon.* Although he did attempt to play the man as an individual, I still see Marlon Brando, not Sakini.

AA *What was your first contact with Desilu in connection with your role in STAR TREK? Were you approached because of your affiliation with the Desilu Actors' Workshop?*

GT No, I don't think so. My agent called, and he said he had an interview set up for me with Gene Roddenberry, so it came through the usual channels.

AA *Do you remember what was discussed in that interview?*

GT It was just an informal talk with Roddenberry. I never met James Goldstone until I was on the set, when we were getting ready for production. I thought it was a strange way of being interviewed, because my recollection is that during most interviews the producer, director, casting director, and a whole slew of other people are present. I met with Gene and no one else.

AA *That seems to indicate that Gene decided whether everybody had the chemistry to get along with everybody else.*

GT That's right. It was a very warm and personal meeting. As a matter of fact, Dorothy Fontana was his secretary at the time, so she was in the front office and she directed me to wait. When Gene was ready, I went in and met with him. He came out from behind his desk, and ushered me to a corner of his office where there was a coffee table and couch-type setting, so it was a relaxed, comfortable setting rather than a formal test with a supplicant chair. It was really a very unusual interview, one on one, and we talked about everything *but* my career. Now, generally they ask you about some of the other things you've done, the other directors you've worked with, and that sort of thing: your background. Apparently, Gene had done his homework and knew about that. So, we just generally "shot the breeze." I can't remember specifically what we talked about, but my general recollection is that it was a conversation about current events and theater. He knew that I had gotten part of my education in England and we talked about that. Frankly, I walked out of that interview thinking I wasn't right for the part, and that's why he was carrying on the conversation in the way that he was. I thought he was just making polite conversation.

AA *In reality, he had probably decided you were professionally qualified, and he just wanted to determine if you were personally qualified to join the production "family."*

GT   Exactly . . . finding out something about the human being, rather than the professional actor, and what makes all of us tick, other than as professionals.

AA   *What happened after the interview?*

GT   I called my agent. I was intrigued by the project, and I said it sounded fascinating and I'd love to do it, but that we had talked about everything but me. So, I told my agent that Roddenberry was probably making polite conversation rather than the standard, cold, "Don't call us, we'll call you," which so brutalizes the sensibilities of an actor. I frankly told my agent that I didn't think I had the part. Two days later he called back to say that I *did* have the part. Hollywood works in strange and totally unpredictable ways.

AA   *Tell me about your experiences during the shooting of "Where No Man Has Gone Before."*

GT   Although the interview was at the Desilu Studios, the pilot itself was shot at Desilu Culver in Culver City, a totally different facility. Thinking back on the shooting of the pilot, one thing I do remember very precisely is that they were so chintzy that we didn't have individual dressing rooms. I shared my dressing room with Jimmy Doohan, so I first got to meet Jimmy as "roommates," and, of course, our conversation was on the prospects of this pilot that we were about to shoot, because our futures were at stake. Being a visionary, I told Jimmy, "This is a real good script. I've met Gene Roddenberry and I have the utmost respect for his integrity and his artistry." Just briefly meeting the personnel on the project, I sensed quality on that show. I said, "This is too good for television. It will probably last a couple of seasons, if that, because television is not known for respecting quality." THE DEFENDERS, one of my favorite series at that time, was canceled and I was outraged by that. That's one of the conversations that I recall sharing with Jimmy in the dressing room while we were waiting.

AA   *Did Mr. Doohan mention James Goldstone? I know that they knew each other prior to that, and Mr. Goldstone recalls that he brought Jimmy in to test for Scotty.*

GT   I didn't know that. Now that you mention James Goldstone, I think that I had done something with him before. Maybe that's why he didn't interview me, because he knew of my work. I remember that when I first saw him on the set we exchanged salutations to the effect of, "It's great to be working together again." I can't recall what I had done with him before the STAR TREK pilot. I'm wondering whether he could have been the assistant director on some of the projects that I worked on before that, because he was a young director at that point. I remember the PLAYHOUSE 90 I did, "Made in Japan," was directed by Herb Herschman, and Bob Butler was the assistant director. Bob Butler subsequently directed me in a couple of other things, including THE TWILIGHT ZONE I did that has disappeared into the "twilight zone."

AA   *How do you feel about your TWILIGHT ZONE episode's having been withdrawn from syndication?*

GT   I think it's unfortunate. I guess it's the climate of the times. As I recall, the story had something to do with my character's father, who spied for the Japanese at Pearl Harbor, and it was considered an inaccurate sort of thing. But the whole thing takes place in "the twilight zone," and if we start taking everything in THE TWILIGHT ZONE as serious, then it becomes highly defamatory, but that's the whole concept of THE TWILIGHT ZONE. As I understand it, the episode was canceled because of some Japanese-American pressure saying that there were no Japanese-Americans who were ever accused of treasonable activity in the case of Pearl Harbor. But there were many totally bizarre things that could never happen being depicted in THE TWILIGHT ZONE. That was the nature of the show and that episode was a wonderful, wonderful opportunity for me as an actor.

AA   *Are you happy with the roles that Sulu got in the series and the feature films?*

GT   Oh, of course not. I'm always lobbying, so they know that when they see George coming, I've got something to lobby them about. And maybe that's not a good reputation to get. They always gird their loins when they see me coming.

AA   *What's your feeling regarding your involvement in STAR TREK? If you had it to do over again, would you do it just as you did?*

GT   Oh, absolutely. No question about it. It's been a very, very full and rich and serendipitous experience in many respects. Doors I never dreamed were there opened up . . .

AA   *What are some of your current activities?*

GT   I'm on the Board of Directors and Executive Committee of the Los Angeles Theatre Center, a four-theater complex. We restored the original Security Bank Building, built in 1906, and in the parking lot next to it we built four theaters wrapped around the restored building. The restored building is a big, classic banking hall with stained glass windows and Ionic columns that go up three stories. That structure becomes the common lobby for the four theaters. It's a wonderfully exciting project, opened in 1965, but our subsidies for the various areas are very troubling right now. So we're heartened by the "product" that we put on the market, so to speak, to use business terminology.

AA *When were you appointed to the Rapid Transit Board?*

GT That was back in 1973, and I left it in 1984. I'm also currently chairman of the El Pueblo State Historic Park, and president of the Friends of Little Tokyo Art, a group that places works of art in public places being created in the revitalization of Little Tokyo. In the business arena, I'm chairman of the board of a bank that we founded, called Golden Securities. It's finding a new niche in unfilled areas. We have a lot of Southeast Asian, Taiwanese, and Hong Kong immigrants coming in to Los Angeles—people who are very thrifty and hardworking, but who also have no credit record. They can't walk into the Bank of America and get a loan, nor can they get a car, the first thing they need when they come to Los Angeles. What we've done is started a bank that meets the unique and specific needs of these people speaking in their own languages. We have two branches now. Where many of these immigrants come to this country with professional resources—bankers, financiers in the old country—what we've done is to harness those professional resources that these people bring and give them jobs, because otherwise they'd be working below their experience and qualifications. We give immigrants a place to make their loans in the languages with which they're comfortable, where people will understand their circumstances and backgrounds. They borrow money from us, and they save with us. Later on, because they're entrepreneurial, they save up a little nest egg and open up their own businesses.

NICHELLE NICHOLS

Nichelle Nichols became a part of STAR TREK in May, 1966, after both pilots had been completed. She portrayed Lt. Uhura throughout the original series' three-year run and the animated episodes, and continued her role in the STAR TREK feature films. But her association with outer space does not end there.

After becoming familiar with the work of the National Aeronautics and Space Administration, Nichelle became active in the space agency's astronaut recruitment program, increasing the participation of women and minorities within NASA.

In this interview, Nichelle discusses how she became part of STAR TREK, and her experiences aboard the Enterprise, in addition to her work with NASA and her observations of this country's space program. She spoke with me on June 9, 1987—only a day after her first direct participation in an event connected with her colleagues who perished in the space shuttle disaster.

AA *You were in an episode of THE LIEUTENANT. Is that how you became involved with STAR TREK?*

NN No. That was three years before STAR TREK, my first dramatic TV experience . . .

AA *Joseph D'Agosta speaks very highly of you in reference to that role.*

NN Well, Joe was responsible for my getting that role in THE LIEUTENANT. Frank Silvera had an acting workshop, and he and I were in a theater workshop together, called "The Theater of Being." We gave young people the opportunity to hone their craft, not only in a class environment, but also within the theater, working out scenes. I was working out a scene from a Tennessee Williams play, I think. Joe was taking some classes and he was in the workshop. He probably saw how hard an actor's life is, and decided to do something else. But he was also working at MGM, casting for Gene Roddenberry. I don't know whether he was casting for MGM in a general sense, or whether he was just casting specifically for THE LIEUTENANT. But he saw the scene that we were working on developing, and he was very impressed with it. There were roles in which both Don Marshall and I would fit perfectly in THE LIEUTENANT episode, in which Don was playing a young private, and Dennis Hopper was the antagonist. [Joe] told Gene's company to see us before they saw anyone else. He got in touch with our agents and asked us to go to MGM to perform our scene. We presented this scene to quite a few people at MGM, and that just started the ball rolling, opening doors. We got the part in nothing flat, and it also got the ball rolling for other things: I did a lot of work at MGM after that. The next thing I knew, STAR TREK was being cast, and I was in Europe . . .

AA *I recently saw you in an episode of the TARZAN television series that was probably filmed soon after "The Corbomite Maneuver."*

NN . . . Everybody did at least one episode of TARZAN.

AA *Did you go down to Mexico to do it?*

NN Yes. I was an African princess. Every week there was an African princess. You were either a chief, a princess, a prince, or a witch doctor [laughter].

AA　*How did you happen to be in England when STAR TREK begin casting as a series?*

NN　I'd just come from singing in England, and I was going to meet some friends in Paris. The day I checked into the hotel I got a telegram from my agent saying, "Come home immediately." This was the first time I'd heard anything about STAR TREK, and I thought, "What's a Star Trek?" I ignored the telegram, and the next day I got another, saying, "I tried to reach you, obviously you didn't get the first telegram, come home immediately." He knew my engagement was up, and it wasn't like saying, "Stop singing, drop everything and come home." I felt, why should I go back to Los Angeles, fly all the way back to the States to go on an interview which I probably wouldn't get anyway. I hadn't been doing that hot, which was my reason for going to Europe. Gene had given me introductory star billing, and now that I had a starring role with a good salary base I was being considered, at that young age, and as a Hollywood newcomer, with the other people of the same caliber . . . people like Diahann Carroll and Eartha Kitt. But when you're being considered for name value, if their names are stronger than yours—if they get there first, it's hit or miss. I thought I was going to fly all the way back and give up all those wonderful times there, only to have the part given to Eartha Kitt. So I ignored the second telegram, too. The next thing I got was a phone call from a very irate agent, screaming, "What's the matter with you? Are you out of your mind? You get over here!" After doing THE LIEUTENANT, I got to know Gene Roddenberry. We got to be friends, and through his recommendation I got a few other things over at MGM.

AA　*Such as* Mr. Buddwing?

NN　. . . *Mr. Buddwing, Maid of Paris*, and a few other things that I don't remember. But these were my chances, my opportunities, and lots of interviews and lots of being seen for top roles. Doors were opening, and as a matter of fact at some time between THE LIEUTENANT and the time I left for Europe, Gene had said to me, "I've got something in mind. If it comes off, there's something in it for you." . . . He had never said it was called STAR TREK, and he had never said, "I have this space picture," or "science fiction picture," just a project. My agent had not said it was a Gene Roddenberry project, or I would have been on the phone and on the plane immediately. But just another interview didn't mean that much to me, to be told I'm not that big yet, yet to be in that category of being called in with those gals. I

was the little fish in the bigger pond, so it was difficult. . . .
My agent said, "I'll make a deal with you. There will be a
first-class, round-trip ticket waiting for you, and if you get
back here and you don't get this part, the ticket's on me." I
thought it was an offer I couldn't refuse, and I returned. I
still didn't know it was Gene Roddenberry's project. I think
that my agent thought I knew what STAR TREK was. I
didn't know anything. I'll never forget that interview on
Tuesday. You go for an interview dressed rather casually,
as if you do this every day. I had been out of the States for
four or five months at least, and I still wasn't used to
California casual dressing. . . . I had this neat little pale pink
and white Chanel suit on, high-heeled shoes and my little
cream leather gloves, I had a new hairdo with my hair
almost all cut off in the back, and with these long, stringy
bangs in the front, long sideburns, and I was reading a big
book called *Uhuru*, a lovely treatise on the history of Africa.
I walked into the office, and there were all of these ladies to
be interviewed.

AA *Do you remember any of them?*

NN I remember that they were gals who were worthy of being
in contention for the part, and young women I had seen at
other interviews. Apparently, he was not looking for a name,
but for good actresses, someone who was not face identifiable as much as some of the others I had been up against. I
walked in and they saw me, and their eyes went, "What?,"
because of the way I was dressed, and I suddenly realized,
"Oops, I'm back in L.A." . . . Nobody was wearing hair
like that, and nobody would come to an interview with eye
makeup like that. Now it's usual. I gave the secretary my
name. There were no lines to read, so I started to read my
book. Finally I was called in, went into the room, and there
were Bob Justman, [Gregg] Peters, Joe Sargent, Eddie
Milkis and maybe one or two other people all in front of me,
sitting in sofas. I turned around, and behind this huge desk
was Gene Roddenberry. I said, "Oh, Mr. Roddenberry,
what are you doing here? How nice to see you again," and
he said, "I have a little something to do with this . . ." I sat
down, and it started to hit me: "I have something in mind,
and if it happens it would be for you," and I started to think,
"This could be it, or not." They asked me to tell them
something about myself. Before we could even get into that,
someone mentioned the book I was reading and for the next
half hour we talked about the book, about my career. We
laughed and we joked, and so far we hadn't even gotten to
the reason why I was there. We were just having a time

talking about Europe . . . Finally they said, "This has really been wonderful," and they asked me to read for them. I said, "I'd love to." They handed me a script and apologized, saying the part I would be playing would be the communications officer, but that they were just changing the whole role, that there was nothing for me to read, and would I read this part here, because that would probably be close . . . , and I said, "Oh, well, tell me about this Spock person, what does she do?" And they explained, "Oh, wait a minute, you're not reading for Spock now. Spock is male, and has already been cast. We just felt that in order to get a feeling . . ." I said, "Why don't you tell me about the character, the person, and I can read it as though I was going after that role, and you can see if I can act." Joe Sargent said, "That's a great idea . . . I'm glad I thought of it . . . He's half alien, has green blood, and he's totally logical about everything." I said, "What do you mean, he's half alien?" They said, "His mother's an earthling," and I said, "Well, then he doesn't have total logic," and we laughed about that. So I read for the role, pretending that I was up for the part of a female Spock. We did a nice long reading, a scene that was several pages long, and when I finished, one of the guys said, "Call down to personnel to see if Leonard Nimoy has signed his contract yet." Of course, they knew he had, but that was their charming way of telling me that I had really done a good job. They asked me to wait, so I went out. None of the poor gals who were behind me had been asked to stay, after they had waited 40 minutes or longer during my visit there. I came out and told Penny [Unger], the secretary, that they had asked me to wait. She said, "Okay." In this business they often will ask you to wait if they're really interested. They may want to see you and two other people, you may be a finalist. That doesn't mean you have [the part]. I'd been through that before, so all I thought was, "Hey, I've got a chance." Penny put me in a little room, and I curled up in the sofa, opened my trusty *Uhuru* book, and proceeded to read for the next hour. The next thing I knew, Joe Sargent popped his head in, looked at me and said, "What are you doing still sitting here?" I said, "You told me to wait," and his face blanched. He said, "Oh, God, hasn't anyone told you?" All I could think of at the moment was, "My bags are still packed, I've got my ticket," and he said, "Well, you've got the part. Let's go to lunch." So he took me to lunch, and that's how I got the role.

AA   *What did you think of the role initially? Were you happy with it?*

NN I was delighted with the role. It was actually one of the lead roles. What happened after that is another matter. Script after script were wonderful parts, and then you'd get the rewrites, page rewrite after rewrite, and I thought it was very cruel to give us the original scripts which had terrific parts in them, and then to see your part get cut, cut, cut. Through all of the time that you're working, you're getting up at 4 in the morning for a 6 o'clock call and not getting off from work until 7 that evening. But being a real newcomer, you don't know what your rights are; you're delighted to be involved. This is the first time you've gotten a big break, and then it's not going to be a big break. You don't know. There's a confusion there, and there's a pain. And then you get thrown a bone . . .

AA *Did you ever want to leave the series?*

NN I was going to quit after the second season. They told me in the first season that everything was going to be different in the second season, that everybody was going to be equal, and the fan mail was coming in like crazy for me . . . But you also have to remember that the thing in 1966 was that everyone was scared to death of having a black and a woman in an equal role. They had just gotten through having a battle with Gene Roddenberry over Majel Barrett in a strong female role, and they were scared to death of the South, and the whole thing. It was all in vain, the fear was all for naught. . . . But when they began cutting, virtually down to "Hailing frequencies open," from really fine, substantial parts, I just couldn't take it. In the second season I went to Gene and said, "I can't take this any longer, I'm leaving the show": I was going to leave the show in the middle of the season. By this time, I think Gene knew a little more than I did, and he said to me, "Don't do it. I have a feeling about this." I think his feeling was that we were only going to last another season, and why blow it now. He said, "I just have a feeling, I'll do the best I can, but in many ways my hands are tied." And things did get a little better, for instance, with "Plato's Stepchildren" [filmed in September 1968] and some of the other episodes.

AA *Was that the first interracial kiss on television?*

NN Yes. So big deal. So much was made of it. As a matter of fact, no fan mail came in protesting it, except from one guy who said, "I'm a white Southerner, I believe in the separation of the races, but any time that a red-blooded American boy like Captain Kirk gets a beautiful gal like Lt. Uhura into his arms, he ain't going to fight it." That was the big, major protest.

AA   *Knowing the character of Captain Kirk, it was strange that the only time he would kiss you was when he was forced into it, although he came close to it in "I, Mudd." I always felt that the character Uhura might have had some closeness with was Mr. Spock.*

NN   Yes . . . I felt from the original reading that Spock was my mentor, and that emotionally they were very much alike. . . . Many times Uhura would just turn and look, and say volumes. She was extremely loyal to Captain Kirk, and was following him to "where no man had gone before," through thick and thin, but it was Spock who fascinated her, and inspired her mentally and professionally.

AA   *Was there an effort to imply an attachment between Spock and Uhura? For instance, he let you play his Vulcan harp.*

NN   He not only let me, but the Vulcan lyre is an instrument that defies the musicianship of any normal earthling, and so he *taught* me to play his lyre. We developed a thing where I was one of the first people to play the Vulcan game of three-dimensional chess. I took it that my mind aspired to where the greatness of where this man's intricate mind was. . . .

AA   *Was any of this supposed to be in any script?*

NN   Yes, yes. And remember the song in "Charlie X"? The spoof on Spock, the teasing of Spock? No one else would dare. It was only she.

AA   *And since he smiled at you, you had his approval.*

NN   Exactly, exactly, or he'd cut her dead. And no one else would have dared. There were a couple of times during which he protected her, for instance when there was something wrong with the electrical systems and she was repairing them . . . showing his great admiration and respect for her in ways that were not given to others than Kirk and McCoy.

AA   *. . . Including that little scene in "The Man Trap," about Vulcan having no moon and Uhura saying, "I'm not surprised, Mr. Spock"?*

NN   That kind of thing. That almost got cut, and I screamed bloody murder.

AA   *There was a scene filmed for "Elaan of Troyius" featuring Kirk, Spock and Uhura in the recreation room that was cut from the final episode.*

NN   Interesting, interesting. Yes. It was shot, but anytime they had to cut, they cut me and George.

AA   *Do you feel that you've been treated better in the movies?*

NN   . . . Fortunately we've become such a marvelous, cohesive, legendary institution . . . I think that they would do very well to build our parts and make us truly a unit, because obviously STAR TREK IV was successful for those reasons, because everywhere I go that's all I hear in audiences. That's why IV works so well for them, because everyone was involved, and the humor was wonderful to see because of the whole cast. . . .

AA *In STAR TREK III, everybody remembers the "Mr. Adventure" sequence.*

NN That was a wonderful scene. That almost didn't get filmed. . . . The day I was shooting that scene was the day of the fire at Paramount; the helicopters kept going around and around, and we couldn't shoot the scene. The sound man, the only person who can cut a scene besides the director, kept cutting that scene. . . . They were evacuating the studio, and Leonard said, "We'll just keep shooting as long as we can." At that time of day it was usually beautiful, bright sunshine, and outside our door from the fire it was black outside. If they had said, "Evacuate," we would have had to evacuate, and our shooting schedule was such that they were already talking about cutting that scene to save time, but Leonard wouldn't let them . . . ; he was trying to get that scene done so he could have it in there, and then this happened. Bill was out there saving the studio with his trusty hose. Boy, we teased him about that the next day. We were in there trying to get this scene down, and this was the only scene of poor "Mr. Adventure." He [worried], "Are they really going to cut this out?"

AA *Wasn't there something else cut? In one scene you're staying behind, and in the next scene you're on Vulcan.*

NN There was another [scene]. I begged for that scene to be written, and they insisted that everyone would understand. They did rewrite the end of my scene when I said, "I'll see you all at the rendezvous point," and you're now supposed to understand that was on Vulcan . . . I think that was one of the big weaknesses in that film. There were a lot of weaknesses in STAR TREK III. They had to achieve something that was totally illogical and improbable from what they had done, and that was to bring Spock back. . . . I love the family on STAR TREK, I love the fans . . . I believe in the original philosophy of STAR TREK. I believe that Gene Roddenberry is a man of great wisdom, and it's a philosophy that if a majority of people based their lives on, we'd have no wars, our species would be wondrous—I think our species *is* wondrous.

AA *Do you think that's a reason for the series' popularity?*

NN Absolutely. I think people still discover it, and discover the high level of idealism, of possibilities. Just the credo of

Infinite Diversity in Infinite Combinations is what makes the world beautiful, the universe beautiful. I know the guy who wrote "I'm Okay, You're Okay" got the idea from that. Suddenly you say, "Whatever I look like, whatever shape, form, size, configuration, capacity, color, mental level that I am born with, I am, in fact, really okay."

AA *Are you planning to write a book regarding your experiences with STAR TREK, and with the space program?*

NN . . . I'm just getting some data together now, so that I have my facts and figures right. I always dread research. I'd rather write fiction than fact. But if you're going to write anything predicated on factual substance, you have to do the research. . . . When I have an interview with someone like you—who incidentally makes it very easy—enough stories come up that I begin to feel what I felt at that time. I feel I should write a book, even if I don't publish it. I'm starting to do that now, to put things together, to research back into things that I did.

AA *Were there ever times in STAR TREK that you felt as if you were a "token black"?*

NN I never felt that I was a token black in the eyes of Gene Roddenberry. I know the man, I know his thinking, I know where his heart is, and I think he tried to achieve something at a time when all of the energies were against him . . . A time when it was really unheard of, and I think that an attempt was made to reduce me to a token black, and to reduce George Takei to a token Asian, but I think it failed because of the manner in which Gene placed us. It was stated over and over that we were the command crew. Now, whether they tampered with that in the production or not is beside the point. Whether I ever took over the ship or not is immaterial to me. The fact of the matter was that I was capable of it, that I was in a role that was not a black role or a female role, as such. It was the role of anyone who was qualified in the area of ship's communications. What was not brought out many times was that there was a whole coterie of people down in the bowels of that ship, doing my bidding, who worked under me. I was head of communications, just as Jimmy was head of engineering.

AA *You always played it that way. I got the impression that when you pressed a button you knew that you would be telling someone else what to do.*

NN Yes, absolutely. Exactly. I certainly did not consider myself a token black, and I don't think anyone else did. I think maybe in retrospect one could see that there was a diminution of my speaking role, but [not of] the manner in which Gene insisted that it be a role of equality, on an equal basis as person to person . . .

AA *Do you think it was also equal on a male and female basis?*

NN There is no such thing [laughter], and that's a contradiction in terms in Hollywood.

AA *I'm recalling "City on the Edge of Forever," when they gave you the line, "Captain, I'm frightened."*

NN They did this often.

AA *I can't picture McCoy saying, "Jim, I'm scared . . ."*

NN Yes, but that's Hollywood: they express the emotion through the character that they feel best expresses it, and who better than a female? There was a point at which I argued that, and they just simply couldn't understand me. There were times of danger in which they were so valiant in taking care of the little lady. The women were always cringing. Are you joking? There is no way that in a crew of 450 people pretty much equally balanced between male and female that the women are not going to be given self-defense lessons.

AA *I always got the impression there were psychological requirements the people had to meet before they were assigned to the starship.*

NN Exactly. Of course. So I argued the point, and they would say, "I know, babe, I know, but we need this kind of almost female gentleness, tenderness. We can't just all be one whole dynamic superpeople . . ." They would argue with me, and I'd say, "Okay, forget it. I'll do it." It was many times a no-win situation. I was very lucky: I won some battles and I lost some battles. But back in that time it also bothered me to say, "Captain, I'm frightened," because I'm really very expressive, but that's Nichelle. I don't think Uhura would have [said that]. So it didn't bother me as much as implying that I couldn't fight. . . .

AA *How does it feel, knowing you're part of a legend?*

NN I'm delighted. I've always been proud of being part of that first and original thing that Gene Roddenberry wrote. Again, I wish that what he wrote and intended had been actualized on the screen, more fully. Enough of it was, for people to see through what wasn't, what was denied, and of course enough of the stories came off.

AA *For you, it's gone full circle, regarding your actual involvement in the space program. What were your feelings at the time of the shuttle disaster, considering your part in the astronaut recruitment program?*

NN Devastation. At least three of my astronauts were on board, and I just went into shock and seclusion, and into mourning.

The press from all over the world called me, and I denied interviews. I just could not deal with it, and although I and every astronaut knew that someday that day was coming, when are you ready for it? You get on that ship knowing, "This could be my last ticket," but would you get on that ship if you knew that if you went on the ship this *is* my ticket? So, it's very, very painful, and yesterday for the first time I took part in anything that had to do with any of the astronauts who were on there, acknowledging that I dealt with the disaster, I should say. I went to a dedication, as a guest speaker, part of a dedication for an elementary school to be dedicated to Dr. Ronnie McNair. I found him in California at Hughes during my recruitment, and he was one of the ones I was most close to . . . But the dedication was wonderful. He was also a teacher. His wife and their children were there. It was a most beautiful experience, and I realized I had to come out of mourning, and join in the celebration of those valiant people's lives, for what they gave, and what they were a part of, that our space program is still a valiant and glorious undertaking, and it's criminal negligence on our part to demean it, to destroy it, to do anything that might short-circuit it.

AA *Do you think the program has suffered because of the accident, or will suffer for it in the future?*

NN It's suffered tremendously, and at a time when this nation should have taken the bull by the horns and moved right back into it, and furthered it, and strengthened it. Congress instead indulges in this infuriating grandstand play and circus investigation. Let NASA do its work, let it find out what's wrong. Yes, find out what's wrong, correct it, and not all of these, "What are we spending all of this money in space for," kind of recriminations, "I told you so's," and, "I don't need it, anyway," until another Sputnik occurs, and then everybody goes hog-wild and crazy and asks, "Where is our space program?" I truly don't think we'll make that mistake again, but there are the nay-sayers who just cannot stand the idea of progress in any way, shape, form or fashion. However, we have some new astronauts, the first black woman astronaut has just been inducted, and our next shuttle, if the politicians leave us alone, is some time in 1988 or 1989.

AA *Are they still planning on building a space platform?*

NN They'd better, because Russia sure is. It's under contract, and I think the President has okayed it, so I think we shall. And, of course, in order to do that, you've gotta have your space shuttle.

AA   *Do you have anything you've always wanted to say to the fans of STAR TREK, but have never had the opportunity to say?*

NN   Oh, I think I say it every time I'm at a convention, and every time I'm with the fans. I think the most beautiful thing about STAR TREK, and the most important, is the fans, because it is . . . they who recognize what Gene was saying, what the philosophy was, the positiveness, and that beauty and that strength that they subscribe to and accept as fact. Non-Trekkers will see it as a fad, or an aberration of humanity, [but] if you're a Trekker, you really understand what it is that has ennobled and enriched your life, and that it's not just because you can paint yourself green or wear some costume or enter some dreamworld. It's a reaching, accepting . . . really a highest good. I believe that, so I would just say, "Keep on Trekking." To me, that's what saves mankind, that ability to dream and to make it real.

AA   *Have you ever thought of entering politics?*

NN   [laughs] Why do people say that?

AA   *Because you're a great speaker, and you'd be a vote-getter . . .*

NN   I see [laughter]. No, I have no aspirations for politics. I'm not that masochistic. If I thought that entering politics would ever make any difference, I might consider believing in it. . . . It's enough to exercise my vote and think for myself, but I think the whole political process is one that eventually eats away and diminishes the person with ideals and dreams with the need to compromise, and then to compromise, and then to compromise, and then to compromise, and finally you've forgotten what it was that you were out there fighting for. I wouldn't last five minutes, because I don't know how to do that, and I'd never want that to happen to me.

AA   *You're not a game-player.*

NN   Not where my values are concerned, and not where the honesty and truth of this situation is concerned, not when I'm playing with thousands, and maybe millions of people's lives and rights. I don't think I have that right.

AA   *So you're making your mark in the scientific community rather than in the political arena.*

NN   Yes, and by being a person . . . It's enough for me . . . All I wanted to do was to be an actress and a singer, and an entertainer, and to travel all over the world and entertain people.

AA   *. . . If someone told me there was an entertainer who started by dancing with Duke Ellington's band and finally worked for the space program recruiting astronauts . . .*

NN   . . . [laughs] Yes, exactly.

AA   *Let's just say you're atypical, very atypical.*

NN   Yes. I probably have always been.

WALTER KOENIG

*Following the production of STAR TREK's first season in Febru-
ary, 1967, it was decided that an additional officer would join the
Enterprise crew. By the beginning of May, when the series' second
season started production, Walter Koenig had been signed to portray
Ensign Pavel Andreivich Chekov.*

*Born in Chicago and raised in New York City, Walter began his
higher education at Iowa's Grinnell College, and earned his B.A.
degree in psychology at U.C.L.A. in Los Angeles.*

*After his graduation, Walter studied acting at The Neighborhood
Playhouse in New York, and appeared in Off-Broadway produc-
tions before beginning his television and feature film acting career in
Hollywood.*

*In addition to his frequent guest appearances at STAR TREK
conventions all over the world, Koenig has written a novel,* Buck
Alice and the Actor Robot, *to be published by Pyramid Books. He
is also the author of* Chekov's Enterprise, *a diary of the filming of
STAR TREK—THE MOTION PICTURE, now a sought-after
collector's item. Koenig stars in the soon-to-be-released feature*
Moontrap, *produced by Magic Lantern Productions.*

AA   *I've heard several stories about why Chekov was created for
the STAR TREK television series. What really happened?*

WK   Well, the facts are that they were looking for somebody who
would appeal to the bubble gum set. They had somebody in
mind like Davey Jones of THE MONKEES, and originally it
was supposed to be an English character to kind of break off
that segment of the audience; however, in acknowledge-
ment of the Russians' contribution to space they made the
decision to go that way. All that stuff about Pravda—you
know, the complaining—that's all nonsense. That was all
just publicity. But it was a very practical decision. They
wanted somebody who would appeal to eight-to-fourteen-
year-olds and they decided to make him a Russian.

AA   *Was it Joseph Pevney who brought you in?*

WK   No, not really. It was Joe D'Agosta, the casting director. I'd
known Joe. We had been friends for years and I had acted
with him. We did a terrible movie called *Strange Lovers* . . .
and he brought me to read for a MR. NOVAK episode
which [was about] a defecting Russian student, in 1964. I

didn't get the part initially. The director went with a very strange, very undisciplined actor with whom he was fascinated. However, they didn't have a completed script. When they finally did, Dean Jagger, who was one of the running leads in the show, became ill and since he was heavily involved in that episode, they postponed it. When they got around to shooting it, that first director was no longer available. They brought in Michael O'Herlihy, and Joe D'Agosta brought me back. I read literally two lines and got the part. Now, I give you all this preamble because three years later STAR TREK was the result of my doing that part as a Russian. Joe Pevney knew my work because I had done a lead for him on an ALFRED HITCHCOCK HOUR. And, in fact, Gene knew my work because I had done a lead for him in THE LIEUTENANT, so it was one of those fortuitous situations where everything came together. . . . I think Joe Pevney was very supportive, but I do believe it was Joe D'Agosta who brought me in.

AA *Mr. Pevney told me that he thought your performance in "Memo from Purgatory" was so remarkable, it was scary.*

WK Well, that's very sweet. Yeah, he thought I was going to be a big star. He told me, "Kid, you're going to be a star." It never happened, but it was very nice to hear it, and working with Joe Pevney on [STAR TREK] was a delight. He had directed every other episode during the second season. My best performances were given when he was directing, simply because he was relaxed, I didn't feel under a lot of pressure, and it was just a good environment to work in.

AA *In reference to "Memo from Purgatory," did you ever get any feedback from Harlan Ellison as to your performance?*

WK You know, Jimmy Caan played Harlan . . . I had gone to school with James Caan—we had gone to The Neighborhood Playhouse together—and I also went to school with Chris Lloyd. We didn't have as much to do together in STAR TREK III as I had with Jimmy in "Memo from Purgatory," but it was great fun. As I say, Joe Pevney was terrific to work for. And it was fun playing opposite Jimmy Caan. He was the protagonist, I was the antagonist, and that was a delight. That's how I got to meet Harlan, and a very volatile turbulent, unstable relationship has followed that is now working on its third decade.

AA *When you joined the show, did you find that you were immediately accepted into the STAR TREK family?*

WK I didn't really know enough to be too worried about all that, because I didn't know what the personalities involved were like. I wasn't too concerned. Nobody treated me badly.

George, of course, wasn't even there for the first eight or ten weeks. I don't even remember when I first started working with George, but I know he wasn't there because he was shooting *The Green Berets*. I remember Jimmy was friendly, De was friendly, and Leonard was always a little distant, because that's the way he was when he was in character. Bill was friendly enough. I never felt intimidated by him. Being the new kid on the block, I knew enough to keep my mouth shut most of the time. But I didn't know it was going to continue. I was told that the role might recur, but I wasn't given any guarantees. I wasn't under contract that first season. So, when they brought me back a second time it was a big bonus, and the third time, et cetera, but I never took anything for granted. It was very pleasant. I always found the people in the show very comfortable to be with.

AA   *So during Chekov's first appearance you thought it might be just a one-shot?*

WK   That's right. [Gene] said to me that there was a chance that it would recur, but actors hear that all the time. They're told that for various reasons—the money is short, the part isn't that big—so I didn't really have a great deal of faith in the possibility of my recurring. . . . First of all, STAR TREK at that point was stumbling, anyway. Secondly, I wasn't aware of the fan support, and thirdly I don't think I *felt* that I was necessarily going to continue, so I didn't have any sense of, "Gee, this is fantastic. I'm on a series . . ."

AA   *Before they told you, for a fact, that you were a regular on the show, what did you think of the caliber of the roles they gave you? Were you content?*

WK   Yes, I was content because this was a bonanza for me. I had never done a series. Like everybody else in Hollywood, I was struggling. I had done some leading roles, guest-starring roles on television shows, but the idea of getting a salary every week, or even every other week or however often they used me, was just terrific. First I had to get used to that before I could start complaining about the size of the roles. It is a fact that in the third season I asked for a month off to do a play in Chicago and in the process lost three episodes that I would otherwise have done, one of which was quite good. George took it, and it had to do with being on the planet—I don't know what it was about, but it was a good episode. In fact, in the episode Kirk says, "If I'd wanted such-and-such I would have had Chekov here." That was the one Chekov was supposed to [be in].

AA   *"That Which Survives . . ."*

WK   But I went off to do a play with Jackie Coogan in Chicago, or just outside Chicago, and I had the best month of my career.

AA   *What was it?*

WK   Oh, it was a piece of fluff called "Make a Million," a comedy, but working with Coogan was . . . working with a part of filmic history: this man had been around forever. He was a delight to be around, an inveterate, compulsive scene-stealer . . . We just had a great time. . . .

AA   *At the start of the second season the opposite had happened. George was off on location in* The Green Berets; *I guess it was only fair that he got "That Which Survives."*

WK   Oh, absolutely, absolutely. It obviously helped me when he was doing *Green Berets*. It was during that period that I got reasonably nice roles.

AA   *When did they tell you that Chekov was officially a recurring role?*

WK   They never told me. I'll tell you when it happened. Between the second and third seasons I called Gene and he invited me over to his house, we talked, and he took out some memos that were sent to him by the heads of NBC, and some memos from him to his staff, all of which said, let's develop the character of Chekov. He's gotten a lot of support, we can make him a vital member of the team and, in fact, he can become the fourth most important character on the show. Let's get him involved with women, girls, and the action, etc., etc., etc. We have a following for him out there. Now, that was Gene's intention; these were the memos that he had written at the end of the second season. That's when he thought he was going to be more directly involved in the show. When the circumstances changed and he withdrew, there was just a general lack of inspiration, I think, regarding how the show would go. The first episode that was shot in the third season was "Spectre of the Gun." That, I believe, was to be reflective of Chekov's participation during the course of the season, had not all these other things happened, had we not been switched from 8 o'clock Monday to 10 o'clock Friday. When that happened, Gene threw up his hands and we had a new producer in and things just changed remarkably.

AA   *In other words, "Spectre of the Gun" was laid out before Fred Freiberger came into the picture?*

WK   Absolutely . . . And there I was, down there with the principals, with the three star guys, Chekov had a love interest—all of that stuff. I believe that's the way the season would have gone. . . . I remember that Jimmy, George and I were out doing a layout on horseback for some fan

magazine when we found out that we had been switched. . . .
It was like a bolt of lightning. I knew immediately that my
situation had changed drastically. First of all, Monday at
eight o'clock the kids, the crowd that I was supposed to be
appealing to, are still up watching TV. At ten o'clock Friday,
they're either in bed or out on dates. As I sat on the horse,
I knew it was all over. It's really weird, but that's exactly
what happened.

AA   *A terrible, sinking feeling.*

WK   Yeah, yeah.

AA   *All the others must have gotten something akin to that, too.*

WK   I'm sure, because that suggested that the network did not
have a lot of faith in us. But my situation was even more
personal, because I knew that the involvement of the character would not develop the way I had anticipated. . . .
When Freiberger came aboard, I wrote him a three-page
memo saying how I thought Chekov could be developed
without subverting the story or other characters, instead of
just saying, "Aye, aye, Captain," and "Warp factor . . . ," to
give me a chance to do a couple of character lines integrated
into the story. His reaction was, "Forget it." However, I
think "The Way to Eden," coming on the heels of that
memo, was his effort to somehow appease me.

AA   *There was considerable pressure in the third season . . .*
Ralph Senesky told me he was fired in the middle of "The
Tholian Web" because he wasn't delivering as many scenes,
as many setups per day as he should have.

WK   Well, I think the network was disillusioned with us. They
weren't happy. They thought we were just playing out the
string and they were cutting costs as much as they could.
They told us they would pull the plug at 12 minutes after 6
because they were paying the craftspeople in units of 6
minutes of overtime and they would only permit two units of
overtime, two 6-minute units of overtime. So, certainly,
that was one of the reasons the quality of the show suffered
in the third season.

AA   *Do you have any favorite episodes in the series?*

WK   Well, "City on the Edge of Forever" is certainly one of my
favorites. I think it was the most moving episode, emotionally. Of the ones that I appeared in, I like "Who Mourns for
Adonais?" and I like "Spectre of the Gun." I wasn't totally
happy with my performance in "Spectre of the Gun," but I
liked the show, and I liked the character. I liked "I, Mudd"
and "Tribbles." Those are the four that come to mind, I
guess, even though I had a big part in "The Way to Eden." I
thought it was a pretty pedestrian show at best and I wasn't

thoroughly happy with that. I wasn't happy with the way it was directed and I wasn't happy with what the show had to say and how my character was depicted. I think I performed it okay but I don't think that's the way the character should have been.

AA *You had a very interesting involvement in the animated series, too. You wrote one.*

WK Yes, I wrote an episode. I don't know how interesting that was. It was a difficult thing to do because they kept asking for rewrites and kept asking me for more strange things . . . you know, talking vegetables wasn't my idea. My idea was simply the cloning of Spock. It wasn't all that wonderful, it was okay. Gene read a screenplay of mine, and on the basis of that screenplay offered me the job. You know, the other side of that was that they didn't involve me in the voices for the show . . . they didn't even draw the character. They had some alien [in place of Chekov]. And then I heard about not being in the show from a fan, which was really humiliating. Gene and Dorothy were at a convention in Los Angeles, and Dorothy had just finished talking to a group of fans about the animated STAR TREK and they spilled out of the room and they came to me and said, "How do you feel about not being in the animated episodes?" That's how I found out about that. It wasn't wonderful. I was upset about that. We're touching on a lot of things I was upset about, but . . . as infrequently as I was upset, I was many more times ecstatic about my involvement in STAR TREK.

AA *How were you first approached to appear in STAR TREK— THE MOTION PICTURE?*

WK . . . Back in 1975 or 1976 a letter was sent out by Gene to the members of the cast saying, Welcome aboard! We're doing STAR TREK again as a motion picture and look forward to seeing you all aboard the U.S.S. Enterprise. There was only one problem with that letter. One was never addressed to me. Naturally, a certain amount of paranoia creeps into one's being under those circumstances, but I was assured by Susan Sackett that that was obviously a mistake, the letter got lost in the mail. . . . She couldn't confirm that because Gene was out of town. However, when he did return, he did call me and it was no mistake. I was not going to be included because the story he had in mind was to take place three years before the five-year mission. Okay? Now, think about the math here. I was playing a character who I was nine years older than. This was six years after the show had gone off the air, so we're talking about an eighteen-year difference. . . . He didn't feel that I could play a character who was eighteen years younger than I was, which was reasonable. Having the disappointment of being told that I wasn't going to be involved in that first script, I was at first gun-shy. So when we were called back in to go into production . . . I was always a bit cynical and a bit skeptical. . . . And then when we were postponed once. . . . In fact, we went in and had costume fittings with Bill Theiss. Bill Theiss at that point was going to be the costume designer. . . .

AA *That's when it was still going to be a TV show called STAR TREK II?*

WK Yes . . . it was a two-hour movie for television, and the day we were supposed to come back—I'll never forget this—we were supposed to come in for the final fitting on the costumes. We got a call saying, Don't come in today. We'll let you know when. I don't remember how many days after that we found out that there had been a change and instead of a television movie, they were going to do a feature, a low-budget feature. Then it went through several other permutations and finally it became what it was. . . . As I related in the book I wrote, *Chekov's Enterprise,* a certain part of me still expected that somebody would say, "Okay: cut! No film. We're not going to shoot this after all." You know, to come back after all those years and make a motion picture . . . But I loved coming back, and I loved doing STAR TREK. . . . It was a great pleasure, and there were certain moments, very focused moments that were thrilling. It was thrilling to do that first setup, not when the camera was panning when we were all at our consoles—that big master shot—but when George, Nichelle and I moved forward to come into the shot with Bill as he stepped aboard onto the bridge and we were standing there as they were lighting it. That was an absolutely thrilling moment, to be back after all those years, to actually have it happen, one time in a lifetime that a dream actually becomes reality and, as I said in the book, I wanted to embrace them. You know, I really had to suppress the desire to give everybody a big hug. That was a glorious moment . . .

AA *How did you come to write your book?*

WK A couple of friends of mine kept telling me that I should, and I think I did it as much from that, from their encouragement, and from the fact that there was so much time to kill on the set . . . and most of the time when you have those really long, long days . . . you sit around, you do crossword puzzles, you play chess, you read a novel, but I thought this was an opportunity to really make use of that time. There was nothing very challenging for me in the role that I had to give a great deal of my attention to, and I discovered that it was really fun to log the things that were happening on the set, and interesting things *were* happening. I don't think I could have written the book if we had been actually limited to our original shooting schedule. We were supposed to work on it—George, Jimmy, Nichelle and I—for four or five weeks. That was our original contract. We ended up working sixteen weeks, but that was very fortunate in terms of writing the book. There was that much more to write about.

AA *How did the others in the cast and crew react to having all these events chronicled?*

WK Oh, they never knew I was writing. I never told anyone else because I was afraid of static from somebody, and I wanted to get as natural a response as I could, one that was not clouded by their concern that their words were going to be immortalized.

AA *Your cynicism came through in the book, but it was so wonderfully funny, the irony that you brought out in so many places. I felt I was on the set while I was reading it.*

WK Good! Good!

AA *What were your reactions during the filming of STAR TREK II?*

WK I was very pleased, very happy with the working circumstances. I loved working with Nick [Meyer], a nice man, incredibly bright, and not only bright but knowledgeable in so many areas and, since most of my stuff was with Ricardo [Montalban] and Paul Winfield, that was super. Total professionals, no ego problems whatsoever . . . I remember watching an early rehearsal and Ricardo would occasionally wax poetic. Nick was almost a neophyte in terms of his involvement with the industry, although certainly he had qualifications to be directing. He was very young in the business. He would suggest to [Ricardo] that he was kind of overdoing it, and Ricardo's response was just as professional as could be: he would say, "Aaahh. I think you're right," and then he'd try it another way. . . . On STAR TREK III I was so unhappy going in that I don't think I would have written a very funny book. . . . STAR TREK IV was wonderful. I don't want to sound like a total malcontent because I enjoyed STAR TREK—THE MOTION PICTURE, I had a great time on STAR TREK II and I had a sensational time on IV . . . I thought it was a joyous film. I think the performances, and the scenes between Leonard and Bill, were wonderful. . . .

AA   *Your best moment in IV has to be when you ask the way to the nuclear "wessels."*

WK   Well, thank you, but you know, Harve wrote for me and Nick wrote for me very specific scenes and I was eternally grateful. . . . I think there was a tremendous amount of mail supporting the relationships or applauding the relationships as they were in STAR TREK IV. The Spock-Kirk relationship was delightful and the McCoy-Spock relationship was really quite exciting, too. I thought STAR TREK IV was a delightful picture. The biggest surprise was seeing Leonard's performance because I'd never seen him work in the picture, except for the scenes in which he was behind us on the bridge, but those individual scenes . . . those scenes with Bill, I'd never actually seen. That was *the* most effective performance he'd given as Spock because he maintained the sense of emotional distance and at the same time there was a wonderful underpinning of compassion to the character—you know, the little moments, just little moments . . . just very touching, when he's chastised by McCoy in the hold of the ship— His response—I mean, just the look on his face was terrific. So, I'm pleased for him, for his success, for the picture's success, and I'm very pleased to have been part of that.

AA   *Well, the odds are that the next one will be funny to an extent, lighthearted, at any rate.*

WK   I don't think so . . . I mean, I don't think we have to do the same kind of picture. In fact, if I had my druthers, if I had been given the opportunity to write a STAR TREK film, I would want to write the ultimate boo!—something that would scare the daylights out of the audience, but without any graphic violence: I don't go for blood-spattered lenses and that stuff. I think you can be much more threatening and scary if it's offscreen. . . .

AA   *You mean like Val Lewton's films?*

WK   Yeah, yeah . . . The greatest scene that I've ever seen in a film that did that so beautifully was the early version of *Oliver Twist,* when the woman is getting beaten up in the room. . . . The bad guy is beating her up and the dog is scratching to get out of the room, and the panic of the dog scratching at the door is more frightening, terrifying, than all of the blood and open wounds that you might have seen.

AA   *To what do you attribute STAR TREK's continued success?*

WK   I think they are myriad, the elements or components of that answer. In terms of sociology, I think there's a "bandwagon effect." I really believe that. . . . It just seems to snowball, like fans. . . . It becomes the "in" thing. I think to a certain degree, that was the case with STAR TREK. I think more important, of course, was the other sociological factor that advertisers, the people involved in promoting products, always adhered to: if you repeat something often enough, people are going to believe it, and we were in syndication so frequently, not on a weekly basis or even a daily basis, but on a multiple daily basis. We were seen in some areas two and three times a day. I think it was very difficult to ignore TREK. I think that those people who might not have had an affinity for it otherwise finally convinced themselves that, well, if it's on this often and there are those people who are enthusiastic about it, it must be good. Now, that's part of the bandwagon effect, I think. Beyond that, I think there are certain intrinsic qualities to STAR TREK that make it a very attractive show and quality show: characters are dimensional, particularly the three most-featured performers; stories are innovative—the best ones have been—good science fiction written by science fiction writers as opposed to people who wrote in other genres and just extrapolated for the "space" medium. We of course suggested a future that was very positive, one in which people could work together and love together and where there would be a one-world society to a certain extent, where ethnicity, cultural differences were not ignored or wiped out—they all existed—we still maintained our individuality, but were able to function as a whole, as a unit. All that, I think, is very attractive. So, I think those things, a very hopeful future, good scripts, well-developed characters, the constant repetition in syndication, the bandwagon effect—all of that, I think, contributes to the success that STAR TREK has had.

AA   *What is the attitude of your own family about STAR TREK? Does you wife accept the phenomenon?*

WK   Well, yes, she accepts it. I think she distances herself a little bit from it. I asked her to attend conventions with me, but with a few exceptions, she generally decides not to go. One of the reasons, of course, is that it's so time consuming there isn't very much time to do anything else. My son's an actor. In fact, he's going to be a semiregular on GROWING PAINS this season. He's had an abiding enthusiasm for the show and he expressed over the last three or four days that he would like a guest spot on STAR TREK: THE NEXT GENERATION. I'm sure his agent will submit him for that. And then my daughter: She's a fan as well. They're all supportive. . . . We went to Australia because of STAR TREK. We went to England twice. I went to the Bahamas, as well as practically every place in this country, so there certainly have been ancillary benefits that can't be denied and my family has also benefited from them.

AA *Is there anything that you've always wanted to say to the STAR TREK fans that you never had a chance to say?*

WK A thing that I always want to say to the fans, and I have on occasion, although it starts to sound a little mawkish or mushy, is the gratitude I think we all feel. You know . . . I think we owe them and their passion and their dedication an enormous debt of gratitude. Sure, there are people as there are in anything, in any popularly supported movement or group or whatever, that stretch one's patience, but SATURDAY NIGHT LIVE to the contrary, generally the fan population of STAR TREK's supporters out there have been a godsend. If it hadn't been for their enthusiasm, the fact that they write letters, that they attend conventions, that they are just there in numbers, that they go back to the films three and four and five times—there wouldn't be any STAR TREK today and I think we must never lose sight of that. I mean, certainly what put us over the top this time in STAR TREK IV, that got us over one hundred million dollars in box office, is the fact that we brought in people who are not STAR TREK fans, but if we didn't have that base of seventy-five million dollars in tickets, then the additional thirty or forty million dollars wouldn't have been very imposing. So, hallelujah to the STAR TREK fans for sticking with us these 20 years, introducing their kids and other assorted relatives and making it a second- and third-generation thing.

[Mr. Koenig can be reached at P.O. Box 4395, North Hollywood, CA, 91607.]

GRACE LEE WHITNEY

Born in Ann Arbor, Michigan, Grace Lee Whitney started singing for Detroit's radio station WJR at the age of 14. Three years later, Grace went to Chicago to become a model and a nightclub singer.

The ultimate dream of a Broadway career came true for Grace at the age of 21, when she was cast in Top Banana *with Phil Silvers, Jack Albertson, and Kaye Ballard.*

After beginning a busy schedule understudying the play's star and training with Jack Albertson, she accompanied the cast to Hollywood to appear in the film version of Top Banana *(1954, United Artists). Other film appearances followed, including* Some Like it Hot.

Grace's work in STAR TREK began shortly before "The Corbomite Maneuver" started production in May, 1966. She was the first one who posed for series publicity photos with William Shatner and Leonard Nimoy.

Although she appeared as Janice Rand in only seven STAR TREK episodes, and the features STAR TREK—THE MOTION PICTURE, STAR TREK III and STAR TREK IV, Grace Lee Whitney is a solid member of the STAR TREK family. A welcome and frequent guest at STAR TREK conventions, Grace is every bit as energetic and enthusiastic as most of the series' fans.

AA   *How did you become involved with STAR TREK?*

GW   I was in a pilot that Gene did called POLICE STORY. I was Lt. Lily Monroe, De Kelley was a lab scientist and Steve Ihnat was the police officer. That did not sell, and STAR TREK did. They took Grace Lee Whitney and De Kelley and put us in the STAR TREK series. I replaced Andrea Dromm, who had portrayed the Yeoman in the second pilot. Why I replaced her is something I don't know. When they tried out the POLICE STORY pilot in the preview theater, they had little audience response buttons. When Sgt. Lily Monroe came on the screen, Gene Roddenberry said all the bells went off, and he saw the reaction in the theater. He took me from there, and put me in STAR TREK because he wanted me to ring the bells. When I got into STAR TREK they tried to change that image, and it never really did get to the point where it was going to go. . . .

AA   *The first portrait photos taken of you for STAR TREK show you with a hairstyle you did not wear in the series.*

GW   That was before they put the wig on: they made the wig after that.

AA   *Who designed that wig?*

GW   Bill Theiss.

AA   *In those photos, you were wearing the same costume worn by Andrea Dromm in "Where No Man Has Gone Before."*

GW   I was in pants. I rebelled, because to me it should have been a big belt with a short skirt, boots, and long legs. That's what I saw. And when I said that to Bill Theiss, he had the same image. Bill designed the shorts with the skirt lap over the top: the famous uniform.

AA   *Whose idea were the pants?*

GW   I don't know. They were in the pilots, before I got there. When we put legs into the format I think that helped sell the series.

AA   *What do you think of the costume you wore in the series?*

GW   I thought it was sensational. It stopped traffic, and being an egocentric actress, the more attention I could get, the better.

AA *Were you happy with what they gave you to do?*

GW Yes.

AA *Did you have any experience with science fiction before you became involved with STAR TREK?*

GW I did an OUTER LIMITS episode, "Controlled Experiment." I didn't do any TWILIGHT ZONEs, but I watched it. I was fascinated with it. . . . I also love THUNDERBIRDS. My children and I were fascinated with that show. And then, of course, SPACE: 1999, with Martin Landau and Barbara Bain. They were on the next stage doing MISSION: IMPOSSIBLE while we were doing STAR TREK, and she would always come over to our set and look at us. She was fascinated with our costumes and the way we were. . . . And whenever I hear a fan putting down SPACE: 1999 I always say, "Don't do that," because Barbara Bain appeared in "1999" due to her fascination with STAR TREK.

AA *Why were you written out of the STAR TREK format?*

GW Well, there are a lot of things that come into it. I see it now. I'm 56 years old now. I'm a recovered alcoholic . . . an addict for five and a half years. I think I was written out because of my alcoholism. I think that I was difficult to work with, demanding and rather unpredictable. And I was on diet pills. When I first began to be talked to about doing the series, a doctor gave me diet pills to lose ten pounds, and I became addicted to diet pills. My behavior was erratic. Now, I'm telling you this out of hindsight. This is just now being revealed to me at five and a half years clean and sober.

AA *What did you think about it then? Did you have any idea of what was happening to you at the time?*

GW I only knew that my face blew up and they couldn't make me beautiful. The first half year of STAR TREK I looked wonderful, and then I came into work one morning to Fred Phillips, and I said, "My God, what's wrong with me?" What had happened was that I'd become anorexic from [having] no food, and when I went home at night I would drink to calm down. Well, we all partied a lot: this was a very partying group. It's just that I had the allergy. I did not know. And I know now that I have an allergy. That's what the disease is. And I came into work and I said, "Look at me," and I was bloated.

AA *Is that why in the last episode you appeared in you're only seen for a few minutes?*

GW No . . . You could not see this unless you actually looked for it. . . . It was very obvious to me in "Charlie X." When I see the reruns, I see my face.

AA *But it wasn't obvious to anyone else?*

GW No, because of this disease. From what I am learning, most people walk around with it and die from it and don't even know that they have it. I think I may be able to help somebody if I come clean and say that I now see.

AA *When did you realize you had a problem?*

GW After I was fired, after they let me go. My agent called and said, "[They] are not going to renew your contract. They're writing you out . . ." I was very popular with the media because I was very glib and very eager. In fact, maybe I overshadowed a few other people. . . . I now see that I may have antagonized a few other people through my desire to please and through my egocentricity. When I was let go, it was the first psychic pain I had ever felt in my life except when my mother told me I was adopted. I was nine years old, and I remember the same pain. I remember realizing that I was not living with my mother and father, and wondering who they were and why I was not living with them. I stuffed all those feelings away when I was 9 years old. I was now 35 years old and I had just been removed from the absolute family that I loved, which was STAR TREK, and I had the same psychic pain. I was rejected again, and that triggered my spiral into alcoholism. . . . I had to drink from 1966 to 1981. I had to go in and out of this disease and try to fix it with all kinds of things. I got sober and clean on April 13, 1981. I was free of everything, the obsession was removed. Through 1981 to now, 1986, my life is being revealed to me, and this is what I'm finding out . . . I am not cured, I am simply recovering, and today I am clean and sober, very much in love with God. And I'm here to serve other people, not to take, anymore. I'm here to give.

AA *Regarding your part in STAR TREK IV, are you content with your participation in it? Would you like to have participated more?*

GW One of the things in my disease that I related to the most was when they said, *"More is the alcoholic's middle name."* In other words, we can never get enough. Part of my recovery is to be grateful for what I do have, so I am going to say to you that today I am grateful that I had the two weeks' work that I had, that I was in whatever I was in, and Leonard allowed me to say, "Commander Chapel, this is Chief Rand." He allowed me to say my name in the film. That's a first! I'm more than happy.

AA *Who approached you to work in the film?*

GW It was Leonard who called me . . . Harve Bennett, I guess, had said "yes," that they wanted both Chapel and Rand in it

. . . and I even had a little cameo in III, which is more than she had. So they put both of us back in and gave us a scene together, and gave us a lot of dialogue of gobbledegook— five pages of it that we had to learn. So the two of us got a chance for the whole week: we were there to read this dialogue. Even though they weren't going to shoot it all, we got a chance to act, actually read this stuff and react to one another, and do it. And it was great. They didn't even shoot one quarter of what we had to read to each other, but it really made us feel a part of it. At least it made *me* feel a part of it.

AA *And may I observe that you look just wonderful.*

GW Thank you. It's been just so wonderful to be able to share this. You're the first person with whom I've shared this, and you know they say that we're as sick as our secrets. I just want to unburden myself.

AA *And I think it will help tremendously if there are any people out there who are a part of the STAR TREK scene who require such assistance.*

GW Yes, yes, yes.

THE PILOTS

THE ARTISTS REPRESENTED IN THIS CHAPTER SUC-
CESSFULLY TACKLED SOME OF THE MOST DIFFICULT
ASSIGNMENTS IN STAR TREK HISTORY WITH THEIR
CONTRIBUTIONS TO THE SERIES FORMATIVE SEGMENTS,
THE PILOTS "THE CAGE" AND "WHERE NO MAN HAS
GONE BEFORE."

ROBERT BUTLER

Robert Butler's direction of "The Cage" (filmed in November and December 1964) involved him in the genesis of the STAR TREK legend. Equally at home directing television comedy or drama, Butler directed eight segments of BATMAN, including the series' pilot ("Hey, Diddle Riddle"/"Smack in the Middle"). Butler recalls preventing the pilot from becoming too funny:

". . . Adam [West, the actor who played Batman] and I had a pleasant running battle. . . . It wasn't conflict, it was fun, but he kept sneaking in jokes and I kept taking them out because I thought they were too cute . . ."

Butler's serious television directing credits include episodes of HAVE GUN WILL TRAVEL, GUNSMOKE, THE FUGITIVE, KUNG FU, and MISSION: IMPOSSIBLE, as well as two genre TV movies, Death Takes a Holiday *(1971) and* Strange New World *(1975).*

Robert Butler remains very active in television today. As of this writing, his most recent assignment was Out On a Limb, *a five-hour television movie (aired in January 1987), based on Shirley MacLaine's autobiography.*

AA   *Congratulations on the Shirley MacLaine TV movie.*

RB   Thanks. The reviews, as you know, were medium on her but they were good to the rest of us, so at least in the professional zone we're all very proud of it. I noticed the reviewers picked on her about her ego, her self-centered stance on the thing. I don't know. I never thought about that much. I was more interested in the straight line between the material and the audience, and making that as clean as possible.

AA   *It reminds me of "The Cage," which also dealt with themes difficult to depict on film.*

RB   Yes. That's interesting, because when I first read the STAR TREK pilot, I hesitated heavily just because it wasn't very clear to me. I thought Gene had done a terrific showcase of the science fiction elements, and yet it was so chock-full of them that it was hard for me to follow. I am not particularly a fan of science fiction but not an opponent of it, either. I was told later by NBC that—I don't remember if this is exactly what they said at the time—their perception was, "We like it, we believe it, we don't get it, do it again."

AA   *I have heard that they said it was "too cerebral."*

RB   Yes, that would certainly be a network approach. I would say that's pretty accurate.

AA   *Is that to say it had no fistfights?*

RB   Yes, it might come to that but as it turned out, the series generically didn't have fistfights. I think they simply thought the audience wouldn't get it, that it was too unclear or too thoughtful. So I would think we're both right on the point.

AA   *How did you first meet Gene Roddenberry?*

RB   He hired me on THE LIEUTENANT to do some episodes. I think I might have done either two or four. He liked my work on THE LIEUTENANT very much, and I suppose that at that green point I was beginning to formulate stuff that I've done since: very real, very dry, and very naturalistic, and I suppose he liked that and responded to it. He was a cop, you know, and he must have a feeling about naturalism in spite of his enthusiasm for science fiction. So he must have thought I was good casting because of my kind of true touch in the science fiction zone, and I got along with him. I enjoyed working with him, and vice versa.

AA   *Do you remember any changes that you wanted in the script for "The Cage"?*

RB   I do remember beginning to try to suggest to Gene that the stuff was impossible . . . terrific and entertaining, but impossible. I remember trying to get Gene into a conversation like that, and as a "hired gun" director one is careful at such points because the producer-writer is usually pretty blind in terms of seeing the forest for the trees. I remember trying to suggest to Gene that we ought to do some straightening out, or that at least we should discuss it, and I remember thinking that Gene was too far into it, so I just gave up. It seems to me we had a conversation as I was considering taking the job, and from my perspective the conversation was, "Are we going to go with this, or would you consider any minor surgery?" and he said in so many words, "No, I wouldn't consider any minor surgery," and the conditions under which he said that were such that he just couldn't see any minor surgery. He was too close to it. It taught me always to speak out, subsequently, but anyway that's the way I remember it. I don't think Gene might remember such a scene. I was political and I was careful about it, because what does it get you to start yelling at the producer-writer about the obscurity of his script?

AA   *Did you have casting approval?*

RB   I think directorially what happens in series work is that you have a veto. It certainly happens today, and I'm pretty sure it was the case then. If you say with conviction and proof, "This person isn't really going to make it in the long pull, and here's why," I think you will be heard. The major roles are really the turf of the network and the producer. After all, they're the ones who get intimately and continuously into a show, and the director is very often a hired gun to give what he can, and then move on.

AA   *Then when you came in, Jeffrey Hunter and Susan Oliver were already cast?*

RB   I don't think so. I think Susan was cast after I got there. I had known her from the PLAYHOUSE 90 period and knew her to be an excellent actress. I did not know Jeff, except professionally from a distance, not personally at all, and I thought he was probably a good, chiseled hero for that kind of part. I remember thinking, "God, he's handsome," and this was sadly the opinion of him at the time. When one is trying to bring reality into an unreal situation, that usually isn't a wise thing to do, to hire a somewhat perfect looking actor. You should find someone who seems to be more natural and more "real." I don't remember saying those things, but that continues to be my view, and I probably prefaced by saying, "But, fellas, it's your ball game, and your money. I just feel that I have to mention that to you."

AA   *Hunter had just finished an unsuccessful series, TEMPLE HOUSTON.*

RB   Yes. I think that the situation then was in its way much as it is now. The scramble for the chiseled, naturalistic, 35-year-old American male is a killer. And to find that guy, around whom you can wrap a series, and on whose shoulders you can place the whole thing, is a task. Whether Jeff was a compromise candidate, or whether everyone believed in him at the time, I don't know. When the eleventh hour approaches, you finally have to take your money and bet it. That's always the case.

AA   *Do you recall anything about Jeffrey Hunter's attitude regarding "The Cage"?*

RB   Only generally that he was an extremely pleasant, centered guy, and maybe decent and nice to a fault. But he was very amenable and very trusting . . . kind of a gentle guy.

AA   *Joseph D'Agosta told me he cast the STAR TREK pilots over the phone because he was at 20th Century-Fox at the time.*

RB   . . . And he was just helping Gene.

AA   *Yes, exactly.*

RB   He had done THE LIEUTENANT. Is that right?

AA *Yes.*

RB That's where I met Joe. He is a very "savvy" guy, and I'm sure that was a satisfactory arrangement. It sounds like the whole thing might have been pretty hurried, and pretty thrown together.

AA *I've always wondered why Susan Oliver is not a more popular performer. She's a wonderful actress and a beautiful woman.*

RB I think that's an accurate comment. It's testimony once again to the big arm of luck being in on all of these things. I think of James Dean dying before *Somebody Up There Likes Me.* He had the part . . . he was cast in *Somebody Up There Likes Me,* and then on a last trip out of town to relax before the shoot, that's when he was killed and Paul Newman was put in at the last minute. It's easy to see now, 30 years later, that Paul Newman is immense and all the rest. But at that moment it could have been that if James Dean had lived there would be no Paul Newman today. He might be doing good TV shows and commercials . . . When we see Paul now, we see not only a terrific actor, which he was then, too, but we see that seasoning, that confidence, that fame, and that wealth all in the guy. And that's 25 or 30 years of excellent work and success. You don't have it when you're a young person. Luck is immense.

AA *How did Susan Oliver react to having that horrifying makeup transformation?*

RB I don't remember exactly, but I think that would be fun for any actress: a real crazy trip, to be able to pose and be lovely one moment, and then a moment later be all gnarled and bent over. I think she probably got a great kick out of it. . . .

AA *Wasn't the Orion Slave Girl sequence considered risqué for television at the time?*

RB I don't know. I remember my reaction was, ". . . Are we doing Hollywood, or are we doing something spiffy here?" That would be my typical reaction. I recall thinking, ". . . Oh, God, those costumes, and that belly dancing: are we doing Victor Mature over again?"

AA *It reminded me of a 20th Century-Fox film called* Princess of the Nile *in which Jeffrey Hunter goes through the same scene with Debra Paget.*

RB I don't think I ever saw that picture, but that was a great Hollywood standard at the time: it was a great chestnut, the bare feet, the little anklets and all that stuff, and I thought, "Dare we?" I remember that generally I was wincing and wondering if we were going to get away with that.

AA *Do you remember anything about the treatment of Spock at that time? Was he just supposed to be a subordinate crewman in the background?*

RB I don't remember very well. I have thought since that a good actor bringing his notion to a cool part with different ears was about the size of it, and whether his detachment and anti-emotionality developed, or whether we were granted that in the original, I don't know. I would rather think that developed, and Leonard brought that and Gene either wrote to it or discovered it, and then it bloomed. I don't know which. But I can remember Leonard saying that he got some pretty weird fan mail because of his ears, and the joke he made was, ". . . and his commensurate organs," or something like that. But that was funny. Because of a lot of reasons, Spock was an extremely attractive character right off the bat. And I would like to think that he was foreign but still not so foreign that he was inaccessible and uncomfortable for audiences. We could make the jump to his planet without its causing us any emotional discomfort. I think that's where the success of his character lies. Leonard was always thought to be a very fine character actor, really. He is a handsome guy, but he is dark, and God knows then that it was certainly more WASP than it is now in terms of our perception of the leading American male, and that might have been why he was thought of as a character man.

AA *Gene Roddenberry has stated that NBC wanted the character of Spock removed from the format.*

RB I do not remember that. Maybe I didn't even know it at the time. That would have been discussed on another level, between Gene and the network people, to the exclusion of myself and others.

AA *Do you recall whose idea it was to have the Talosians played by actresses?*

RB It think it might have been mine. When I saw the characters in the script I thought that it would be interesting to get a difference, and one easy difference is to cast women just because of their size and grace, and then add voice-overs later. Therefore you get an oddness, an antisexuality that certainly might be more the case in other galactic cultures than our own, and I think that might have been my notion. But at the same time I remember that when I mentioned it to Gene he had had a similar feeling that we should go bizarre, so there was not much discussion if it was my idea. If I said, "Hey, let's do that," he might have said, "Yeah, I get it, it's a good idea," or vice versa.

AA   *In an earlier draft of the script the Talosians were described as crablike creatures that would have required stop-motion animation or special costumes.*

RB   Yes, yes, and I think that probably even then I didn't trust all that stuff because the zipper can show so easily.

AA   *Is that why you didn't show too much of the other creatures in the cages?*

RB   I think that's accurate, because I'm so terrified of the zipper showing in every job I get, in whatever discipline it is. That's one of the big directorial preoccupations. That's what you get paid to prevent from showing.

AA   *Had you worked with Meg Wyllie before?*

RB   I had worked with Meg, and I thought she was a terrific actress. I once told her that I thought that maybe she would have been better than the actress who opened *Death of a Salesman*. I had worked with Meg on other episodes, and she is really an exquisitely gifted gal. When the femininity idea came up for the Talosians, I thought of Meg because I thought it would have been challenging to her, and amusing to her to do that, and I just thought she'd do it really well.

AA   *My favorite in the cast, other than the leads, is John Hoyt.*

RB   Yes, as a matter of fact, I'm not really proud of this, but as I was casting the doctor, I was against DeForest. As a younger guy I guess I felt that he was somewhat more of a heavy. At the time, I remember thinking that he was somewhat earthbound. Maybe I thought his youth at the time defied reality somewhat, whereas if we got a seasoned veteran in there, that might bring us a great spread of reality in our main people.

AA   *Joseph D'Agosta recalls discussing an "old country doctor" image.*

RB   That might have been it. It sounds typical of me to say, "Look, let's don't cast anybody heroically. Let's cast some characters in this bunch, or it's going to look totally synthetic." I remember Gene stood up for DeForest to the end, but ultimately he backed me and went with John Hoyt. . . . Hoyt's a really nice actor. I think every spring he's in a festival in the San Fernando Valley. I think he's always over there doing a lot of Shakespeare recitations and so on.

AA   *Along with Ian Wolfe?*

RB   That's probably right.

AA   *Do you recall anything about Peter Duryea [who played navigator Joe Tyler]?*

RB   I think Peter was simply a good choice from casting. I think we had seen a lot of people, and I remember that he had terrific energy. He was a spark plug type, I liked him a lot, and he has disappeared. That could be luck, too, because he was a good, young actor.

AA *So was Adam Roarke [who played the young, dark-haired geologist].*

RB Yes, that's right. I see Adam once in a while, and he hasn't fared as well as a lot of people, and he's damn good.

AA *You had another interesting character in there, Clegg Hoyt as the transporter chief.*

RB I remember. He was always a freaky, funky western character. That was a good move, I think, because he always brought a reality to anything he did. . . . I have a feeling that he is not with us, and hasn't been for maybe ten years.

AA *Were you involved in the discussions regarding the designs of Franz Bachlin and Pato Guzman?*

RB Only to this extent: I remember pleading to get some vertical structures in the bridge, because that was just too clean for me . . . I remember thinking that either Franz's heritage was such that he wanted to do "clean," which is to say maybe older Hollywood, or Gene's [heritage] was, and that he had been brainwashed by some futurist who had forgotten to consider that stuff wears out in the future, too. I remember trying like hell to shake up that bridge, and it fell on heavily deaf ears, and that clean set was the result. I remember that it was dense with people and opinions, because it was science fiction and it was the future, and there was the problem of getting it through the lens, and the problem of being true to what might be a fact in the future, and also it's so free that everybody's insecure. [In science fiction] you can do anything: it's just absolutely free. You can do virtually anything you want to in your design, and that always makes for lots of discussion, lots of committees and lots of ideas: tediously, in my view, but I remember that was a part of being involved in that show. I don't remember much about it, and I'm not particularly scarred by it, but I do remember that it was pretty dense with people and opinions, which I always find a little tedious. . . . I remember thinking that when Bill Snyder shot it, he made it too pretty. But as you hear, that's my view generally. Anytime I get into a clean situation, I start grinding my teeth. And obviously STAR TREK was a clean situation. So I really can't accuse *it* of being wrong, I can more accurately say that I was in a situation that makes *me* less than comfortable. I'm also reminded that in rehearsal I wanted to remove the exclamation point from the melodrama. Instead of something like, "Harry, I've just found the *key*!," I wanted to remove that exclamation point and play the show more the way *The Thing* that [Howard] Hawks produced was played. It was extremely dry and verité, and all the rest of it. And in Gene's enlarged reality it simply did not work. It was flat as hell. . . .

AA   *That's odd, because Mr. Roddenberry later stated that you mustn't get overly preoccupied with "the immensity of it all." I'd have thought he would have appreciated having the Enterprise crew act as cool and seasoned professionals.*

RB   Well, that actually happened in my secret domain. I didn't tell anybody what I was doing. I probably expressed it to the actors as we were rehearsing, and then we got to whatever was the equivalent of a run-through. . . . I never stage, the staging of the cameras has never bothered me, so I just sort of play radio in my rehearsal, to get the tone, the sound and the behavior right . . . and as we finished our rehearsals, I remember starting to think, "I'm wrong. I don't think I'm right about this," and I rechecked and fiddled for a while, and then finally I just said to the actors, "Hey, folks, this was a noble experience, but all I can tell you is that it's death, so let's bring to it what we normally bring to it," and that's a certain intensity and a certain elevation of the dramatic moment, a certain hyperbole and exclamatory quality, and all that. And I was OK discovering that and saying that to them, because I'm very self-conscious about size, and oversizing things. So I was satisfied that what we should do is just bring it back up a bit so it wouldn't seem quite so dry and flat, and ultimately that's what we did. I suppose in the eyes of others it was still kind of realistic and not overly stated, and so on.

AA   *I think that if the series had been done that way it would have been gorgeous, but it would probably have lasted for half a season at the most.*

RB   Yes, that's interesting because it underlies that in that heightened, melodramatic situation you have to lift the performances up into that style.

AA   *Were you there when they were doing the early costume and makeup tests?*

RB   Yes. I don't remember much about that. I remember Susan's transformation was certainly laid out and discussed and worked out ahead of time, and then it was very time-consuming to do, of course. I remember there was a glitch on the uniforms on the first day: something was really corny, and the first day of production with the meter running heavily, Gene just shut down for a couple of hours, or whatever time it took to fix this particular thing in the wardrobe.

AA   *I recall seeing some early test shots with very simple costumes that looked almost like coveralls.*

RB   You remind me that there was a lot of discussion about what the look should be. It's interesting . . . I pride myself on this thought. I remember to some extent begging Gene and company not to do a new show, a new world, a new bunch of costumes, a new craft. I begged him to do a timeworn craft that had been up there for twenty years, a captain who had been out there for seven, etc., and it all fell on deaf ears. I really like that much, much better. Not long ago, I got into heavy discussions with Harve Bennett about doing the second feature. The first movie was very expensive, and was run through the feature department at Paramount. Then Harve was hired to run the subsequent movies through the television department with greater economy applied. And though Harve didn't offer me the job, we talked about my doing the thing, and I've known him forever, so it was easy to say, "Harve," in so many words, ". . . Let's save time for both of us and don't hire me if you want to do it clean, because I want to do it dirty. I want to do weathered uniforms, and all the rest of it," and he said, "Well, it's good we're having this conversation because in my view the fans are going to expect what they've seen, which is to say a clean show," and I said, "Well, it doesn't sound like I'm your best guy." So we just agreed to have dessert and forget it. But I still like that idea, and it was certainly proven in STAR WARS . . .

AA   *. . . And in almost everything they've come out with since . . .*

RB   . . . and it brings a great reality and a great frailty and humanity to what is potentially sterile stuff. Anyway, I'm satisfied that I was right and they were wrong at that point, but it didn't have much to do with the success of the show. I understand they did the last STAR TREK movie a little raunchier. They returned to Earth. Whether or not I was the source of that idea, I don't know. Anyway, that was one discussion we had.

AA   *Did you have anything to do with the postproduction processes of editing the music and effects into the film?*

RB   As an ex-musician I'm usually into the music discussions. I don't remember specifically on that gig. Because of my general conscientiousness I'm usually heavily into editing, which in that instance would have been partially governed by the special effects requirements, and I remember after doing that show thinking, ". . . I've got to stay away from science fiction for a while," because there are constraints. When you feel like moving the camera and you need visual tricks, you just can't move the camera because of the visual effects that have to be applied later, so you're a little hamstrung here and there.

AA   *What was your overall impression with the finished product?*

RB   I think I was probably provisionally happy with it. I always wonder about synthetics: the zipper showing is just a real dread of mine, and I think I probably worried about that. I probably felt old Hollywood here and there as we used a camera crane, or as Franz Bachelin brought his perspective to it.

AA   The film was also shot on the old Selznick lot.

RB   Yes, that's right, it was. I'm pretty sure I probably thought to myself, "Well, if they understand it, great, but wow—we should have made it easier for them." I'm pretty sure I persisted in that feeling, although it would just have been negative to have said that to Gene at that point because, alluding to the script discussion again, he just wasn't entertaining other thoughts. STAR TREK was ultimately a heavy success. So I guess we've got to assume that he was more correct than I was on that point. I'm pretty harsh for about a year. It takes me a year to get kind and to get a little perspective. So I think during the first year, and after the assembly and the answer print [the first complete print of a film] and all that stuff I think I was probably still thinking to myself, "Well, I hope they understand it, because it is a . . . difficult trip to get from A to Z in a straight line on that particular story."

AA   *I'm looking forward to your seeing "The Cage" for the first time in years.*

RB   Yes, that will really be a wild kick!

JAMES GOLDSTONE

A native of Los Angeles, James Goldstone majored in English literature at Dartmouth College. After serving in the Army, he earned his Masters in drama at Bennington College.

Goldstone's work as the director of "Where No Man Has Gone Before," STAR TREK's second pilot, began before it was filmed in July, 1965. He participated in the discussions that determined some of the most important aspects of STAR TREK, and recalls those preproduction decisions ". . . did establish the style and form of the series, which I'm sure changed greatly, because all series do . . ."

Goldstone returned to direct "What Are Little Girls Made Of?," the tenth STAR TREK segment (filmed in August 1966). ". . . I don't have any memory of it," he says. "It was really done as a favor to Gene Roddenberry."

After signing a contract with Universal Pictures, Goldstone directed his first feature, Jigsaw (released in 1965 and featuring James Doohan).

With a year and a half after completing "Where No Man . . ." he directed three television pilots, all of which reached series status: Goldstone and his close friend Stephen Kandel cocreated the TV movie Scalplock for Columbia, the pilot for THE IRON HORSE series. Kandel wrote the teleplay and coproduced the film. He and Don M. Mankiewicz co-wrote the teleplay for the IRONSIDE pilot (based on a story by Collier Young), which Goldstone directed. He earned an Emmy nomination for his direction of "A Clear and Present Danger," the pilot for the series THE SENATOR.

Mr. Goldstone also directed the classic two-part OUTER LIMITS episode "The Inheritors" (which costarred Robert Duvall, Steve Ihnat, James Frawley and Ivan Dixon)—still one of the most beautiful science fiction films ever created for television.

AA   *How did you first meet Gene Roddenberry?*

JG   I met Gene at Ziv [television studios], when I was doing other things. He was with the Los Angeles Police Department. I did many shows at Ziv while I was cutting my teeth, and he was the police contact when I began. After he quit the police force he wrote for us. I later did THE FUGITIVE with Gene, and I had been doing a lot of shows at MGM at the time: DR. KILDARE, THE ELEVENTH HOUR, and THE LIEUTENANT. I did the "feature version" of THE LIEUTENANT, too. They expanded one as a feature. Gene and I got along marvelously, and we'd known each other for years.

AA   *How did you become involved with STAR TREK?*

JG   Gene, of course, did "The Cage," which I hadn't seen: it had not sold. When they got the green light to do another pilot, he asked me if I would direct it and I was thrilled to do it. When I said I would do it there were other scripts, and the choice was made by Gene, the network, and me. The one that showed the best potential was "Where No Man Has Gone Before." I know that Steve Kandel, who's one of my closest friends in the world, wrote one of the others ["Mudd's Women"] Once we selected "Where No Man . . . ," then Gene went to work, and we all went to work, and—this is not in any way discounting the writer—everyone went to work to make it . . . and that's true of almost any pilot . . .

to make it say all the things that had potential in the series within the number of minutes an hour show then ran. Work continued on it, memos were written, but there were a lot of things that we just didn't know how we were going to do. Gene asked me many times if I would produce the series, and I said, "Gene, it's like every other series for which I was doing episodes as well as pilots: if I produced it, I'd have to watch it." The lovely thing about doing a pilot is that you're involved in the inception of a series, and you don't have to worry about the day-to-day and week-to-week problems, the fact that it doesn't live up to what the original concept was. That's somebody else's headache. Indeed, I'm sure that STAR TREK probably has as high a record of living up to its promise as any other. That's one of the reasons it's [a] perennial [favorite]. It's the same thing with both THE NAKED CITY and ROUTE 66: I worked on episodes of both. Series don't always come to what you hope for when you start: something that will work, succeed, and continue . . .

AA *Who had been cast when you came into the production?*

JG As far as I know, the only person already cast when I came in was Leonard Nimoy as Spock, because he had been in the first pilot. And again, I've never seen "The Cage" in its entirety, but there were great differences. We made great changes in makeup, hair, ears, and other things between the two shows. Largely through Leonard, but also through Gene and me and a lot of people, the character matured in "Where No Man. . . ."

AA *I know that Robert Dawn did the makeup in "Where No Man . . ."*

JG Yes. It was really from scratch. There was talk about really changing him, making him humanoid in a different way. I remember the jokes, such as, "Maybe we should do something with his nose—Pinocchio."

AA *Did you have a hand in casting William Shatner?*

JG Yes. Bill was one of a number of people talked about. I liked Bill: I had worked with him before. Actually, I think Shatner was the choice partly of the network, partly of Desilu, partly of Gene, but I don't know whether I had approval technically within contract. I was a creative partner as the director, I thought he could play it marvelously, I liked him very much, and thought he was a marvelous balance for the Spock character, as time has shown he is. The whole thing was getting [a "Kirk"] who could work with Spock. I've continued to be both socially and professionally very friendly with Leonard.

AA *Did you bring anybody else into the series?*

JG Well, actually, I brought in Scotty, James Doohan, with whom I had worked a couple of times before that and who was a friend. There was this Scottish character "Scotty" in Gene's concept, and I called Jimmy before he came in and asked if he could do a Scottish accent, because Jimmy's not Scottish. And he said [imitating the dialect], "Of course I can do a Scottish accent." And he came in and did a Scottish accent. We did the casting of that pilot on weekends for a number of reasons. First, Joe D'Agosta, the original casting director, was under contract elsewhere, so he couldn't come in and we would have our casting readings and meetings on Saturdays and Sundays. I brought Jimmy in, and Jimmy was cast. In fact, as I recall and you'll have to check with Jimmy on this, I think I told him to speak [with a Scottish accent] when he first came in, and not just read in Scottish, because I wanted them to think he *was* Scottish.

AA *Jimmy also remembers reading in Italian and Yiddish dialects.*

JG I think that was with me, fooling around, but I'm not sure of that. We also read an actor named Richard O'Brien for the "Scotty" part.

AA *I know that George Takei was a member of the Desilu Actors Workshop.*

JG I think it was through that that it happened. We also had the idea that it would be a multiracial crew. We were doing this at a time when racial violence in the United States was rampant, and we were saying that in the future that will not be a pressing problem, that we will have transcended that, thank God. The notes I wrote about George Takei were, "Excellent, Arkansas and Japanese." I also read Mako, James Hong, Bob Doqui, Ray Shigaki and Dennis Iwamoto. Those were probably all for the same parts, but they might not have been.

AA *I think it was also you who brought in Lloyd Haynes.*

JG Yes, I did bring in Lloyd. I had worked with Lloyd. Lloyd was a friend. I had taught him in acting classes I had given at the Film Industry Workshop. He was a sweet, lovely, and very bright man. There were also other people I had worked with that I'd brought in.

AA *Was Paul Fix one of them?*

JG Yes. As a matter of fact, I had done a DEATH VALLEY DAYS with him, and it was my idea that he be in.

AA *What about Gary Lockwood and Sally Kellerman?*

JG Gary, of course, had been THE LIEUTENANT. I had a very good relationship with Gary, as did Gene, and when we did the pilot Gary was our unanimous choice because we wanted that almost animalistic, very physical person . . .

We read a number of other actresses for the role played by
Sally Kellerman. I, along with Gene and whoever else, did
cast Sally, but again, Sally went with Gary beautifully. There
was a marvelous kind of physicality to her.

AA *To what extent were you involved in the various technical
aspects of the film?*

JG As direct a hand as a director has on everything: at the
least, approval and at the most participation in the conceptual meetings with Gene and everybody. The whole [look of
the] picture was really designed by Matt Jefferies. It was a
great deal of fun, working out the practical as well as the
conceptual and making sure that the practical was not only
practical, but was also the echo of the concept. The starship
bridge was designed in such a way that it was practical to
shoot. It was made in either four or six slices, each one
independent of the others electronically and electrically so
that you could slide one out on wheels and everything else
still worked. You didn't have to plug in a lot of wires. In
other words, practicality has an influence on concept, and
concept tells you what path to follow. That's true in everything, but it was the seven-day requisite that created a lot of
things which became perennials that people have waxed
very eloquently on, as if everything done in film, feature, or
television is done because it is the ideal. It is very often
done because it is within the budget and within the schedule.

AA *What are your recollections regarding the design of the costumes?*

JG The costuming concept: we brought [William Ware] Theiss
in, and the whole velour look was "the thing" that had just
started that week. You didn't see shadows on it, you didn't
see wrinkles in it, and it had a sense of ease, comfort, and
practicality. [1]

AA *You had a great cinematographer on "Where No Man . . . ,"
Ernest Haller.*

JG Ernie Haller. It's interesting. I tried to get Bill Fraker, who
was not yet a cameraman, as director of photography. He
was Conrad Hall's camera operator. Both of them are very
dear old friends. Richard Brooks, who since then has become a friend but wasn't at that time, said that he would not
use Connie Hall on the picture he was about to make unless
Bill Fraker was the operator. So I couldn't get Billy. I
wanted to start him new. Ernie Haller was my choice, and
the reason I opted for him is that I wanted a real old pro,
since we were doing some very radical things with color,
attempting some things that were not conventional. I wanted

---

[1]Unfortunately, it also shrank. Later STAR TREK episodes used other fabrics.

someone who really was a black and white cameraman, and who could deal with depth and things of that kind. Ernie was hardly known as a fast cameraman, but he was marvelous. Then, when the series was about to go, I recommended Jerry Finnerman, with whom I had gone to high school, and Jerry ended up doing the series. He took whatever we had established with Ernie as a beyond-the-Earth reality of colors, and played very interesting games with colors.

AA   *Most of the colors in "Where No Man . . ." seem to be on the brown side.*

JG   That, of course, could be time, too. We weren't going for brown colors, and I doubt sincerely that they were brown then.

AA   *Were you going for bright colors?*

JG   Not bright, no, but variations in pastels, and using color based on the lights, to have changes of mood as well as depth based upon colors, to get out of the "Earth" look. And that's why a black and white cameraman was so essential, because it's easy to shoot in color, much easier than black and white, and depth is created by light and shadow. It was something that Jerry was hired to do, and of course it was a great opportunity for him and it established him as a cameraman.

AA   *Ernest Haller had photographed* Gone With the Wind.

JG   No small cameraman, he.

AA   *The positions of associate producer and assistant director aren't usually the same, although Robert Justman is credited as both in "Where No Man . . ."*

JG   No, they aren't . . . I brought Bobby in, having worked with him on OUTER LIMITS, because he understood that kind of shooting, understood the meticulous preparation I wanted. Obviously, he was made associate producer out front, too, or his name wouldn't appear that way. It is very unusual for that to happen.

AA   *He later became a full producer on the series.*

JG   I haven't seen Bobby for a couple of years . . . but we worked together many, many times before then.

AA   *Do you remember discussing any other design or production concepts?*

JG   Well, I recall scouting locations. They were talking about shooting in a chemical factory downtown in regard to the [scenes on the] planet. All sorts of elaborate stuff, and we determined to do it all onstage.

AA   *Are you referring to the exterior establishing shot of the lithium cracking station?*

JG   Yes. We did those in postproduction, actually.

AA   *Was that matte painting the work of Albert Whitlock?*

JG   It was painted by Al Whitlock, with whom I worked many times after that, he is the master . . . There were all those complex and wonderful things. Very often it was sheer shooting time and budget that dictated the things that have now become the standard by which other people make films. They came up to me: the cameraman, the effects guys, Matt [Jefferies], Gene, and everybody else. There was marvelous cooperation, marvelous colleague work and collaboration, which produced such things as the famous "beam me up" and "beam me down." For this photographic effect we did the simplest possible thing, and just locked off the camera and had the person there, then had the person walk out, snip the in-between part, and he was gone. Then put in some kind of optical effect. I know my words were, "Make it sort of like a shower." And in fact, as I recall, that's what it was sort of like—you know, the little twinkling stuff like you're standing in the shower, then you're going down the drain.

AA   *Almost that same effect was used in the first pilot.*

JG   Well, again, I don't recall seeing the first pilot. I have vague memories of a tremendous number of elaborate optical things and mechanical effects things that were discussed. We didn't have time for all that. Very often, aesthetically, the simplest thing is the best thing. . . .

AA   *There are also some very subtle things in the film, such as Mitchell's hair turning progressively grayer: also changes in his personality.*

JG   Yes. I participated in the collaborative process, and again, as I say, it was Gene Roddenberry's movie. Here's one of my production notes: " 'Where No Man Has Gone Before,' Goldstone notes on June 16, 1965, second draft. . . . A major point, which applies all the way through the script, and to which there might be specific references below, concerns the character of Mitchell and the evolution of his mutation toward god status. The purpose is dramatic, to create a subtext . . . My proposal is that from the time Gary suffers the first realization of what is happening to him . . . once he begins to give in to it, to enjoy it, even, he moves from his human status toward the status of a god within all and any of the criteria we place on such dieties in our Christian-Judaic culture. Specifically, I propose that he become oracular, in the sense of Moses or even Cotton Mather. I propose he do this in his stature, his way of using his hands and arms and eyes, silver or normal, his attitude as it applies to the script, aside from those specific stage directions, perhaps physical actions, that pertain to the dialogue. I don't mean to suggest that it become so stylized as to become a symbol rather than a human being. I suggest it happen on a more symbolic level. This can be done by starting him more on the flip, swinging level of articulation so that we don't even notice at one moment that this drops, but it does, on its way to becoming more formal, then more laden with import, more self-declarative, and finally downright miraculous." Anyway, I'm not going to read it all, it was a four page memo from me, and I obviously went into it in great detail.

AA *Were there similar notes on other concepts of the production as well?*

JG I have "Notes for Gene Roddenberry on June 28 draft, Goldstone July 8," and these are long, long handwritten notes on technical things, dialogue, and everything else. For example, there's an undated carbon note: ". . . The drama does not stop for introduction of characters, and introduction of characters does not stop for drama and information. . . . I have a feeling all the way through that Spock, once again, is top banana, instigator of ideas for Kirk, rather than Kirk the HERO who draws upon Spock when he needs him. Added suggestion: that conflict between point of view between Spock and Kirk be laid in early and played dramatically in terms of character, rather than just when it is convenient in terms of plot." Another note says: "From page 44 on, my feeling in the Peeples draft is that if the subsequent action comes out of the character relationships and internal character conflicts, then dramatically it continues to run uphill rather than merely coast along on a succession of physical tricks, and even offers a climax that might make them a dramatically moving point while still a simple *western in space*." So we were talking at that time about the mythic properties of this piece. . . . Now here's another series . . . the shooting order for maximum security area scenes. These are directors' notes, a shooting list, which I assume varied from the way we had originally laid it out, which is what a director does. You discover as you go along that things will go faster or more efficiently in other ways, and it has every setup that I intended to do.

AA *Do you recall any problems during shooting?*

JG There are a couple of marvelous anecdotes in that question, and I remember them quite distinctly. I hope I have not embellished them with age. The first is that we shot it at what was then called the Desilu Culver Studios, which was formerly the Selznick Studios. The soundstage had not been used in a long, long time. It was enormous, huge, and high—which was to our advantage—high fly areas, a big, vast place. And we, of course, had all these modernistic things and people in modern costumes. And in addition, at the speed at which we were going, as the two guest characters mutated forward, we had an opthalmologist on the stage because we kept putting different opaquenesses of contact lenses [on them] leading up to and eventually becoming ones out of which they could not see at all. They were literally silver. We would have to rehearse with them off, then we'd have to take the time to get the contact lenses on the actors. Contact lenses were not common then. They had to put them in, rehearse, "Take three steps, reach out, and you will pick up the so-and-so." Now, that led to many, many situations where they would reach out and pick up the camera, or they would go to sit down in the chair and miss the chair: things of that kind. But during that time, say the third or fourth day of shooting, the presence of a company shooting on that stage after all those years dislodged and disturbed a huge nest of wasps 'way up in the flies. So here we were in the 99th century, out in space with two blind actors and wasps zooming all over the set, people getting stung. But, for the two blind actors— when you can't see, your other faculties become that much more acute—it sounded like bombers were coming at them. And it was a very, very funny idea that there we were, pretending to be in this future world that has become famous, and we had a nest of these things. That night they called in exterminators, and, as I recall, the exterminators made it worse, because they really disturbed them—and all of this on that time schedule where we had to keep a good sense of humor and make jokes. As I said, it was very important that NBC know that we had done it in seven days. On the last day we got a little behind. We did do it in the seven days, and they were going to have a wrap party when we were finished: you know, the champagne was there, the food was there, and everything was there. We were scheduled to finish at a certain time, and I still had some additional shots. So everybody was waiting around impatiently. As I recall, Lucy [Ball] was there, all dressed up as only Lucy can dress, waiting for this party. And she kept coming up to me and saying, "Jim, when will you be finished, because the party is supposed to start." And I kept saying, "Just one more shot, Lucy, just one more shot." We were doing a big dolly shot on the surface of the planet, and the set was made largely of styrofoam. When the actors moved around the styrofoam it chipped and flaked, and it would get all over the dolly tracks. The sound man would say, "You can't use that take," because you could hear "crunch, crunch, crunch." Lucy finally asked if there was anything she could do to help speed it up. And I said, "Yes, Lucy. We only have one craft serviceman." We had a forty- or fifty-foot dolly shot, and he was walking in front of the dolly sweeping the styrofoam out from under the wheels, but he could only get one side or the other. So I gave her a broom, and there was Lucille Ball in her party gown, on the last shot of the pilot of STAR TREK, sweeping the styrofoam from in front of the craft dolly. Incidentally, I told that story to Lucy about two years ago, and she broke up. She remembered it . . . there's also an anecdote about my [copy of the] script. During the height of STAR TREK's popularity before the first feature was made, I bumped into Gene at a Christmas party, and he said that he had been asked by somebody who buys and sells artifacts if he [Gene] knew what had happened to the direc- tor's original screenplay, with all his notes in it. I asked, "Well, what is it worth, Gene?" And he said, "Well, I don't know, but I would guess you could probably sell it for ten thousand dollars." Now again, this was at a Christmas party. I said, "Gene, you realize that's more money than you paid me to do the pilot? I can sell the piece of paper for more than you paid me to direct the show?"

AA   *I'm afraid he was exaggerating a bit.*

JG   Of course, there's no question: it *was* a Christmas party. But as a result, I dug this out of a big box of old television episodes I did, a couple of hundred of years ago, and I've never given it to anyone, copy or not. In a sense, maybe it does have some value, and someday I'm going to give it to a library or something, if I ever get around to doing that. I guess when I see the end coming, so I'd just as soon not make it available.

AA   *Things like that belong somewhere where researchers can get at them.*

JG   Available for students. And I've missed the time when I could have made some money by doing so, but that's not the point. I'll probably give them to Dartmouth, where I got my B.A. in English before I got my Masters at Bennington.

AA   *What's your Masters in?*

JG   My Masters is in drama. Personally, as far as my career is concerned, there have been jokes about STAR TREK. Jay Cox, who was at the time the film critic for *Time* magazine, and an old friend, when I was getting nominations for mov- ies and that sort of thing, said, "I don't care what you do. On your tombstone it will say, 'James Goldstone, the date, directed "Where No Man Has Gone Before." ' " It's looming very large in my career, but obviously it hasn't dominated it in that I have never seen it again.

AA *I know you started as a film editor.*

JG I was a film editor in college, during summer vacations, and for the first six to eight months after I got out of college, before I was drafted into the army. After the army, I got my Masters and I came back to Los Angeles to make my living at it. Then I sold a script, and never went back to being a practicing editor, [although I] have never left the cutting room as a director. So I never saw "Where No Man Has Gone Before" for the first time, because I was working on it *all* the time. The way I got into this was that I would work in the cutting room on this picture while preparing the next picture, and the postproduction was rather long because of the opticals, and I kept working on it all the way along, along with Gene, once I had done my cut. So there is never a "first time" a director sees a picture.

AA *You're compared to Robert Wise at times, because you both came from a film editing background.*

JG As a matter of fact, we were both assistants to the same man: I think I learned more about filmmaking from Merrill White, who was one of the great film editors of all time. Robert Wise, Mark Robson, John Sturges, and David Lean were all his assistants. He was a genius, and he was the godfather of my oldest child, who had just been born, and that son has just become a father. A great percentage of the people who were Merrill's assistants, at one time or another, became directors. He was also the first man who ever cut sound on film, but that's a whole other story.

AA *When I first saw "Where No Man . . ." at a science fiction convention in 1966, before it had ever been aired, I recall thinking that although we'd been told it was a TV pilot it screened like a feature.*

JG Well, I've been told that about a lot of television films I've done. I hadn't yet made a feature. But though you have more time and more money for features, and you get paid more money, too, I don't see any difference, except for the limiting factors of time and facility money, and I still do television. I did a show this year called *Dreams of Gold . . .* and except for the fact that I shot it in 23 days plus underwater work, I attempted to make it a feature.

AA *I guess that's one reason your television work is so good.*

JG Well, that's a matter of opinion. It's also why I have become increasingly selective in what I will do, either features or television, because five years ago I finally came to the conclusion, after doing a feature that I hated, that if I don't want to see it I don't want to shoot it. And so, I've become known as someone who turns down a vast amount of work, whereas in those early days in television you'd take whatever came along trying to establish a career.

AA *How does that attitude make people think of you?*

JG They think of me as peculiar, as a craftsman, or crochety. I don't know. My feeling is that a director is a collaborator with the producer and the writer.

AA *Then you don't subscribe to the "auteur" theory?*

JG No, I don't. The only true auteur is somebody like Woody Allen, who not only produces but writes and directs a film. It is collaborative. The director is the person who actually implements the work, but if he doesn't work with the writer, and if he doesn't work with the producer, the technicians in the preparation, then he's being cut off at the knees and so is the film. Television, especially, has just become a producer's medium. People would probably rather not have me, because I'm a pain in the ass: I want to do the things that directors, as I understand it, are supposed to do.

SAMUEL A. PEEPLES

Samuel A. Peeples has explored both man's past and his future during his career as a Hollywood writer and producer.

His TV productions include THE TALL MAN, a 74-episode series concerning deputy sheriff Pat Garrett and outlaw Billy the Kid, OVERLAND TRAIL, which chronicled the operations of a stagecoach line, and CUSTER.

When he produced the latter, Peeples (whose family is part Native American) treated the Indians with respect, and was careful to ". . . show their attitudes and some of their feelings about what was happening . . ."

Moving from the wide open spaces of the American west to the outer reaches of the galaxy, Peeples began his association with STAR TREK before the series' first pilot was written. After assisting Gene Roddenberry with his early STAR TREK research, Peeples wrote "Where No Man Has Gone Before."

AA *Did you always want to be a writer?*

SP I think so. I was born into a circus family. My mother and grandfather were circus performers. I grew up in show business. My mother was out in Hollywood making films in 1919: that was my earliest visit here. I had made a couple of silent films as a kid, and mostly we traveled with circuses, and "tab shows."[1] My mother, billed under the name of Trixie Lee, was in half a dozen of those shows. I've tried for years to find prints of her films: she worked for Pathé for three or four years. I've never been able to find them, and I collected 16mm films for about 20 years.

AA *I read your column many times in* Films in Review . . .

SP That's right: "Films on Eight and Sixteen."

AA *When did you start writing?*

SP I came here in January of 1958.

AA *How did you first meet Gene Roddenberry?*

SP I was producing three series at Universal, and his agent had sold me a writer. I asked about Gene Roddenberry, and he said that Gene was tied up doing HAVE GUN WILL TRAVEL. We had both been nominated for Writer's Guild Awards for shows, I for a WANTED DEAD OR ALIVE, and he for a HAVE GUN WILL TRAVEL.[2] I remember that the first time I met him we had lunch at the Brown Derby, and he said, "Hey, you know I voted for your script," and I said, "Well, I voted for yours." I was producing THE TALL MAN, THE OVERLAND TRAIL, and FRONTIER CIRCUS. They were all mine: I created them and produced them.

AA *Did you buy Dorothy Fontana's FRONTIER CIRCUS script, "The Lippizan"?*

SP That's right. She was my secretary at the time she did that, and she had ambitions to be a writer. She came up with this idea for a story, and I bought the story. She became, and is, a very fine writer.

AA *How did you become involved with STAR TREK?*

SP Gene Roddenberry and I were friends, and he was doing research on what would become STAR TREK. At first, I remember, he borrowed a copy of *Odd John* by Olaf Stapledon. Then he came out to my house. I have a collection of science fiction magazines, probably one of the most complete around. He and I waded through them, and photographed some of the covers, and we discussed every ele-

---

[1]"Tab shows" were condensed versions of Broadway plays, performed by traveling troupes of actors.
[2]Gene Roddenberry won the Writer's Guild Award for "Helen of Abajinian."

ment of what he was doing. I thought it was fascinating and fun, because he was going to try to do what I considered to be science fiction, which is not often done in Hollywood. Most so-called science fiction movies are horror plays, and similar stuff that dates back to the silent days. Gene actually had an idea, a plan, a dream of making a genuine science fiction series that would be very much like the better science fiction magazines. I think he wanted to do a more realistic, a more earthy version of Olaf Stapledon's concepts that were so enormous and staggering, especially the idea of pursuing a far-flung empire in space. It's space opera, which is I think exactly what he had in mind, and of course they are sort of a perfect western. I wrote enough westerns, I should know.

AA *This was before either of the pilots were shot?*

SP Oh, yes . . . I had been at MGM in 1963. I knew him when he was doing THE LIEUTENANT. . . . I had met him a long time before that.

AA *Was the Enterprise captain based on Captain Horatio Hornblower from the beginning?*

SP Well, we talked about that. I think that Gene's idea was to have an authoritative figure, not a father figure, but someone like an adventurer in high places who had a sort of daring that was unquenchable. . . . One of the things was a training program where they'd pose almost insoluble problems . . .

AA *So Kirk was originally a combination of Odysseus and a Ship of the Line captain.*

SP Well, he didn't have as many of Hornblower's failings, but he did have some of his sense of humor. We tried to keep that alive, and to point out that Spock kept insisting that he had no sense of humor. He kept insisting Kirk wasn't funny, and at the same time he would occasionally betray himself with a remark that showed he had his tongue in his cheek. I always thought that was a humanizing part of Mr. Spock. It wasn't in every episode, but it was carried in many.

AA *Do you recall anything about Gene Roddenberry's earliest ideas about the nature of Mr. Spock?*

SP Yes . . . as originally conceived, Spock was a red-skinned creature with fiery ears, who had a plate in the middle of his stomach. He didn't eat or drink, but he fed upon any form of energy that struck this plate in his stomach. I told Gene that I thought this very effectively destroyed him as an interesting character, because he was no longer human, and that he should be at least half human, and have the problems of both sides.

AA   *Do you recall what Spock's native world was at that time? I've seen early references to the character as a "red-skinned Martian."*

SP   That's possible, because he was red in the earliest version that I can recall discussing with Gene. And remember, Gene worked alone. I didn't work with him on this stuff. He spent endless hours going over my magazines and we were talking, having drinks, and just shooting a lot of bull about what the possibilities were.

AA   *This is certainly the first reference I've heard to the plate in Mr. Spock's stomach.*

SP   Like I say, it was a totally alien creature, and Gene humanized him. I won't take any credit for it, because I think Gene was working in this direction; we had talked about it and how it evolved from the very first time he came out to my house. I don't know what he had on paper at that time, but certainly the first script had not been written.

AA   *I understand that when Roddenberry first discussed the Enterprise's motive power, the vessel was run by magnetic propulsion rather than the familiar matter/antimatter.*

SP   That's right. The idea here was that he wanted a universal form of energy that might be tapped in outer space and magnetism, of course, is one. So I think it was a valid concept. Whether it was practical or not is something else, but the concept is valid: it's possible, like the solar winds that blow. They do exist. We're aware of them. Would there be enough plasma involved in them to drive a spaceship? That's something else again. But I think that if we're ever going to visit planets that have people on them, it will be in our own solar system and it will be our own people who have been transplanted to those planets. That's my personal opinion.

AA   *Do you recall how Roddenberry arrived at the matter/anti-matter concept?*

SP   No, I don't. We had many discussions over a considerable period of time, and Gene was very much into this. He must have researched very heavily before we first discussed anything. As I recall, he was very knowledgeable, and he understood the paradoxes that are involved in faster-than-light travel, and this business of whether or not it's possible to warp in and out of this plane of existence. We are at least pretty sure that null matter does exist. If there are universes in which you cannot achieve the speed of light, then obviously there's another universe where you cannot go slower than the speed of light. On that concept, if you can

just shift over into that other universe, at that point there is
no limit to how fast you can go.

AA *I believe that Gene Roddenberry discussed all of this with
Harvey Lynn, Jr., of the Rand Corporation, so he really
wanted to get a valid picture of the possibilities.*

SP A lot of fun has been made about "Warp One Speed," and all
of this, but theoretically, there's nothing wrong with it. If
you postulate a problem, then you have to postulate an
answer in a framework that makes some sort of common
sense. Antimatter is simply the reverse of everything we
know. In other words, creatures in that plane of existence
couldn't go slow enough to enter ours, and we can't go fast
enough to enter theirs. If you could warp between the two,
find a hole to get through, obviously we can exceed the
speed of light.

AA *Was "Where No Man Has Gone Before" the first script idea
you worked on for STAR TREK?*

SP It was the first. What actually happened was that Gene had
produced "The Cage" and he wanted me to see it. I went
down and saw it at one of the very first screenings down at
Desilu-Culver, the old RKO Studios. I liked it, but I thought
it was too much of a fantasy and not enough science fiction,
which is what we originally talked about his doing, and he
said he thought so, too. My understanding was when it was
submitted to NBC they felt much the same way, that it
should be more hardcore science fiction than fantasy. . . .
Gene told me that he had an okay from NBC to do three
more scripts and from those three, if they liked them, they
would pick a second pilot to be shot. Mine was the one that
NBC picked, so technically I wrote the pilot script that sold
the show. There was a lot of rewriting on it, and with my
blessings: Gene and I are still very good friends. . . . And
that title is mine, incidentally, if you're curious. . . . That
was the original title of the very first copy of the very first
version of the story that was submitted to Gene Roddenberry.

AA *It's a very poetic title.*

SP I always thought it was. Today we forget that people should
be a little larger than life when you're dramatizing them. I
think the boldness of an explorer, of a person who challenges the unknown, is what I liked about the concept of the
series, and about "Where No Man Has Gone Before."

AA *Do you recall hearing about alternate casting choices for your
pilot?*

SP Not to my knowledge. I was involved in producing some
other shows on another lot, so I wasn't active in the production of the show. Gene was kind enough after it sold, and

was going to become a series, to offer me the job of producing it. I had to decline, because I had two series of my own at 20th Century-Fox: CUSTER and LANCER, and I was under contract there, so there was no way I could work on it with Gene.

AA *The triple personality of Kirk, Spock, and the Doctor wasn't at all evident in "Where No Man Has Gone Before," so I guess that evolved later.*

SP Yes, because it was a different doctor . . . Paul Fix played the role, and in my opinion he was a little too old for the part. Although I knew Paul for many years, and he appeared in some of the shows I did, I just felt he wasn't right for the part. Apparently Gene felt the same way, because he was replaced.

AA *I have been told that Gene wanted DeForest Kelley initially, and Paul Fix got the part because the concept that was discussed with Gene, director James Goldstone, and casting director Joe D'Agosta was an old country doctor.*

SP Well, that's a point, and he did a good job, but the physical element, I thought, required every crewman of the U.S.S. Enterprise to be active. He had to be not only mentally alert, but the traditional images of a country doctor would hardly have fit the images of a man who would say, "We've got an unknown disease, and there's a cure on this planet. Our only choice is to try it. It might kill you," and I don't think Paul Fix's interpretation of the character would have been able to do that.

AA *He seemed distinctly twentieth century.*

SP That's right.

AA *In the first pilot, John Hoyt portrayed the doctor. He was a bit more energetic, and was able to interact with the Captain.*

SP That's true. And DeForest Kelley, in my opinion, in this role, is better than anyone else. I'm not saying he's a better actor than Paul Fix, [who] in my opinion is a splendid actor. He just wasn't right for this part, in my opinion.

AA *Were you at the studio while it was being done?*

SP No.

AA *How did you feel when you first saw it on film?*

SP I liked it. I saw it with Gene and Jimmy Goldstone, and I do not remember if it was a rough cut or not, but I liked it very much. I felt that he kept much to the essence of what we tried to do, and we worked very hard on its gimmicks and gadgets. They all had to be extrapolations of things that existed in the 1960s. It had to be possible, nothing fantastic. The hospital bed, which you may remember, was carefully designed. I think Gene even told us that at the Jet Propulsion Lab he determined that a radiation field in space would be a possibility.

AA   *Did you want to do anything in "Where No Man . . ." that you couldn't?*

SP   Not really . . . There is nothing that I can think of that was cut out or left out. One thing that was put in that I didn't particularly like was the fight at the end. Although I thought it was staged very well, I was opposed to it because I felt that an all-powerful man like Mitchell wouldn't have to resort to physical violence. Gene wanted this physical action at the end of the script, and that's the way it worked out.

AA   *When NBC rejected "The Cage," the first STAR TREK pilot, one of the things they complained about was the lack of action in the episode.*

SP   That's a point, yes . . .

AA   *Why didn't you ever write any other live-action STAR TREK episodes?*

SP   I didn't particularly want to. Science fiction has always been a hobby of mine, and I still have a very large collection, although I've shipped literally thousands of books to the University of Wyoming as contributions over the years. Since it's something I like very well, I've never considered myself a science fiction writer. I've published 28 novels, and most of them have been historicals, westerns, and mysteries, but I never considered the notion of writing science fiction novels. My last novel was *The Man Who Died Twice*, which is something of a fantasy: it's a Hollywood murder mystery. I enjoy writing, and I've always been a buff on Hollywood's history. As a science fiction fan, I feel that I could not write science fiction as well as it was written in *Astounding* many years ago. I knew so many of the people personally, including John W. Campbell and Horace Gold. Both of them had asked me to write for their magazines, and I always said that I felt that science fiction wasn't my field . . . I did the animated version of *Flash Gordon*, too. We wanted to make it a little different from the strip, to give it a little more meat. *TV Guide* ranked it as one of their top movies of the year. I enjoyed that one, that was fun. I say I never write science fiction, and every once in a while somebody will say, "Well, didn't you write . . ." and I'll say, "Well, yes, I did." Why, I don't know. Just because it was something I was fond of, I guess.

AA   *What do you think of the original STAR TREK episodes?*

SP   I have watched a few . . . I thought some were great. I've seen all of Robert Bloch's—he's a close friend of mine— I've watched all of Dorothy Fontana's, and those of other writers who are friends of mine. Some of the episodes I've liked and others I have not. For example, I thought that the one with the fuzzy little creatures wasn't my idea of what the show should be. It was awfully cute and awfully nice, but it covered an area that I felt was unnecessary for that particular type of series. We all have our favorites and our nonfavorites. I've always been a "Jack the Ripper" buff. Bob Bloch and I have both been to London and walked the same streets and been to the same sites where the killings took place, so Bob's version of a science fiction Jack the Ripper of STAR TREK has always amused me, and I enjoy it very much. . . . Bob's story, "Yours Truly, Jack the Ripper," has been reprinted a hundred times at least. Over the years, many writers have used the same gimmick: something that has to kill in order to stay alive, and it's funny because if you think about it, Bob's, if it is not the first, is one of the very first to use that premise.

AA *What do you think of "City on the Edge of Forever"?*

SP Harlan Ellison is someone I know quite well, and we've never particularly gotten along. He's quite avant garde and I'm not: I think tradition is something you should observe, at least. I've enjoyed many of his books, and I even like the short story collections that he has put together, because I think his taste is impeccable. I thought his version of his script that won the Writer's Guild Award was far better than the script that was shot. So here, Gene and I disagree. But I think Gene, in thinking back, would probably agree with what I've just said. When you produce a series there are circumstances . . . hundreds of reasons why you may have to change a script. The original writer of that script is not aware of these, and even if you tell him he doesn't necessarily believe you, because he likes what he did, and he wants to see exactly what he wrote. I've felt the same way as a writer, and I feel the other side of the hat as a producer, so in my opinion there is no blame attached to the fact that "City on the Edge of Forever" was shot from a script much inferior to Harlan's. . . .

AA *. . . But one that was more adaptable to the continuity of the series?*

SP That's right. So I agree with Gene. He was forced to do some things and also sometimes you run across writers who are very much in love with something they've done and don't really want to change it, although you feel it's not right for the show. It's a matter of personal taste. So I think Gene did what he felt he had to do. At the same time, in my studied opinion as a man standing on one side, I preferred the original version of the script to the one that was shot.

AA *You also wrote a STAR TREK animated episode, "Beyond the Farthest Star."*

SP That's right. It was the pilot for that show, too, as a matter of fact. Dorothy was the associate producer and story editor, and she and Gene both said, "You did the one that sold the live-action version, so how about doing this one?" So I wrote that one.

AA *As an expert in science fiction, what do you think of STAR TREK? Do you have any opinions regarding its popularity?*

SP I think it's something that caught on. The ratings of STAR TREK were never very good. . . . NBC played the fool and scheduled it at night when younger kids who might really have loved it couldn't stay up that late, and older kids were out, so it was bad scheduling in my opinion. . . . Frankly, after 30 years in Hollywood STAR TREK is not a big thing in my life. The first script I wrote for it was a favor to a friend, for which I was paid $5,000. Now, at that time my normal fee was $6,500. I just did it. I worked harder on that script with Gene than I did on anything else. I went over to THE GIRL FROM U.N.C.L.E. at MGM, and on that I not only got $6,500, but I also got a $2,500 bonus. In other words, I got $9,000 for doing that GIRL FROM U.N.-C.L.E. script, and it took me exactly 23 days. Now with "Where No Man . . . ," I worked with Gene a long time, willingly, and I enjoyed doing it. I liked working together with Gene, we got along great, and we did another picture together, years later: *Spectre*. We even did a third one which you never heard of, about a futuristic police department. . . . *Spectre* was made into a "movie of the week" and was the pilot for a series. . . . It was our attempt to do a horror story, sort of a tribute to *Weird Tales*. We both like that sort of thing, so Gene and I did it. It is basically Gene's story. We went through two or three drafts on this. Fox shot the final version in England. Gene rewrote because I was busy doing something else, and I couldn't help him with it. As far as I know, both our names are on the script. One version of the script had one name at the head of the credits, and another had the other's, so as I recall we flipped a coin to see who would come first, and I probably lost. But I think that any good quality of the picture is directly attributable to Gene, because he really did a magnificent job of producing it, and he worked awfully hard on it.

AA *It screens like it was meant for theaters rather than for television.*

SP That was the idea: to try to do something a little better than average. It was originally written for Warner Brothers and it bombed out there. Gene was a good enough salesman to finally get it made at 20th Century-Fox.

AA *Did you have anything to do with* The Questor Tapes?

SP No. I remember working on something else in Gene's office, and I read the script with Gene Coon, the gentleman who produced it. The three of us were in Gene's office, and they had run into a slight problem. I think I made a suggestion or two on the script, and I don't know if they used any of them. I liked the book version that Dorothy Fontana did. She really did a fine job.

AA *How many scripts do you estimate you've written?*

SP I used to secretly number all my things. I wrote 327 screenplays and scripts for Hollywood, and I would guess close to 300 were actually produced. I think my top favorite is the CUSTER pilot. I wanted to do a "John Ford" cavalry picture, and since I was involved in its production, that's exactly what I did. Henry Hathaway, the director, was kind enough to call me and ask to have lunch with me on the Fox lot, and said, "I want to tell you, Sam, I've seen a lot of westerns, a lot of cavalry pictures, and I've made a lot of them myself," and I said, "A lot of this goes back to your *Lives of a Bengal Lancer*, I wanted to do that kind of a picture," and he said, "You did. I want to tell you you did it as well as John Ford or I could have done it."

AA *I recall that was released theatrically in foreign markets.*

SP Yes, it was. It's funny: do you remember a big, huge, multimillion dollar Cinerama film, *Custer of the West*? Ours outgrossed it in the United States, I think something like two and a half times. The pilot, I think, cost very close to three quarters of a million dollars. The second episode was written by a very good friend of mine, and we put the two together to make the theatrical feature called *The Legend of Custer*.

AA *Have you ever heard from STAR TREK fans in reference to your contributions to the series?*

SP I've received letters for many years from Trekkies. And I'll go somewhere and someone will say, "Are you *the* Sam Peeples who wrote 'Where No Man Has Gone Before'?"

AA *What do you think of the likelihood of anything like STAR TREK really happening in the future: going out into space and contacting other civilizations if there are any out there?*

SP One, I doubt if there are any out there that are within our reach. In fact, when you called I was watching a discussion of Einstein's Theory of Relativity, which talked about the possibility of faster-than-light travel. In other words, if you're on a ship that's approaching the speed of light and fire a cannon forward, would that cannon shot exceed the speed of light? It won't, mathematically, but the idea is the sort of thing that I think is a stumbling block in any realistic pursuit. To get to the nearest star system, which to the best of our knowledge has no habitable planets, would take four or five years. On a round trip, who's going to waste eight or ten years of his life?

THE WRITERS

EVEN A MOTION PICTURE WITH THE MOST EXPENSIVE PRODUCTION VALUES IN THE WORLD WOULD AMOUNT TO NOTHING WITHOUT A WORKABLE SCRIPT. NOWHERE IS STAR TREK CREATOR GENE RODDENBERRY'S CONCERN WITH QUALITY MORE EVIDENT THAN IN THE ROLL CALL OF STAR TREK WRITERS: FROM AWARD-WINNING SCIENCE FICTION AUTHORS SUCH AS NORMAN SPINRAD TO ESTABLISHED INDUSTRY PROFESSIONALS LIKE STEPHEN KANDEL.

JERRY SOHL

Jerry Sohl, journalist and fiction writer, began his science fiction career in 1952 with the publication of his first science fiction short story ("The Seventh Order") and novel (The Haploids). His television writing includes the TWILIGHT ZONE segments "The New Exhibit" and "The Living Doll" (1963), and "Queen of the Nile" (1964), for which writer Charles Beaumont received screen credit. He scripted "The Invisible Enemy" for THE OUTER LIMITS, and that series also adapted his 1959 short story "Counterweight."

Mr. Sohl's association with STAR TREK began with "The Corbomite Maneuver," the first STAR TREK script written for the series following the network acceptance of "Where No Man Has Gone Before." He also submitted the earliest outline and script for "Power Play," the title of which was first changed to "The Way of the Spores" and finally filmed as "This Side of Paradise." His story for "Whom Gods Destroy" was scripted by Lee Erwin.

AA *Do you recall how you became involved with STAR TREK?*

JS I had heard that Gene Roddenberry was going to do a science fiction show. I had no idea of what it was about, and I didn't even endeavor to contact him. He contacted me. We met, he picked my brains, we had a very good time, and he said he wasn't at all near to having the thing done. The network sale hadn't been made yet, but he hoped that it would be. At that time, he was writing his original conception of "The Cage." We talked about that, and we talked about science fiction in general, and I gave him a few [caveats]. Then he saw a lot of other people, like A.E. Van Vogt, Ray Bradbury, and all the people that he could think of. He would have lunch or dinner with them. I didn't hear from him again for about a year after that. NBC turned down the series after having viewed that first pilot, but it wasn't all bad news. They said he should take into consideration certain points that they gave him and have it redone, and it was redone. I was the first writer he called, and I did the first [series] script, "The Corbomite Maneuver." It was during the making of "The Corbomite Maneuver" script that a lot of things had to be solved. We were originally going to have [each crew member] carry a language translator, which would fit on the wrist like a beeper, and no matter what area of the universe they were in, the thoughts that the people were thinking would automatically be translated into English as they spoke. We got rid of that idea, and assumed that everybody did speak English. It was a lot simpler that way. [Leonard Nimoy] did not like the idea of having those pointed ears. He was uncomfortable with it. And the idea of the clothes: my word, the number of different kinds of wardrobes that were suggested! The size of the ship was also a big problem. Roddenberry's conception was that it would be hundreds of stories high, and you'd take an elevator that would zoom you around the whole thing. Well, he kept that concept. And we never do learn when we see the series just how big the starship Enterprise really is. I don't think there's any necessity to know. I think one of the things wrong with television is that it's too visual, and that it inhibits your own thinking. STAR TREK left things to your own imagination. Also, it allowed us some sort of free reign that over the mountain and out there among the stars could lie anything, rather than visually portraying it all like a bunch of screwdrivers and hammers.

AA *In other words, while you were writing "The Corbomite Maneuver" you were visiting the studio?*

JS Oh, yes. We had story conferences. Bob Justman, who was one of the producers, and Gene Roddenberry and I went over "The Corbomite Maneuver" with a fine-tooth comb to determine whether or not the things that were in it were things that we really wanted to use from that point on.

AA *Then the script for "The Corbomite Maneuver" was used as a standard for establishing the format of the series?*

JS That was my understanding . . . Gene Roddenberry told me himself that he would have liked "The Corbomite Maneuver" to have been the first one aired, but that was impossible because of the special effects. They were having such a difficult time with the special effects for the starship Fesarius . . . such an enormous ship . . . and this held them up for so long that it became the tenth episode to be shown. Gene Roddenberry told me that when they received the script of "The Corbomite Maneuver," on the basis of that script [the network] ordered nine more STAR TREKs, and they were well on their way. Now, whether or not he was telling the truth, I don't know. He may have been making me feel good; I don't know whether that's absolute fact or not. But that's what he told me, and it could very well be true, because I do think it was a good script.

AA *Do you recall any concepts that were discussed or abandoned?*
JS Yes. One of the things we were going to put in was a
       commander who was going to be on the ship and second-
       guess Captain Kirk's decisions about things. In this particu-
       lar instance he was going to call him on the carpet for risking
       the lives of all the people on the crew with his poker
       maneuver. We decided, and rightfully so, to take that out,
       because . . . the concept of the series, as Roddenberry told
       it to me, was based on C.S. Forester's "Hornblower," and
       that if you have somebody above him on the trip, then that
       person, and not Kirk, becomes the protagonist.
AA *Whose idea was it to have this person over Kirk on the ship?*
JS It was my idea. It got voted down, and I can see why. I see
       now that it would have been a move in the wrong direction.
       But all I was looking for was more tension. In other words,
       here's this young Captain Kirk going out there and trying to
       make really far-out decisions, and here's this older man
       saying, "This is your first trip, son, and you have to learn
       some things, and I'm here to help you," which kind of
       emasculates Kirk. I agreed, yes, it did, and so we took him
       out entirely. But that gave them a basis for using such
       characters in ensuing episodes, and they did, as I recall, in
       quite a few.
AA *Did any of the tension between Kirk and McCoy in your script
       come from that?*
JS It could have. One of the things that I failed to do was show
       interaction among the people on the ship. And that's what
       they wanted to create: some kind of tension that would be
       there permanently. In other words, how do the characters
       interact with one another? Well, I hadn't really given that a
       great deal of thought. In the rewrites, and as we put in the
       color pages for first, second, third, fourth, fifth and sixth
       rewrites, we got onto what they would say, what would
       make one rub the other the wrong way. It gives them some
       kind of dimension. I must say that first script was a difficult
       one to do.
AA *Were you asked to work on more of the episodes?*
JS Well, at that time I had just had a best-seller out, called *The
       Lemon Eaters*, which was the definitive book about the
       encounter group movement, marathon group therapy. There
       were a lot of nibbles on that. I had to go for a lot of
       interviews, and I did not assume a posture of ready availabil-
       ity to the show, which of course then prevented my being
       appointed to any big position in it. I did go to Cleveland with
       Gene Roddenberry for a science fiction convention. . . . At
       that convention Roddenberry introduced me as the head

writer. Of course, there were no head writers: we were all equal on the show. He did, however, hire John D.F. Black, who did have an office there, and who did more than the normal scriptwriting. He changed the scripts of some of the science fiction writers who had never written scripts before so that they were useful as television scripts. And I think he did a good job. I don't know how long he stayed there. If anybody was the head writer, he was.

AA   *Do you recall whether or not Mr. Shatner had much say regarding the character of Captain Kirk?*

JS   Well, that was pretty firm in Roddenberry's mind. He wanted Kirk to be that "Captain Horatio Hornblower" character, and he tried to make him as much of that cloth as he could, without borrowing too much C.S. Forester, and still make him believable. It caused him to create a complete genealogy for him, and I think that was some of the material he handed to potential writers: something about Captain Kirk's background, and what we should be alert for. He had the character pretty well worked out, and of course Spock could be just about anything. We had no idea of what he would eventually turn into.

AA   *Do you recall what he was approximately during the time you were writing "The Corbomite Maneuver"? Was he just someone to serve as a sounding board for Kirk?*

JS   Oh, sure. Here was a person who was a living computer, a Vulcan. He had no emotions. He was just like the Oracle of Delphi. You would ask him a question and you'd get a very erudite, cerebral kind of answer, the kind of answer that a machine would give. That was the way that his character came about, and of course Kirk would make fun of him in the scripts. Leonard Nimoy is a perfectly normal, funny fellow, very friendly and warm, but on the set he was supposed to be very cold, very analytical, and it gave writers an opportunity to play off that particular thing, so many of them did—to good effect, I think.

AA   *"Corbomite" was also the first script in which Dr. McCoy appeared.*

JS   . . . I've always been fascinated with the idea that in the future it's going to be possible to take out your appendix without even intruding in the body: just do it somehow without actually piercing the flesh. I don't know how that could be done, but we were all thinking in terms of what Dr. McCoy would do, and what kind of medicine he would have. Well, he just holds the instruments up to you, and he tells you everything he needs to know about you: your white blood count and all of these things, the state of your health, blood pressure, the state of your liver . . . and I think anybody seeing the starship Enterprise would certainly buy that because it's so far in the future. . . . It's hard to put all these things in chronological order. What I did whenever I had any free time at all, was to run over to Desilu and see what I could do. I had no difficulty in getting an assignment. The difficulty I had was in completing the assignment in view of all the things that there were to do. Among other things, I had to go on a tour to promote my book, and I don't know how long I was gone for that. And so it was very difficult for me to do what I would really have liked to have done. I was considered a staff writer for the show. I don't think there's any doubt of that, if there are such things, although I don't think anybody was designated as a staff writer. Anyway, I had an open sesame there, and so did Ted Sturgeon, Robert Bloch, George Clayton Johnson, and Harlan Ellison. The special photographic effects were sub-contracted. Roddenberry was furious with the slow pace they were making. It was before the time of George Lucas and that great big studio up there in San Francisco where they do all these things now.

AA   *Can you recall any humorous things that happened while you were around there?*

JS   Well, one thing that will give you an idea as to how he was received by fellow writers and production people was . . . it was his birthday, and so he had no idea what was going to happen, but the door opened and this naked woman came in, and of course he was absolutely flabbergasted. . . . I don't know who she was, but she came in and sat on his lap and gave him a big kiss. And his face was all red. But everybody really enjoyed and liked him, and he loved this kind of thing. He said, "That's the best birthday present I ever had," and the woman left. . . . I was not there for it, and I didn't see it, but this is what I heard.

AA   *It sounds as if there was an informal atmosphere between Mr. Roddenberry and his staff that might explain why no one seemed to be afraid to contribute to the series.*

JS   That's true. On the set you could talk to anybody, you could make your suggestions known to whomever you felt like. Roddenberry wasn't always on the set, but if you knew the director you could make suggestions. William Shatner and I were good friends before the series even started.

AA   *You receive credit for writing the story for "Whom Gods Destroy," with Lee Erwin.*

JS   I don't know who he is, or whether or not he did any other scripts. I think it was about that time when things really began to start popping for me, and I was busy doing the script for *The Lemon Eaters* for Embassy Productions, then I did another *Lemon Eaters* for Paramount, and still another for CBS, one after the other. None of them were made, but I made a lot of money out of it. . . .

AA *When you finally got to see "Whom Gods Destroy," did you like the completed episode?*

JS Yes, I did. I really did . . . I shouldn't have taken the extreme position that I did, that if you're going to do it this way, then go ahead and do it and I'll take my name off it, and all that sort of thing.

AA *"This Side of Paradise" certainly went through many changes. In fact, you only used your pseudonym on the screen credit.*

JS Yes, I did. D.C. Fontana, who was then Roddenberry's right-hand woman, you might say, was sitting in on all of the story sessions, and I didn't like the way that they were going.

AA *The first script I saw called "This Side of Paradise" had your name on it as Jerry Sohl, but you used Nathan Butler on the subsequent drafts after D.C. Fontana had introduced an emotional side to Mr. Spock.*

JS That is true. I don't know whether it was that particularly, because I originally had it so that the spores did get to him. She tidied it up. She made it more of a complete entity. It had less philosophy, less preaching in it, and it wasn't so polemicized. She made it more STAR TREKish, which was all right, and I put my other name on it: I've written many books and screenplays under the name of Nathan Butler, so I decided to put that on just out of spite. And it really doesn't matter, one way or the other. . . . I think she did a good job. I've seen it recently, and I think it holds up very well.

AA *Why do you think STAR TREK is so successful?*

JS I really don't know. I think it's an anomaly. It certainly is strange. Truman Bradley used to introduce SCIENCE FIC-TION THEATRE with, "Let me show you something inter-esting . . . ," and he'd always show you something interesting and a little story to go with it. Well, it's a wonder to me that it and ONE STEP BEYOND and several others like that did not become "cult favorites" but they didn't. STAR TREK is now bigger than ever, and I'm really surprised.

STEPHEN KANDEL

Stephen Kandel is a veteran television writer, with countless scripts to his credit, yet he is perhaps best known for his development of one particular character—STAR TREK's Harcourt Fenton Mudd, the Federation's beloved rogue. Working from a story outline by Gene Roddenberry, Kandel wrote his earliest draft in 1965 as one of two unfilmed possibilities for STAR TREK's second pilot. Mudd languished on the shelf until Kandel's first draft script of "Mudd's Women" was submitted on May 23, 1966; the episode went before the cameras two weeks afterward.

Two other chapters were added to the filmed Mudd saga: "I, Mudd," written with the contributions of David Gerrold and the animated "Mudd's Passion."

Kandel is currently a production executive for the MacGYVER television series being filmed at Paramount.

AA *How did you first become involved with STAR TREK?*

SK There was an initial pilot script written for STAR TREK that was rejected by the network, but nevertheless enough interest was retained to move forward with the project, and several other scripts were commissioned. I wrote one of them, "Mudd's Women," and on the basis of those scripts they went ahead and did a second pilot. The rest is history. I created the character "Harry Mudd," and basically that's what I wrote for STAR TREK.

AA *You did two episodes of the animated STAR TREK as well.*

SK Yes. I did several "Harry Mudds." There was one that was written but never filmed. I still have the story somewhere.

AA *Can you tell me anything about it?*

SK It was called "Deep Mudd." In one that I wrote, "I, Mudd," Mudd was trapped on a planet of robots who elected him king. "Deep Mudd" involves Mudd's escape from that world, after he tricked these particular robots into revealing to him the location of a cache of scientific equipment and weaponry left by their makers. Suddenly Mudd found himself with very, very advanced armament, which he used to bribe a group of pirates into helping him escape. The problem was, of course, that he could control neither the weapons nor the real heavies he was supposed to be in control of, the pirates. They tangled with the Enterprise, on a planet with a surface of molten, viscous mud. And it went on from there. That was basically it: bailing Harry Mudd out of his own problems, getting control of this weaponry they couldn't destroy, and sending it into a sun.

AA *Did you ever submit any other story lines that were bought but not produced?*

SK Yes, there were a couple of others, but I just don't remember them. "Deep Mudd" got to the story stage: I wrote it as a story, and that's where it ended.

AA *Had you ever worked with Gene Roddenberry before STAR TREK?*

SK No. My first involvement with Gene was when he first called me. We had a meeting and got along famously, and it went on from there. It was really very uncomplicated, and very pleasant while it lasted.

AA *Why do you think the show is so popular?*

SK It personalized science fiction, and gave a relatively literate television audience a chance to watch an adventure series that didn't insult them. It raised a great many ethical, cultural and social questions that the stories made palatable. The network, I think, had no idea that there were serious issues being raised. But I think it found an audience for those two reasons. It offered escapism with a tinge of reality: it found that audience, clung to it and held it, because here it is again, launching forth.

AA *Did you ever keep in touch with Roger C. Carmel?*

SK I did from time to time. It was an ideal part for him, and there was a brief talk at one time of doing a two-hour Harry Mudd thing, but I think this was fantasy on his agent's part. We talked about it, and it was terrific, but nothing ever came of it. He was a gifted but difficult man, and he found a part that suited him so well that I think it frustrated him a little. The rest of his career was mostly doing bits. And there it went.

AA *You also did some work on BATMAN.*

SK I did the work on BATMAN because (a) a friend of mine was producing it, (b) I had small children who desperately wanted to get on the set, and (c) [the producer] said, "Okay, even though it's a closed set, I'll be delighted to have your kids as guests: one script, one kid, a ticket of admission." It was a joke, but that's how it started. Listen, STAR TREK was fun. They hardly do science fiction anymore.

AA *Did you ever submit any ideas for STAR TREK II, the TV series that was never produced?*

SK   I was at Paramount when Harold Livingston was producing it. I was going to do several. I ran into Harold and he seized my arm in a grip of death and we kicked around a few ideas. But I had a "movie of the week" that I had to deliver, and by the time that was finished, so was STAR TREK II, the TV series.

AA   *Instead, they decided to produce it as a feature film, STAR TREK—THE MOTION PICTURE.*

SK   And that, of course, spawned all kinds of good things for Paramount. Anyway, that's really it. A short—and happy— relationship. I was really sorry it went off the air, and I'm delighted it's going back on.

GEORGE CLAYTON JOHNSON

Born in Wyoming in 1929, George Clayton Johnson enlisted in the army at the age of seventeen. After studying architectural drafting in the service, he relocated to California.

Five years after deciding to become a writer he sold his story "All of Us Are Dying" to the TV series THE TWILIGHT ZONE. With the encouragement of fellow writer Charles Beaumont, Johnson later sold the series four full scripts: "A Penny for Your Thoughts," "A Game of Pool," "Nothing in the Dark," and "Kick the Can."

In 1967, Johnson and William F. Nolan wrote the novel Logan's Run; a film and television series both followed. (The story editor on the series was Dorothy C. Fontana, and the series' writers included Fontana, David Gerrold, Shimon Wincelberg, and John Meredyth Lucas.)

Johnson recalls seeing his first STAR TREK episode and thinking, "How do you write a show like this?," adding that ". . . Many guys who were writing other shows reacted strangely to this new format . . ." The STAR TREK milieu, though, was no surprise for Johnson, a long-time science fiction fan. ". . . All those things were standard to me. . . . Whether you dial your destination in a phone booth, or somebody says, 'Beam me up, Scotty,' it's all basically the same thing."

His sole STAR TREK script, "The Man Trap" (filmed in June 1966) became the first STAR TREK episode televised (on September 8, 1966).

AA   *How were you contacted to work on STAR TREK?*

GCJ John D.F. Black was their associate producer. He was one
of the first people Gene Roddenberry had called in after
Desilu gave him the go-ahead on the series. He's a friend of
mine. He called me and said, "Hey, I just saw Gene
Roddenberry and I did about 15 minutes on you." He meant
that he recommended me to Gene. I told my agent about it
at the time and the next thing I knew, I had an appointment
to see Gene. We didn't talk 20 minutes before he hired me
to write an episode. . . . What I proposed was that we [use]
the book by C.M. Kornbluth called *The Syndic*, about gang
bosses taking over America, and I suggested the title "Chicago II."

AA   *That was one of the ideas Roddenberry mentioned in his
treatment to sell the series, and it was later written as "Mission Into Chaos," and filmed as "A Piece of the Action."*

GCJ Well, "Chicago II" was almost like an assignment: It was as
though Gene had thought up the idea. I didn't feel it was
really original. Many times an episodic writer will go into a
show waiting to see where *they* want to go before suggesting any brave new ventures. He suggested some of these
ideas, and I followed up on it, saying, "Okay, I'll do the
plot." I worked "Chicago II" out and I turned it in, but
before Gene even responded to me about *my* treatment, he
told me that he wanted me to work on something else. He
was perfectly prepared to pay me for what I had done, but
he had [someone else] working on a similar story and asked
me to do something else. So I said, "Sure," and I thought up
the "Man Trap" plot which I called "Damsel with a Dulci-
mer," influenced by the poem *Kubla Khan*. I had written a
story for THE TWILIGHT ZONE called "All of Us Are
Dying" and it was about a face changer, someone who could
take a look at a photograph and become a different character
. . . part of the fun of it was watching someone transformed
into someone else. So, that transformation thing was still
sort of fresh in my head, and I think almost every writer
tries to get some more mileage out of anything that works.
So that was, I think, why I thought of the idea of trying to
do a story about a creature that could appear to be anyone.
He liked it and we went ahead. What's interesting to me is
that I finished the first draft and I knew something wasn't
going right with the plot . . . John D.F. Black was the
story editor, and when I went to see him . . . I told him
I wasn't happy with the way things had gone with the story.
He asked, "Well, what have you done?" I told him my
plotted out tale, and he said, "Oh! I see what you're doing

wrong: You've got to get the creature aboard the ship faster. You're doing it in the third act and it should be aboard the ship almost at the beginning. That's where all the jeopardy is, and then you could do this and that." We started talking [and] five minutes later I left. I rewrote it, and about two days later I was back with a new script, almost completely rewritten. Gene liked it, or claimed that he did. Then he hid it from me for a while, and the next thing you know I got a copy of the xeroxed final script and it had been rewritten quite a bit—the business with the chili peppers had been added, a couple of things that I had put in were taken out, but it was basically the same story, and so they shot it.

AA *How did you feel when you saw the finished product? Were you content with it?*

GCJ I loved it. *I* loved it and . . . one of the things about that is that it's the very first one America saw, so that almost all the critical reaction to STAR TREK came off that first show, and the things that I read, the basic attitude of America's reviewers was one of total bewilderment. I had watched the show myself and I was wondering, "Is anybody going to understand this?" I mean, a long-eared alien charac- ter . . . I didn't like the [Spock] character in that I never quite understood it. After "The Man Trap," Gene offered me another story. At first he wanted me to do a rewrite of Robert Bloch's story, the one about "Little Girls."

AA *"What Are Little Girls Made Of?"*

GCJ Yeah, "What Are Little Girls Made Of?" I tried, but I couldn't do it without throwing Bloch's work away . . . and Gene didn't want a real rewrite. He wanted it polished. It didn't work very well for me. I told Gene I was sorry, and that I'd like to work on the show. I think he was considering *me* at the time for a story editor to work opposite John D.F. . . . And then he wanted me to do another story, so I wrote one called "Rock-A-Bye Baby." It was a story about the ship coming alive. In the opening scene something comes from outer space, strikes the ship, and the next thing you know switches start swinging around and we hear the sound of a baby crying. I turned in this outline at the end of the first season. Gene Coon, who was a friend of mine, became the line producer—I used to party with him and go on vacations in Mexico with him and his wife—I thought it would be smooth sailing, but Gene called me in after I turned in the outline and said he wanted to make it more of a science fiction story. He felt that what I had done was a fantasy, that my concept of a creature taking over the computer, and my treating the creature as a little boy did not work for him. It worked very well for me. I was really, really happy with what I had done. With the ship coming alive, becoming an interesting little baby kind of a character and identifying with the Captain as his mentor, there was a great deal of opportunity to play out the myth of the young prince who sacrifices himself to win his father's love kind of a story.

AA   *Were you going to have the ship idolizing Captain Kirk?*

GCJ   Yes . . . At the very end of the story the ship was headed for the sun to coerce these people who had taken over the command of the ship to give it back to Daddy, so to speak, and when they finally do, the kid breaks their nerve, but he can't pull out of the dive and he burns up whatever connects him to the ship and the ship reverts to being just a plain ship, no longer alive. Mr. Spock's attitude was that it was a very rare and wonderful thing to have a living ship, and he wanted to take it back to Earth to the Academy and have them research it. The baby's idea was to live up to its father, but it was also very naive. . . . In the story [the Enterprise] was taking some prisoners to a prison colony, and these prisoners were the ones who managed to talk the naive ship to get it to turn against the Captain. At the end of Act I, the ship was diving toward the sun, saying, "Pretty, pretty, pretty": It was a little baby seeing a pretty sun and they couldn't get the damn thing to pull out of the dive . . . and that same scene was recreated in the fourth act when the ship managed to kill itself saving Father, wanting Father to be very proud of it. . . . I thought it was a very touching piece. I thought it would have been a great part for Captain Kirk the Childless One, who sublimates [his needs through] the ship, who doesn't want anything to hurt the ship, and now the ship is a baby boy and it loves him and wants to stand tall in his eyes and wants to learn to be like him. . . . I'd already walked all over their sets and I knew everything that they were doing from having watched them shoot the first few shows, so I really did feel like I had a handle on how to dramatize that vessel.

AA   *And I guess that's why you never submitted any other ideas.*

GCJ   After that, no more work for the series. When the first movie was to be done, I wanted to use my idea for it . . . but somehow, again, there was some kind of a misconnection. I couldn't get through to the right people. . . .

AA   *What were your thoughts at that time about the STAR TREK format?*

GCJ [When I first talked to] Roddenberry—I don't think this pleased him, either—I reminded him that you're talking back and forth with a producer, you're trying to convince him that you know everything about science fiction. You want to get this job, so you're laying it on pretty heavy about how wise you are in the area. So I was telling him about a series of pulp magazines I read, called *Captain Future* . . . there you have the ancestor of STAR TREK. You have Simon Wright, the brian, all intellect. His body has been removed, and his brain is in a glass case. . . . You have Grag, a robot, and Otho, an android, then you have Captain Future, and these four form an ill-assorted team. Well, there's Captain Kirk, and there's Mr. Spock, and there are a couple of other assorted crew members who have a remarkable talent and the kinds of stories that Edmond Hamilton, one of the original writers of *Captain Future* had a handle on doing . . . stories in this rocket ship with this strange crew that was always becoming involved with different kinds of desperados in outer space. I told Gene about that, trying to hint to him that I was very familiar with this format because I'd seen other people using it. He was seeing the U.N. of outer space—mixed cast, crew—no Russia any more, no Red scare, none of that stuff, and that was where *his* emphasis was. I think he also liked that thing that I did because it was a case of . . . the last of the buffalo. That was the scene that interested him in my presenting the idea. The thing I can say about Roddenberry is that I never saw a harder working producer, a producer who stayed until midnight or one o'clock and rewrote everything, [who] couldn't leave things alone . . . When I listened to him and Nimoy talking about this Mr. Spock character, and Nimoy taking it all very seriously, I just couldn't quite fathom it. Later on, I saw that the main thing Nimoy was doing was speaking very slowly and very deliberately, and that came to mean wisdom, also very straight-faced, no humor . . . real cold. He speaks with great authority, he is not afraid that anybody's going to interrupt him no matter how much time he takes to say something. He knows when he's right. If you want a meta-phor for it, it is this: Spock represents thought, the con-scious mind and all its power, and the subconscious mind and all of its power. Captain Kirk represents the action, the body with all of its power, and the soul, or emotion, with all of its power. We like to have the body and soul in charge, and we're perfectly prepared to have the mind, the subcon-scious, to be the second officer, but we don't ever want him in charge. We would rather trust the emotions of people than the cold analytical mind. That TV series really illustrates that.

AA   *Did you ever see the movie* Metropolis?

GCJ   Yes.

AA   *In it, someone points out that there can be no communication between the brain and the hands, unless the heart acts as a mediator.*

GCJ   Well, that's good . . . Bradbury said that about his own stories. He said your average doctor knows more about the musculature and the size, specific tension and diameter of the human heart, but he said, "I can reach out and touch it faster." And I think that's one of the things I've always liked about his stories: those moments of heart that could touch you, that could bring a lump to your throat, like those so-called two handkerchief movies. I used to like those. I used to love sitting there, watching and learning to care, and a lot of good science fiction is the same way. In fact, a lot of people said that about some of the stories that I did for THE TWILIGHT ZONE: they had heart, like "Kick the Can." They are very touching little stories, and they did the same thing for me. When I was writing them I got myself terribly emotional over them. I still mist up when I read the work I'm doing right now. . . . Of course, I have several rewrites to go through until I get it exactly the way I want it. Mr. Serling, by the way, was a remarkable man. He was really a super gentleman. I admired him, and I was also intimidated by him: and I think he was intimidated by me. When we met at agents' offices we'd be very polite to each other, but he always seemed in a hurry to rush off. He was always very sweet and very polite to me, a very nice man. I never had a harsh word with him, or with Gene Roddenberry, either.

AA   *Do you have any opinions about why STAR TREK is so popular?*

GCJ   . . . I think part of it is that the American public wants to see something they've never seen before. They don't care what it is, but they know what the back lot at Universal looks like, they know what westerns look like, they know what deserts look like, and they know what everything looks like, and they want to see something new. I think that what they got [with STAR TREK] was something new, all those cardboard universes and alien presences, and even in their third season they were still coming up with good shows . . . I did find something interesting. Later on, the plots used by SPACE: 1999 and LOGAN'S RUN were all the same plots that had been done the first season or two on

STAR TREK. They kept repeating, recycling all those same ideas and that must mean that there's a limited number of them, because I know that a lot of the STAR TREK plots and ideas came from other sources, from other pulp sci-fi, from different kinds of stories that had been around for a long, long time. . . .

AA *Well, there are some similarities between "The Man Trap" and* The Voyage of the Space Beagle.

GCJ Yes. I'm not at all surprised by that. Van Vogt has always been a heavy, heavy influence in my life, although I always think of the Space Beagle as that hostile creature that's prowling the ship. . . . You know, generally speaking, STAR TREK has really been good to me. I've really gotten a lot of mileage out of the fact that I wrote STAR TREK, TWI-LIGHT ZONE, KUNG FU, and LOGAN'S RUN. They're all generic, so it's made me fairly well known in that area of fantasy and science fiction. So I really am glad I worked on the show, but it is a damn shame that something went wrong between me and Gene because I could have written a dozen episodes. I had ideas for plots for that show that just spill out of me. I can't talk to anybody for three minutes without coming up with some new angle on it. I'm glad to see it succeeding. I can see what an icon it has become. . . . I also have to admire Gene on another level, which has to do with the man's character and training. One night we were both at the Writers' Guild, and there was a little flareup: one person threatened another. I was talking to Roddenberry, and it was amazing how quickly and quietly he interposed himself between these two guys, how fast he had them quieted down. . . . He just knew what he was doing there, even though he was in a situation where he could have gotten brained. . . . That was one moment in which I looked at Roddenberry and said, "You know, this guy is not an overgrown boy, which he seems to be sometimes."

NORMAN SPINRAD

Norman Spinrad, born in New York in 1940, is one of science fiction's best-known and most honored writers. His novels include Bug Jack Barron, The Void Captain's Tale, *and* Little Heroes.

Spinrad submitted his first draft script for "The Doomsday Machine" to the STAR TREK staff in May of 1967, and the episode was filmed toward the end of the following month.

AA   *How were you first approached to work on STAR TREK?*

NS   I had seen both STAR TREK pilots at a science fiction convention. I had met Gene Roddenberry a couple of times, and I did a long feature piece in *Cinema Magazine* on 2001: A SPACE ODYSSEY in which I compared STAR TREK favorably to that film. Gene Roddenberry called me, thanked me for the nice mention, and said that perhaps I'd like to come in and talk about doing a STAR TREK sometime. I was working on the first draft of *Bug Jack Barron* and I said the perfect thing, not trying to be cunning about it: "Call me back in six weeks. I'm working on a book, and I can't do it now." Gene did call me back. I went in, and we talked about a STAR TREK.

AA   *Was "The Doomsday Machine" the first treatment you submitted?*

NS   What happened was, I went in just to have a meeting with Gene, to pitch whatever was going to be pitched. That's the way I do these things, and that's the way Gene was doing it, too. That was the first time we talked about this. I really didn't have anything particular in mind at the time. Gene said, "We're having a little budget problem, so could you think of something we could do entirely on the ship without having to build any planet stuff," because they always had to maintain the balance between planet stories and ship stories, since the planet stuff was expensive. It happened that I had a novelette that I hadn't been able to sell, which took place on a starship very much like the Enterprise. I resurrected that, and it became "The Doomsday Machine."

AA   *In the first draft of your script, the machine itself is described as a metallic object covered with menacing devices, a very different concept from the filmed version. How did you feel about their interpretation of your descriptions?*

NS   Not at all good. Damon Knight called it "the giant flying turnip," and somebody else called it "the windsock." Gene had actually asked me to draw the thing when I handed in the script. I'm not much of an artist, but I did a drawing of a concept that was a little more complicated.

AA   *How did you feel your script translated to the screen?*

NS   Maybe it was in the story conference, but when I was telling Gene the story I was told that they were looking for something for Robert Ryan. So the part was originally conceived as a Robert Ryan type of character. . . . Whatever happened, Ryan wasn't available. So they cast William Windom, and there were other things in general that changed the character of Decker.

AA   *Were you ever part of any of the campaigns to save the series?*

NS   Oh, yes. I was one of the original people who was on that letterhead, "The Committee to Save Star Trek."

AA   *Do you feel that it was worthwhile saving, based on what you saw after that?*

NS   Well, the first time around, that was in the middle of the first season, so there was still some good stuff to come. I thought the third season was crap.

AA   *Tell me about "He Walked Among Us," which I know progressed from outline to first draft script status but was not produced.*

NS   There were two versions of that script. One was mine, the other was by Gene L. Coon. . . . What happened was that when I did the first draft, Gene Coon felt it needed work. This happened to many scripts. In the case of "He Walked Among Us," he took something that was rather complicated sociological science fiction and turned it into what I thought was extremely unfunny comedy. When I read the thing I kind of freaked.

AA   *The draft I read had Bane, the central figure, as a social misfit who had gone to a planet to try to implement his private theories.*

NS   That was the same. That really wasn't changed. It was played for some laughs. It was completely turned into an atrocity. And it was such an atrocity that I called Gene Roddenberry and I said, "Gene, you've got to read this thing. You can't do this: you've got to kill it." That's why it was never done, because Gene [Roddenberry] agreed with me.

AA   *There was no hope of going with the original version at that point?*

NS   No, because Gene Coon was still the producer. Roddenberry was the executive producer.

AA *So you didn't submit anything after that.*

NS No, I didn't. But not because I was afraid to submit it. I did do a treatment years later, for the first attempt to revive STAR TREK as a TV series.

AA *STAR TREK II, for the Paramount Network?*

NS Yes. I think they commissioned 13 treatments, and I did one of them. Gene commissioned one from me.

AA *Do you remember the name of it?*

NS No. It was about the crew of the Enterprise somehow becoming a hive mind, due to contact with some alien presence.

AA *If you were asked to submit anything for the new series, would you?*

NS Yes, I would. It depends upon what the "bible" [writer's guide] comes out to be. . . . I wouldn't mind, assuming they come up with a viable format.

AA *Do you have any opinions about the popularity of STAR TREK?*

NS I have a lot of theories. One is that the whole of STAR TREK was a created phenomenon to begin with. When the show was first being canceled, Gene got together a committee of science fiction writers who did a letter, which was then widely sent to fans, and dumped all this unprecedented stuff on the network. But as to the whole phenomenon, why this has lasted so long, it's really hard to put your finger on it. I'm not sure. Perhaps because it was the only real science fiction on television at that time. That might have had something to do with it.

AA *You mean other than anthologies?*

NS There were anthologies before, but what was there afterward, when STAR TREK was around? I think maybe it began because it at least filled a niche that was empty. I think that in many ways STAR TREK is a unique piece of American history.

JEROME BIXBY

Jerome Bixby was born in 1923, and although most of his literary output is not science fiction, he has made many contributions to the field.

His first science fiction story, "Tubemonkey," was published in 1949 in Planet Stories, *a magazine he edited from 1950 to 1951. He also worked on the staffs of* Galaxy *magazine,* Thrilling Wonder Stories *and* Startling Stories. *Anthologies of his work include* Space by the Tale *and* The Devil's Scrapbook, *both published in 1964.*

Bixby wrote the screenplay for It! The Terror from Beyond Space, *a motion picture very similar in concept to the later film* Alien. *His most famous story is "It's a Good Life," adapted by Rod Serling as a TWILIGHT ZONE episode.*

Bixby submitted his story outline for STAR TREK's "Mirror, Mirror" in March 1967, and the episode was filmed in July and August of that year. Another outline submitted by Bixby became the segment "By Any Other Name," scripted by D.C. Fontana and filmed in November 1967. His outline for "The Day of the Dove," submitted on June 3, 1968, was scripted by Bixby and filmed in August of that year. "Requiem for Methuselah," his last produced STAR TREK outline, was completed in October 1968 and filmed two months later.

AA *Were you approached to work on STAR TREK?*

JB They didn't approach me: I approached them. I saw the show, liked it, sat down and wrote a script cold, which they later told me would have cost a great deal to produce. But they were impressed with my [feel] for the show and said go home and come up with a story, which I did.

AA *Do you recall what the script was?*

JB It was called "Mother Tiger." Basically, it concerned finding a suspended animation ship in space, with a rather lovely alien female aboard who was the sole survivor of her race: a racial mother, sent into space to recreate her race.

AA *Was that during the first year of the show?*

JB Yes, toward the end of the first year.

AA *There was an episode called "The Devil in the Dark" concerning a racial mother.*

JB   I always found that rather a curious coincidence, about six months after I submitted "Mother Tiger."

AA   *Did you ever submit any additional stories that were considered but not bought?*

JB   Three or four others. One thing I've always desperately wanted to do was to land the Enterprise on a water planet. I don't know how I would have worked it in terms of physics . . on a low-mass, aqueous planet so that it would have floated, but not collapsed. I just wanted to see the Enterprise floating, and they were intrigued by the idea, and I came up with a number of story lines based on that, but it never went.

AA   *One that did is "Mirror, Mirror." Your outline for that is more complex than the filmed episode.*

JB   Well, I'm a wild man in outlines, and very disciplined in scripts. A long time ago I did a parallel universe story called "One Way Street," and I thought of a parallel universe for STAR TREK . . . a very savage counterpart, virtually a pirate ship, into which I could transpose a landing party. I submitted the outline, they loved it, and I did the script.

AA   *In your outline, Kirk was being slowly poisoned by the other universe.*

JB   I must have had my story "One Way Street" in my mind, because that angle does exist in that story, which was published in *Amazing Stories* magazine back in 1952. I think it's about to be reprinted by Marty Greenberg in a forthcoming *Amazing Stories* anthology.

AA   *What do you think of the episode?*

JB   I thought Marc [Daniels] did one hell of a directing job on it. I virtually clocked the last act, stop-watched it, because I got sick of other stories in which there are only 3 seconds to get to the transporter, and 19 seconds later they're still talking about it.

AA   *Some years ago, the Museum of Modern Art showed "Mirror, Mirror" to represent STAR TREK in a science fiction film festival.*

JB   So I've heard, and that pleases me very much. You know . . . I collaborated on "By Any Other Name," too. I wrote a story, they liked it, then I did a first draft and they didn't like it, and looking back I can see why. I did the one thing that Roddenberry was most against: "Don't become obsessed with the immensity of it all." And I did. The Enterprise was hijacked, and was being taken to the Andromeda Galaxy. Our crew was leaving behind their own galaxy, which they would never see again because they would die in space and their descendants would complete the trek to Andromeda. I dealt extensively with all this subjective stuff that this produced in men: loneliness, disorientation, grief . . . and I gave them 45 pages of the immensity of it all. And so Dorothy Fontana, without my knowledge, darn it, started to do a rewrite. Apparently they felt that I was so committed emotionally, and I probably was at the time, to my own vision of that story, they felt it had to be rewritten, and so it was. And it came out kind of a lightweight episode. The drinking contest with Robert Fortier was a funny, funny bit. When he collapsed, I thought it was the best part of the story. . . .

AA *Warren Stevens is a fine actor.*

JB . . . But I don't think he was a particularly good Rojan. I thought they needed an actor with more venom. "Rojan," by the way, was originally "RUSSjan." My two oldest boys are named Russell and Jan. . . . The episode finally came out as "Teleplay by D.C. Fontana and Jerome Bixby, Story by Jerome Bixby." So if anybody asks, I did three and a half STAR TREKs.

AA *The outline for "The Day of the Dove" began with a peace celebration aboard the Enterprise.*

JB I do recall that. In fact, it was very much late sixties, and I ended it with a peace march which, thank God, also came out.

AA *What do you think of the finished product?*

JB I do enjoy it very much. I enjoy Mike Ansara in his performance as Kang. . . . I originally wrote "The Day of the Dove" for Kor, the Klingon in "Errand of Mercy," but John Colicos was unavailable. He was abroad doing a film, and he said that when he first read the script he wept and threw himself at walls and nearly jumped off a balcony because he wanted to play the part so bad, but he was committed to that other production and he couldn't play Kor. So they changed it to Kang. They were looking around for a Klingon, and they almost hit on Joe Campanella, but they didn't think he could draw quite enough fire. So they hit on Mike Ansara, who just ate up the part.

AA *Did you originally have James Daly in mind for Flint in "Requiem for Methuselah"?*

JB My own first choice for Flint was Carroll O'Connor, but unfortunately he turned it down. My second choice was Jim Daly, who was perfectly OK in the part.

AA *Do you like the filmed episode?*

JB Yes and no. For one thing, I had a Beethoven sonata being played by Spock, instead of a Brahms waltz. They said that no composer on earth can counterpoint a Beethoven sonata with any kind of waltz that Kirk and Rayna could be dancing . . . and I said "I can. I'm a trained composer: I went to Juilliard," but they said, "We don't have time for masterpieces," and so they changed it to a Brahms waltz. I wouldn't say it infuriated me, but I sure was unhappy about it. There are two other things that stick with me about "Requiem . . ." One is that in the last act, Kirk and Flint are trading words, and all of a sudden Flint, this totally wonderful immortal, an overwhelmingly educated man, goes right off the wall, he goes Neanderthal and attacks Kirk. Well, I had a page and a half of heated dialogue leading up to that, and they threw it out. He just gets mad. I couldn't do anything about that, either, except grind my teeth. Then, at the very end, Spock says "Forget." I wrote a mouthful of words for DeForest Kelley that De just couldn't handle, because he felt it was just too filled with poetry: he couldn't get up there and utter it with a straight face. So I sat down there on the set, under a Kleig light, and rewrote about a page and a half of that dialogue. It worked OK, but I hated to take out all that alliteration.

AA *How did it feel being on the set and seeing the episode take form?*

JB I got a kick out of it. I've always enjoyed the filming end of it. I probably would like to direct, and I still may do it. . . . I also had to rewrite one act. I guess at this late date the Screen Writers' Guild won't kill me, but I did it off the cuff, much against Guild regulations. They needed a rewrite of the third act of "Methuselah," and they needed it tomorrow. I said "Fine. Give me a desk, give me a typewriter, give me a fifth of Chivas Regal and leave me alone," and at four o'clock in the morning it was done, and I headed for my place in the mountains. I agreed that it was necessary.

AA *Did you feel that the STAR TREK staff was like a family?*

JB At first, yeah. They were very protective of the show, particularly during the first year. The first guy I dealt with was Gene L. Coon, and then I remember Fred Freiberger. The only change that I could see was that it just became less STAR TREK, and more what was going on down the hall: MISSION: IMPOSSIBLE and the others in that same area of Desilu. It no longer had that unique flavor that just pervaded the offices during the first couple of years.

AA *It's a shame you couldn't have sold them a script during that first year.*

JB At that point I was virtually semiretired, working on a whole bunch of personal handles.

AA *Do you have any theories regarding the enduring popularity of STAR TREK?*

JB One of the things that was going around in the old days was the myth of Spock's sex appeal, but speaking seriously, I think it's just likable characters, and dealing openly with provocative ideas that were very radical at the time, and also very topical. It was really the first decent all-out science fiction show in the television industry, excluding anthologies. OUTER LIMITS is about the only one aside from STAR TREK that really played seriously for content.

AA *Is there anything that you care to mention regarding your participation in STAR TREK?*

JB Simply that it was a high point. I was rarely involved in anything that was that enjoyable, and just agreeable in general. . . . I never found anything to bitch about aside from stuff like what I've mentioned.

AA *Weren't you one of the writers approached to do work for the STAR TREK II television series that was never produced?*

JB Right. That was about ten years ago. I went in and talked over some stories with whoever was there. I sent them a couple of outlines, but we didn't connect and it all fell apart.

AA *Have you been approached in connection with the new series, STAR TREK—THE NEXT GENERATION?*

JB It could be something . . . to start doing idea stories again. I don't think Gene Roddenberry would do it unless he could do it on his own terms. I think I'll give him a call and find out what's going on.

William Shatner (Captain James T. Kirk), in the first portrait session taken after STAR TREK achieved series status.

A portrait of Leonard Nimoy (Mr. Spock) taken before the production of "The Corbomite Maneuver." Note the command insignia.

Grace Lee Whitney (Yeoman Janice Rand).

James Doohan (Scotty) tends the transporter in "Where No Man Has Gone Before."

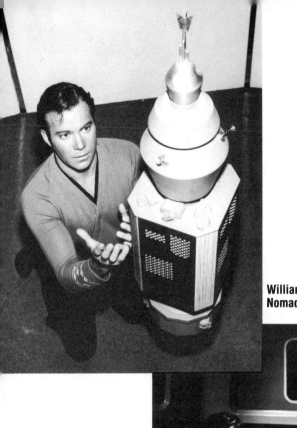

William Shatner (Kirk) appeals to Nomad, in "The Changeling."

George Takei (Sulu), Walter Koenig (Chekov), Nichelle Nichols (Uhura), and James Doohan (Scotty) man the bridge.

DeForest Kelley (Dr. Leonard McCoy) in a gag shot taken during the filming of "Spectre of the Gun."

A third-season portrait of George Takei (Sulu) and Walter Koenig (Chekov).

Leonard Nimoy in his MISSION: IMPOSSIBLE days, playing a magician in "The Falcon."

An imposing study of Admiral Kirk taken for STAR TREK: THE MOTION PICTURE.

Mr. Spock on Vulcan: a sketch by costume designer Robert Fletcher for STAR TREK: THE MOTION PICTURE.

George Takei (Sulu) during a tense moment from
STAR TREK III.

Walter Koenig (Chekov) in STAR TREK III.

DeForest Kelley (Dr. McCoy) and William Shatner (Admiral Kirk)
contemplate Spock's future in STAR TREK III.

Nichelle Nichols in a publicity
portrait taken at the time of STIII.

THE PRODUCERS

AS THE TITLE INDICATES, THE PRODUCERS ARE THE INDIVIDUALS ULTIMATELY RESPONSIBLE FOR THE SUCCESSFUL COMPLETION OF A TELEVISION SHOW—THEY MUST CHOOSE THE SCRIPTS AND THE DIRECTORS, BUDGET THE AVAILABLE TIME AND MONEY, HELP CAST THE GUEST STARS, AND KEEP TRACK OF ALL PHASES OF THE POSTPRODUCTION PROCESS, FROM SCORING TO SPECIAL EFFECTS. IT'S A TRULY HERCULEAN TASK, AND STAR TREK WAS VERY LUCKY TO HAVE PEOPLE LIKE ROBERT JUSTMAN AND FRED FREIBERGER ON THE JOB.

ROBERT JUSTMAN

Robert H. Justman began his film career as a production assistant and assistant director, and has worked on more than 35 feature films and at least 550 television productions.

His feature films include the mystery thriller The Scarf *(1951, United Artists), the science fiction adventure* Red Planet Mars *(1952, U.A.), and the eerie "Mike Hammer" vehicle* Kiss Me Deadly *(1955, U.A.).*

Justman served as assistant director during the second production season of THE ADVENTURES OF SUPERMAN in 1953, and was also connected with ONE STEP BEYOND (which ran from 1959-61), THE OUTER LIMITS (as assistant director and unit manager on the 1963-65 series), SEARCH (producer of the 1972-73 series), and THE MAN FROM ATLANTIS (as supervising producer of the concept's two TV movies and pilot, all aired in 1977).

His long association with Gene Roddenberry began with the two STAR TREK pilots. He was later associate producer during STAR TREK's first two seasons, and coproducer during the final season.

Before STAR TREK achieved series status, Justman was the associate producer of Roddenberry's 1965 pilots, POLICE STORY and THE LONG HUNT OF APRIL SAVAGE, and worked in the same capacity on the Desilu pilots THE RECRUITERS, AL-FRED OF THE AMAZON, and MISSION: IMPOSSIBLE.

He produced Roddenberry's 1975 TV movie Planet Earth, *and the two-hour pilot for STAR TREK—THE NEXT GENERA-TION, and is now producing the series STAR TREK—THE NEXT GENERATION.*

AA *How did you first become involved with STAR TREK?*

RJ Through James Goldstone, with whom I was doing a two-part OUTER LIMITS. Jimmy and I got along very well: I was his assistant director, and he liked the way I worked. He knew Roddenberry . . . and he recommended that Gene see me with an eye toward hiring me as associate producer on the STAR TREK pilot, and so I went to visit Gene on the Paramount lot. The western side of it at that time was Desilu Studios, the old RKO lot. I was shooting OUTER LIMITS nearby at another independent studio, Paramount

Sunset, and I left my assistant in charge of the set for an hour or so while I went to visit Gene. Gene and I talked for a while, and he offered me the job of associate producer and assistant director on the pilot. I turned him down because I felt I didn't have sufficient knowledge of postproduction optical effects. Although it was during the second season of OUTER LIMITS, I didn't have enough actual postproduction experience, especially with respect to opticals and special effects. I knew how to do a number of them from the production end of it, but I didn't know how I would [work] it with the lab and the optical houses. So I turned the offer down, and at the same time I recommended Byron Haskin, who had worked on OUTER LIMITS and with whom I also had a very nice relationship. I liked him personally, and he had all the experience in the world.

AA *He had headed Warner Brothers' optical effects department.*

RJ Yes. He had directed a number of films, some of which were quite good, and he had handled that kind of area for a long time. He really knew it, so I recommended "Bun" Haskin to Gene before I left, and as I left the Gower entrance of the studio I bumped into Byron Haskin who was going to see Gene because he had also been called in. So Bun got the job as associate producer on the first pilot and I got the job as the first assistant. We shot the show, I worked very closely with Gene and with Bun, and when the studio decided to make another pilot, Gene called me and told me that he wasn't going to have Byron Haskin back. He and Byron didn't get along. Gene again asked me to be the associate producer, and this time I felt that I had enough knowledge that I could get by, and so I accepted. This time, it *was* Jim Goldstone directing, and we shot the second pilot together.

AA *You have dual billing on that, as assistant director and associate producer. Was that unusual, to have one man in both capacities?*

RJ Quite often nowadays, the unit manager will also get the credit as associate producer. For an assistant director to get it is another matter, but I was heavily involved in the show and I knew how to do it. . . . That's how I got to do the first and second STAR TREK pilots.

AA *Was everyone happy with "The Cage" after its completion?*

RJ We were . . . Yes, Gene and I felt we could have done it better, but considering the circumstances under which we had to work we thought that we did a good job. Frankly, NBC's reaction to the first pilot stunned us because when they rejected it they said they wouldn't accept it because it was "too cerebral." That's an exact quote. What they were saying was that the audience wouldn't understand it. What they really meant, although they didn't know it, was that *they* were too dense to understand it. Certainly the American public wasn't too dense, but the network executives didn't know that because they considered themselves to be head and shoulders above . . . It bears fruit, when you think that later on when Gene wrote the envelope to make "The Menagerie" a two-parter, that the two-part show ended up, I believe, to be the most popular STAR TREK we ever aired. So much for cerebration.

AA   *I've heard that the sets for the first pilot were designed to be shot from only one angle, and that a lot of refurbishing had to be done in preparation for "Where No Man . . ."*

RJ   We did refurbishing. I worked very closely with Matt Jefferies on laying out not only what the sets would look like, but where they could be spotted on the stage so we could make the most use out of the small amount of space that we had. Everything was very carefully done. It took us weeks to figure out how to do it, and there was not a square inch that we did not take advantage of.

AA   *Franz Bachelin had left by this time?*

RJ   He was long gone. Franz didn't even finish on the first pilot, as I recall. He was involved in the first pilot, and then on the second pilot it was only Matt . . . Certainly on the series it was only Matt Jefferies . . .

AA   *Did the network specifically tell you to put more action into the second pilot?*

RJ   I believe so. They always wanted action. James Goldstone had a very difficult job to do. The first pilot was a longer show. I think we had 14 or 15 days to shoot it. We shot the second pilot in either eight or nine days. The last day of shooting we did two days' work, and we really worked very hard in general to get it accomplished.

AA   *Did it have to be done within a certain number of days to prove to the network that you could do that on a regular basis?*

RJ   No, it had to be done within a certain number of days so that Desilu didn't go broke doing it.

AA   *What did Oscar Katz have to do with the pilots?*

RJ   Oscar Katz was the president of Desilu Television at the time . . . the person who really ran things was his second-in-command, Herb Solow: Herb is the one who really got those things moving. Oscar was dealing with the network, but Herb was actually instrumental in getting not only STAR TREK made, but also MISSION: IMPOSSIBLE. He was hands-on with Gene Roddenberry and with Bruce Geller, who created MISSION: IMPOSSIBLE . . . I was involved in both.

AA *When everything had to be moved over to the Desilu lot after STAR TREK went to series status, was it a difficult task?*

RJ Yes, it was. There was also a good deal of refurbishing that needed to be done, and we also had to make the bridge come apart so that we could pull any section of it.

AA *It was not "wild" in either of the pilots?*

RJ Well, it was kind of wild, but we needed it to be wilder. We made it so that each pie-shaped section of the bridge could come out in three pieces: the bottom, the middle, and the top. We'd usually leave the top in, if we possibly could.

AA *Each section's wiring was completely independent?*

RJ Right.

AA *What a job that must have been to design it that way.*

RJ Yes, especially in those days when we didn't have the techniques available to us now.

AA *When I asked Eddie Milkis what you did on the show, his response was "everything."*

RJ Yes.

AA *Did that entail elements of production and postproduction as well?*

RJ Right, and preproduction as well. In other words, I fulfilled the function of line producer despite my title for the first two seasons of the show, and was called associate producer. I actually functioned as the line producer of the show. I did all of the preproduction, production, and supervised all of the postproduction, hands-on, until such time as Eddie Milkis came on the show.

AA *At first, the Howard Anderson Company was handling all the photographic effects, the opticals. You then called in other companies as well.*

RJ It was too much work for one optical house to churn out. They just couldn't do it, so it soon became apparent to us that we had to recruit other houses. We ended up with about five or six different optical houses in that first season, and kept them all busy.

AA *Each episode must have been like a jigsaw puzzle.*

RJ It was, and without Eddie Milkis we couldn't have gotten it done. He came along at just the right time. It was Gene and myself doing the show, and there was no staff. There was nothing. We were physically, emotionally and mentally exhausted by the time we were halfway through the first season.

AA *Were the network executives always behind STAR TREK, or were they skeptical about the series from the start?*

RJ My feeling is that the network executives never understood what the show was about. I don't think those same people understand it to this day. If they do, they've learned after the fact. The audience who watched the show knew what it was about. They understood it. It's too bad that everytime we had a new season we'd have a new air date, a new time and a new day. The network considered it to be action-adventure, not science fiction.

AA *That's how it was classified in the* TV Guide.

RJ That's right. It was billed in the daily papers the same way. . . . One nice thing about the fact that they didn't understand the show was that they didn't understand that we were dealing with present-day issues by masking them into something that occurs in the future. We were doing something allegorical, dealing with the issues of the late sixties, and luckily the network didn't pick up on that. That's another reason why I feel that the people at the network are not as cerebral as they would have us believe they are.

AA *For a while during the middle of the first season it looked as though the series might be canceled.*

RJ Well, our ratings weren't very good, according to the network. They just looked at mass figures, and how much of an audience share we had, as compared to whatever our opposition was at the time, and, in fact, if the more rabid fans hadn't demonstrated and written and carried on, it would have been canceled at the end of the first season. There's no doubt of that.

AA *It wasn't only the fans, it was also the writers. Some of them got together and mounted a letter-writing campaign.*

RJ . . .There were a lot of people who were not officially connected to the show, as I recall—famous people, writers, science fiction writers, people who had [a] philosophy [bent]—and they helped a lot . . . Our literate audience, composed of high school and college students and young marrieds, was very important. They were the people in the audience that did it. They were our audience, the people with the most buying power, the people who the networks should have been attempting to reach, and who they *were* reaching but didn't know it, and they were the people who saved us two years running. But by the time they saved us the second time, the handwriting was on the wall. By the third season we knew it was never going to go again.

AA *Mr. Freiberger told me that it was a foregone conclusion that the show was dead no matter what he did with it.*

RJ Well, evidently. Each year we had less money to make the show, despite the fact that we had cast salary escalations.

So we had to start trimming . . . on what we could. By the third season, when Freddie came on board, we were reduced to practically doing a radio show. We couldn't go on location, we could hardly build any sets, and the quality of the writing declined, too, because Gene [Roddenberry] wasn't as heavily involved with it by then. He was exhausted.

AA   *When did Gene L. Coon join the STAR TREK staff?*

RJ   Gene Coon came on halfway through the first season, and lasted until about halfway through the second season. Then he was worn out, he had to go. When Gene Coon left we had other people on it. John Meredyth Lucas came in and helped for a while . . . he also directed, and he was a very, very nice man. But then the studio brought in Freddie the third season. Gene [Roddenberry] was not that heavily involved in it anymore.

AA   *Was that because the show's time slot was changed?*

RJ   Yes. Our audience, as I said, was college people, high school, young marrieds. Thursday at 8:30, when we were on the first season, was a wonderful time and the ratings during that first summer rerun season started improving. The ratings kept on piling up, getting bigger and bigger. The second season they moved us to Friday night at 8:30, and Friday is a night when these people go out. The third season they moved us to 10 o'clock on Friday night, and only a few audience die-hards would stay for that. That's a very important time in a young person's life: it's date night, it's getting out, and it's also too late for the younger kids. So they really cut into our audience very heavily. . . .

AA   *At one point, NBC had issued a publicity pamphlet called "STAR TREK Mail Call," in which they talked about the diversity of the letters the series had received, the volume of the mail . . . It's incredible to believe that they would acknowledge these things while shifting the series into such a time slot.*

RJ   The people in programming were the bane of our existence. In attempting to sell the show to their affiliates the first season, they put out a press kit, and they were so frightened by what we were doing they thought that Leonard Nimoy as Spock looked demonic. So they airbrushed the photograph of him, airbrushed out his ears, made him look normal . . .

AA   *I had also heard that NBC, at one time, wanted Spock dropped from the STAR TREK format.*

RJ   Yes, that's what I heard. Lots of things the network does out of fear. Networks are corporations, composed of people who live a highly dangerous life in that they're subject to being fired for making the wrong decision. When you live that kind of a life, it's only natural to avoid making any decisions at all, or to try to make the decisions that will be acceptable to everyone. In other words, as a network executive you don't want to do something because it might be a mistake, because you might get letters, and it might affect the advertisers. That's why you operate out of fear rather than out of conviction. I've bad-mouthed these people for many years, but I can understand how it came to be. These people were afraid, and I don't think you can live your life being afraid. You've got to take a stand sometime. If it's what you believe in . . . go ahead and do it.

AA *Was STAR TREK ever under any pressure because of its minority regulars?*

RJ That would have come to Gene, and not to me. I do know that we did have a lot of pressure from Broadcast Standards on every show, as to what we were showing, what we were saying, what we were intimating. They made our life very uncomfortable at times . . . fighting us and saying, "You can't say that, you can't show that."

AA *Were you content with what you did get across?*

RJ Never. But that has nothing to do with the network. People who are in a creative profession should never be content with what they've been able to accomplish because they always could have done it better. They could have done it worse, too. . . . It has to do with economics, it has to do with many things. I've never been satisfied with anything I've ever done. I've been happy with some things I've done, but not totally satisfied.

AA *When did you first learn that STAR TREK was successful from a critical point of view?*

RJ Years after the series was pronounced dead. The phenomenon started happening, the whole Trekkie phenomenon started happening, people started watching the reruns and stations kept buying the reruns and showing them, over and over and over again. We turned into something famous and cultish. There was great surprise, because when we were making the show we were sort of like pariahs: nobody in the business thought anything of the show, and we were made fun of. We thought we were doing something that was important, at least we felt it: we knew we were doing something we cared about. We were really intent on that, but we felt that nobody else in the world knew except those fans who were so vocal. We were always told, "Oh, that's just the lunatic fringe. That happens on every show, there are people who feel that way and the majority of the public doesn't buy what you're offering to them."

AA *Were they frightened by a show that seemed to attract intellectuals?*

RJ Yes.

AA *I imagine that the sponsors thought that intellectuals were not their main market, either.*

RJ I imagine so, but I can't say that for sure because I wasn't there when they discussed it . . . I don't think it was just intellectuals who were attracted to STAR TREK. I say that in retrospect. Some of the intellectuals, if you want to characterize them as such, wrote in and let us know how they felt. But I think that the word "intellectual" connotes a very small segment of our population, the only real keen thinkers. So I don't think we appeal only to intellectuals. I think we appeal to the morality and the humanity of people. That's what the show is really about: it's about morality . . . the simplest person, the person with the smallest amount of education, the most nonintellectual person you could possibly imagine, has some kind of morality which motivates him. . . . Intellectuals are all well and good. That's fine. Intellectuals have feelings just as uneducated people have feelings. A person reaches a certain age and that person knows whether something is right or wrong. In legalese, in courts, it's "voir dire"[1]—knowing right from wrong. That's a test of whether a witness is competent to give testimony in court, and "voir dire" is used with young people to determine whether they are to be examined, or to give testimony. But I think that almost everyone, unless they're a moron, has "voir dire." Kids know what's right and wrong. Kids know what's moral and what's immoral. . . . they know it from their parents and from their peers. They knew what we were saying with the show. The show dealt with age-old precepts: what's right and what's wrong. The show dealt with mankind's attempts to better mankind, to be better than we were before. It's a constant search for perfection, and to retain it we have to keep on trying, otherwise what's the use of our existence? Why should we even be here on Earth if we don't try to make things better for the next people who come along, so that *they* can make things better. I think man has come a long way, and we have a long way to go. That's what we're saying on this show now [STAR TREK—THE NEXT GENERATION] as we did 20 years ago. The future is bright, things can be better and will be better. All we have to do is work at it. There's no apocalypse coming, otherwise we might as well all give up.

---

[1] Literally translated, "voir dire" means "see speak." As an idiom it means saying what one sees, or speaking the truth.

AA *Is there anything you want to say to STAR TREK's fans?*

RJ I did it a few months ago. There was a small science fiction convention . . . and I went to that convention on purpose. I've never been an official guest at any of them . . . I've gone and I've left. . . . I went to that convention to say "Thanks" to the people who used to watch the show and still watch the show, because without them we couldn't have made it. Let's see if I can find the exact words. [He consults his office computer terminal] Yes, there it is. In short, I said:

> *"There are a lot of people in this room, a lot of people representing a whole lot of people, a whole lot more than could be counted by surveys, census-takers, or perhaps— now I don't want to sound bitter—perhaps even more people than once were counted by the scientific survey called 'Nielsen.' Perhaps you've heard that name before. Certainly we did. Constantly. We heard that name often, 20 years ago. Gene Roddenberry and I were told that according to Nielsen nobody was watching. Well, somebody was watching, because we're still here. You were watching. Your friends were watching. The fact is that millions of people were watching, watching and responding to what our message was then, and what it continues to be now: truth, morality, tolerance, and human kindness. Truth, morality, tolerance and human kindness on television? Damned right, and we're going to do it again. Let me qualify that. We will attempt to do it again. If we fail, it won't be for lack of trying. So please bear with us if the new STAR TREK doesn't always meet your expectations. Our little show has become a legend, and it's hard to live up to a legend. People's perceptions of what used to be sometimes conflicts with the actual reality of what was. We try hard, we want to succeed, we want to excel, we'll do what we can. We're sure going to try. Just hang in there with us, please. The runner stumbles now and then but, if he's any kind of runner, he'll get up to run again. That's human nature: our nature, your nature. Which brings me to why I'm here today. This is my first appearance at an event of this kind. For years I've stayed away, but now I feel the time has come for me to say something to you, and it's about time that I did. A few minutes ago, when my colleagues and I were introduced to you, we were applauded. Applause is a sweet sound. It nurtures the ego, feeds it, but unfortunately it often makes it grow to astounding proportions. Well, somebody else deserves applause, somebody who really deserves it. You deserve it, you and all the millions of people around*

*the world who supposedly weren't watching. You kept our
spirit alive, you kept STAR TREK alive, you refused to let
it die. And that's why we're here today, to thank you and to
applaud you. STAR TREK lives, the future is bright. Tell
your friends."*

FRED FREIBERGER

*New Yorker-born Fred Freiberger was in the U.S. Air Force when
he was shot down over Germany, in November 1943, and confined
in the prison camp represented in the film* The Great Escape. *"At
one time we were in the same compound with the RAF guys," he
recalls. "Then they separated us, and the escape took place . . . It
started to trickle in to us how the guys were being killed by the
Gestapo. Very nervous times . . ."*

*Following his release he went to California, hoping to enter the
advertising/publicity field. He sold one story to a production company, then found himself out of work. "Then it was a question of
finding out what Hollywood was all about . . ."*

He remembers reading Amazing Stories *magazine, and ". . .
trying to hit them with short stories, which I don't think I ever
succeeded in doing . . ." In 1953, Freiberger and Lou Morheim
(later story editor for THE OUTER LIMITS) wrote the screenplay
for* The Beast From 20,000 Fathoms, *based on a short story by
Ray Bradbury. Four years later, working with Lester Gorn, he
cowrote* The Beginning of the End *(1957, Republic), a drama
concerning giant, mutated grasshoppers.*

*In 1968 he became the producer of STAR TREK, working with
coproducer Robert H. Justman on the series' third and final season,
which included the episodes "The Paradise Syndrome," "Is There in
Truth No Beauty?," "The Tholian Web," "Day of the Dove," and
"Requiem for Methuselah."*

*Seven years after his affiliation with STAR TREK, Freiberger
produced the second season of SPACE: 1999 in Great Britain.*

AA *How did you become the producer of STAR TREK?*

FF Gene Roddenberry had interviewed me about producing the
first year of STAR TREK, and I had seen the original pilot
with Jeff Hunter, which I fell in love with, but I was going to
Europe and I didn't want to cancel my trip. I told Gene,
whom I've known for years, that if the job was still available

when I got back from Europe in about six weeks I'd love to do it. Well, *it* wasn't available; Gene Coon was assigned. And in the third year *I* was available, Gene called me again, and I produced it that year.

AA *NBC rejected "The Cage."*

FF Is that right? To me, "The Cage" was pure science fiction. That's what the show should have been. William Shatner was an excellent replacement, and I think he was fine. But "The Cage" was what the series was all about. At that time people didn't accept it.

AA *Did you find doing STAR TREK a pleasurable experience?*

FF Oh, yes. It was very interesting. A very high morale in the company. We had a "happy set." Everybody was very gung-ho on the series. We'd never had any ratings on national television, on network, but everybody was very happy working with the show.

AA *Did you feel nervous about taking over a series that already had such a reputation?*

FF No. It didn't have any big reputation at the time. It had a very strong "cult following," if I can use that word. I remember being concerned about why we weren't increasing our ratings, and, as I understand it, a survey was done and they discovered that although we did have many female fans, women generally seemed to be terrified of outer space. The survey seemed to indicate that women were more comfortable with boundaries rather than the endless expanse of space. At least, that was what was reported to me in terms of the survey. I was doing *anything* to try to increase those ratings, because we were always on the edge. . . .

AA *Did you ever get specific directives to do things in certain ways to increase the ratings?*

FF No, no. In some cases, I tried to do more "standard stories," within the science fiction framework, but the ratings remained the same whether we did a bad show or a good show. Today, a 25 share is a hit. In those days if you did a 30 you were right on the borderline, and we used to do about a 25. In those days the networks had a 90 percent share of the audience. Now it's down to 69 percent or less . . .

AA *Do you feel that Paramount and NBC were in back of you?*

FF Yes. The cooperation was very good. The third year they cut the budget down, which hurt a little. . . . We'd just fight to get whatever we could, but they required every fourth show to be done on the ship within the Enterprise sets, instead of using planet sets on the one sound stage, and that cut down a certain scope.

AA   *Did those reductions also influence the amount of time you had to do each show?*

FF   No. The time was a standard six days per show. There was no complaint from my viewpoint concerning the network or Paramount. Certainly, everybody wanted to get the show down on schedule. We all hoped STAR TREK would be picked up for a fourth year, but the ratings just stayed the same, and it was only the devotion of the STAR TREK fans that kept it on after the first six months of the first year. They went down and picketed NBC, and wrote letters of protest when it appeared the show would be canceled. That pressure influenced the network, which was very helpful when STAR TREK was teetering on the brink.

AA   *Did you attempt to emphasize Mr. Spock in the third-season episodes?*

FF   No. We tried to keep a level between both [Kirk and Spock]. We tried to go with the best stories we could, with the best casts we could get, and the best directors who were available. There were really no directives. Nobody interfered, and I must say it was a very pleasurable experience from that viewpoint. As I said, the morale was high, although there was always the concern about the ratings. We are all very proud of the show.

AA   *I've always thought that one of the most bizarre bits of casting in STAR TREK was attorney Melvin Belli appearing as an alien in "And the Children Shall Lead."*

FF   Ah, yes . . . That was a show I did. He wasn't the greatest actor in the world, but was very cooperative. Using him was an exploitation shot to boost our ratings. He was fun to work with, but the ratings stayed the same.

AA   *Do you recall any other specific incidents that occurred while you were producing STAR TREK?*

FF   One show that I did, "Plato's Stepchildren," had aliens forcing one of our characters to kiss Uhura. Now, remember, that was in the days before the civil rights marches, and we had a problem. I talked to my story editor, and I guess it was Bob [Justman] who said that if I put Spock in the scene people would say that we were too scared to have a white man kiss a black woman. If we put Kirk in there, and we didn't let them kiss, they would have said, "You didn't have enough guts to go so far as to have him kiss her." I gave it a lot of thought, and then I figured, "To hell with it. Let's have it with Kirk, and go as far as we can in terms of censorship and all the rest of it." When the reviews came out on the show, Dave Kaufman in *Variety* picked up on whatever we did with that. So I called Kaufman and I

said, "Look, we had this problem of what we wanted to do."
We were only in touch with the show and what it meant, but
we were aware that there could be criticisms of these kinds
of things. [Kaufman] had said that they wouldn't go so far as
to allow a white man to kiss her, and I said, "The reason we
didn't do it is that Kirk didn't want to *humiliate* her. It was
out of *respect* for her that he fought against the pressure." I
said, "Now, Dave, suppose we had Spock do that, would you
say that we didn't have guts enough to let a white man kiss
her, that we had to have some alien do it?" And he said,
"Gee, I guess you're right." But he never printed a retrac-
tion. I did another show where the aliens were half black
and half white ["Let This Be Your Last Battlefield"], which I
thought was a pretty good touch, but then we had the
problem of whether we should put a black man in the role
and paint him half white, as opposed to Frank Gorshin and
Lou Antonio, who we finally settled on. We went crazy, and
talked to the makeup people, who said that to make a black
man half white was going to be tougher than making a white
man half black. These types of things were always upper-
most in our minds. Not that we were afraid to do things that
we felt would be daring in terms of the context at that time,
but in terms of not doing anything unnecessarily offensive to
anyone. Those are problems that you face that have nothing
to do with the script or the production. "Let This Be Your
Last Battlefield" was one of my favorite shows. Not that it
was one of the best that we did, but in terms of what it had
to say—the differentiation of, "I'm better than you are
because I'm white on one side and black on the other, and
you're white on the other side, instead." In the old days, we
used to do these types of things in westerns, and then we
did it in science fiction when you couldn't get away with it in
normal, everyday situations. In science fiction you could zap
a whole planet and knock out four billion people, but in an
everyday situation you couldn't show a six-inch knife in BEN
CASEY. You'd throw up your hands, or you'd go crazy. On
shows where you were trying to make a statement it was
very difficult. It was always frustrating.

AA *I remember that you were also on BEN CASEY and THE
WILD, WILD WEST.*

FF BEN CASEY was doing a 65 share. And then I was asked
to go over to SLATTERY'S PEOPLE, which was also a
Bing Crosby Productions show. After I left BEN CASEY,
Wilton Schiller remained with the show, but the format
changed. I did the first show of THE WILD, WILD WEST,
with big ratings, and I was over there on the first season.

WILD, WILD WEST went on to be a smash hit for five years.

AA *Tell me about the second year of SPACE: 1999.*

FF They brought me over to SPACE: 1999 hoping that I could save the show. I streamlined the set, and created the character of "Maya," the alien who could change into different animal forms, and I thought we did some wonderful things on that show. They were fantastically cooperative over there, just amazing. Before I came up with that character, they were going to dump the show, and they brought me over to England for the most part just to talk about it. They asked me to give them an analysis of the show. I came up with the Maya character, and they said, "Okay, go ahead and do it," and we did 24 . . . I think that if it had been on network we could have made it, but we couldn't get the ratings in syndication. . . . The special effects stuff was just great: a lot of people who did special effects worked on *2001*. The producer, Gerry Anderson, was an amazing guy in that area. . . .

AA *What type of show do you like the most?*

FF Well, I love BEN CASEY and SLATTERY'S PEOPLE, and I love a failed show called BIG SHAMUS, LITTLE SHAMUS [1979] and KAZ [1978] . . . unfortunately, it only lasted a year. I was on a show called THE SENATOR that also lasted only one season [1970–71]. . . . I also did THE SIX MILLION DOLLAR MAN its final year [1978] . . . I enjoyed the show. I liked Lee Majors. I wasn't crazy about the content of the show, but again, there were a lot of very decent people on the set and it was very pleasant working on it. Very often I found that people were not too pleasant on shows that were highly rated. You can either work on a show that is aesthetically the greatest thing in the world, where certainly the working conditions are very pleasant, or you can be on a show where the ratings are great and the critics acclaim you, and it's not the most pleasant show in the world to be on. I suppose it all balances out in the end.

AA *What does your wife think of STAR TREK?*

FF My wife? Well, she's no big science fiction fan, but she likes to watch it because my name is on it, and it's another show that I've done that she loves and is proud of. . . . We had people coming down to the STAR TREK set: all types, from kids who came with propellers in their hats, to astronauts, who were fans of the show. . . . This is a very peculiar business all around. You just do your best in whatever show you're in: be a professional.

THE DIRECTORS

THE STEREOTYPICAL IMAGE MOST OF US HAVE OF DIRECTORS IS THAT OF A LOUD, DOMINEERING INDIVIDUAL, SHOUTING AND HOLDING A RIDING CROP— WHICH BEARS LITTLE RESEMBLANCE TO THE REALITY. THE DIRECTORS I SPOKE WITH WERE ALL ENTHUSIASTIC ARTISTS WHO RECALLED THEIR CONTRIBUTIONS TO STAR TREK IN SURPRISING DETAIL.

LAWRENCE DOBKIN

Lawrence Dobkin began his Hollywood career as an actor, appearing in many feature films including The Day the Earth Stood Still, Riders to the Stars, *and* Illegal, *which also featured DeForest Kelley. He acted in many television series as well, including episodes of THE ADVENTURES OF SUPERMAN, SPACE PATROL, and HAVE GUN WILL TRAVEL ("The Great Mojave Chase" [1957], written by Gene Roddenberry). Among his many TV directing assignments are episodes of MY LIVING DOLL (1964-65, featuring Julie Newmar as a robot), THE MUNSTERS (1964-66), and THE SIX MILLION DOLLAR MAN (1973-78). His only direct involvement with STAR TREK was as the director of "Charlie X," generally considered one of the most successful episodes of the series.*

AA   *How did you first become involved in STAR TREK?*

LD   I was in Europe, helping an old friend with a spaghetti western. I was playing a villain, and helping to rewrite it as we shot it . . . I'd been there for about two and a half months. The arrangement to direct the eighth [STAR TREK] episode was made through my agent sometime during the period when I was away, and he wired me and told me that I had to be home by a certain date. I got home two days late, as I recall, after being delayed in Spain.

AA   *Nothing in the episode indicates that you were under such pressure.*

LD   No. The film was very good. All the people in the cast were perturbed either by me, or by the work, and they had to be reassured by the producers that my personal problems of that period, the stress, weren't reflected in the film, and apparently they weren't. I ran into young Bob Walker just a couple of months ago at a restaurant, and we had a glass of wine together. All of his memories of that period are the same as mine: a fruitful job, a fruitful two weeks of hard work. . . .

AA   *Did you have anything to do with the casting of Robert Walker?*

LD   Well, only in the sense that they said, "We think we'd like to use him, unless you object." You know, "Do you object to . . . ?" And even after all these years, saying, "Whoops, wait a minute, that's an actor I won't work with. If you have to use that actor or that actress, get another director," that's very, very rare. When they talked about Charlie Evans, I welcomed it when they said young Robert Walker. And I said, "I don't know him, except from the photographs. Is he like his father in the qualitative sense?" And they said, "Yes, very much," so he's got to be splendid. I think they had interviewed him: I don't remember if he was in to read or not, because, as I say, I was a couple of days late by the time I showed up, and everybody was panicked. I couldn't relieve anybody's anxiety that they were not going to have to find another director three or four days later at the last minute, and settle for someone whose work they didn't know. I was trapped. I didn't have a go-ahead for the flight out of Madrid until the last dailies on our feature film came out of the lab free of scratches. When I came in, I had so much to do: getting used to the effects team, the cameraman, the lighting design that one had to make room for, the resident cast, the sets, and then digesting the storyline. I don't believe I got involved in the casting.

AA   *Did you confer with D.C. Fontana at all?*

LD   No, not at all. I don't remember meeting D.C. on that show: I met Fontana another time. No, my contact was with the resident story editor who was shaping the show, John D.F. Black. His presence was very real, and in a sense he represented the writing and the writer. . . .

AA   *Do you have any recollections of the climate on the set of "Charlie X"?*

LD   The sense of cooperative effort was very, very strong. Shatner's ability to envision shots was evident even though he hadn't started directing yet. Leonard Nimoy's ability to visualize, even though *he* hadn't started directing yet . . . all of those came into play. It was a case of "Uh, oh, an actor who directs, so we have to talk to him about *the* scene, *the* moment, *the* relationships . . . ," that kind of work relationship builds well. . . . Probably my best memory of STAR TREK is all those people, that young in the series: they did not yet have the approval of the crowd. They hadn't any support for what clearly was an attempt to bring the humanities into another time zone, to graph today's relationships in some fashion onto a different time frame, and keep the simplicities and the realities and the human interaction going. My God, what a talented bunch. Wow! It was a very fruitful period in so many ways, fruitful for all of us. It was a fortunate time, and people took chances, people took grave risks. In looking back, I think that if you were to say to Leonard Nimoy, "Would you try to base the rest of your acting career on a pair of ears, and a very introverted character?," I think probably he wouldn't risk it. . . . It's very hard to know. But I had the same conversation with Lorne Green one day on a backlot at Warner's. He said, "Next week I'm supposed to be testing to play the father of three grown men in some western . . . ," and I asked who the producer was, and I said, "That's all you have to go on. If the producer has some presence, and can be depended upon to exercise taste and judgment, and this man can, then have a shot at it." At the time they made the initial test, Lorne was probably between 45 and 50, and he was worried about whether or not he could photograph old enough to make the audience believe he was the father of those kids. That would have meant he fathered those kids when he was between 18 and 25, which is reasonable.

AA *Then it's your feeling that STAR TREK is so popular because of its concern for its human elements?*

LD Well, I think so, because like all the actor-directors around I had played with science fiction in one form or another, and it's very difficult to empathize with something quite strange, quite out of the way. It's difficult for an audience to come to terms with even as human a creature as Captain Nemo in the Jules Verne science fiction . . . But here, Roddenberry's thrust made very real people and very concerned relationships. These were reinforced by John D.F. Black, an enormously talented fellow who became a close friend for a while. I watch my kids and they're Trekkies because to them it's a soap opera, but in a different time frame. It's very real.

AA *Did you find that your creative input was welcome?*

LD Yes, it's always welcome to a greater or lesser degree, depending on who got out on which side of the bed, and who had eggs. When you add to a scene and you are playing "daddy," when you're the director, you throw in material and it is both welcome and unwelcome. You find it necessary to contribute your ideas, and the actors are obliged to at least give them some credence, some pretense of welcoming it. Sometimes the actors can genuinely receive development or growth or a suggestion from another; a fellow actor who had turned director, or a fellow actor who is acting with them, and sometimes they can't. Sometimes they are troubled by the intrusion on their own creative entity, their own creative posture. And it's difficult. Under the best of conditions, you are, in effect—you know it as a writer—you're being rewritten. The actor is being rewritten, and he's being rewritten within a time frame that is out of his control, and there is no time to sit back and digest it, calm yourself, and stop resenting the intrusion. It must be done *now!* Now, granted, actors are schooled to accept and relate to a director, but there is frequently some sense that you have put your foot into an unfamiliar show. At the very least, you have to work with it. There are times when the relationship is absolutely superb, it couldn't be improved on. But those are relatively rare moments, and they are fragile, and they don't last terribly long. For example, I worked on THE WALTONS over a period of five years, and that was also like a family situation. People felt free to come back as though I were Mommy or Daddy, and ask, "Should I really do that . . . All right, I'll *do* it!" And then they trade you, like, "I'll eat my peas, if . . ."

AA *So you literally wind up being daddy.*

LD You're in a parental situation: that's as close an analogy as I can make. It varies.

AA *What are your impressions of Gene Roddenberry?*

LD In terms of Roddenberry's aggressive posture relative to STAR TREK and his creativity, I think Gene probably assumes a Cagney-like pugnacity as a permanent life-form. It's well justified. If ever a man took his lumps to get something across, Roddenberry did. He didn't have Arthur C. Clarke's applause from effort one. He had all the other things, with people saying, "Lucky Roddenberry," like he had never had an idea or a concept or fought for it and struggled with it. It would have been so easy to follow the well-established ruts: everybody's a monster, and everybody's a cold-blooded derivative of a lizard, and on we go as sci-fi, treating the characters as symbols. Everybody was doing it in "cartoons." We're talking about 1964, when the first pilot was shot with a different cast. I acted for Ivan Tors in *Riders to the Stars,* long before that, and we were sitting there snickering about this thing. We were going through space in it, and it opened its jaws like a digging machine.

AA *You also did a bit of acting: I remember you were in a MISSION: IMPOSSIBLE.*

LD I had come back from Europe with my head shaved, and I kept it that way, like Telly Savalas. We were at Desilu, I think directing a MOD SQUAD for Aaron Spelling, and someone looked out the window of the casting department, and said, ". . . Wait a minute. How long have you had your head shaved? Come in here." I don't remember if it was Joe D'Agosta or the casting lady, but the schedule worked out that I could act for them for five or six days in between my MOD SQUAD assignments.

AA *The earliest film I've seen you in is* The Day the Earth Stood Still.

LD . . . Yes. My wife bought a copy of that and put it on the machine and my twins, who are now 17, refused to believe that that young man there was any relation to the old man they know. I think I had hair . . .

AA *I also remember you standing in front of a blue screen in* The Ten Commandments, *when the Red Sea was beginning to part.*

LD Yes, that and the wind and the spray . . . All I did was done on the Paramount lot, on the sound stages. There are some things I get surprised at. Someone sent me a photograph . . . and there I was with Boris Karloff. We were both made up as some kind of Hindu princes . . .

RALPH SENENSKY

*Ralph Senensky joined the staff of PLAYHOUSE 90 in 1957, becoming part of what is often called "the golden age of television."
". . . People forget the incredible work that was done on live television," he recalls. "Jerry Goldsmith conducted his scores for PLAYHOUSE 90, live . . . In film you can record the score afterward, measuring exactly how long things are going to run, but in live TV it varied from rehearsal to rehearsal . . . He was down in the basement with his earphones, a little monitor, and his orchestra, leading the music . . .*

"The two directors I admire most are Franklin Schaffner and George Roy Hill," he says. "Frank used to do every third [PLAYHOUSE 90] show, and he was a consummate master of cameras. George Roy Hill was not far behind him. We've remained close friends."

Senensky directed six segments of STAR TREK, and part of a seventh (Herb Wallerstein finished "The Tholian Web").

AA *Who approached you to arrange your first STAR TREK assignment?*

RS It was done through my agent. I'm not too sure, I have a feeling it was Gene Coon who brought me over there because I had worked with him before on THE WILD, WILD WEST. The first STAR TREK I did was "This Side of Paradise," although the first script I was sent was "The

Devil in the Dark." I went back to Iowa for Christmas, and while I was there they sent out the second script . . . "This Side of Paradise." At the time I was very disappointed because I liked "Devil in the Dark" better.

AA   *Joseph Pevney got that one to direct.*

RS   Maybe Joe had been assigned "This Side of Paradise," I don't know. I just know they made a switch. And of course it turned out fine, because "This Side of Paradise" was quite a good one.

AA   *It went through many changes along the way. Originally it was Mr. Sulu who got the girl.*

RS   I was not aware of that at all. By the time a director is booked he usually gets the final draft. It's very seldom they see the earlier version. . . . By the way, I later directed George Takei in an episode of COURTSHIP OF EDDIE'S FATHER.

AA   *James Komack, who produced that series and acted in it, directed a very funny STAR TREK episode, "A Piece of the Action."*

RS   Star Trek IV is a throwback to that, very much so.

AA   *It has elements of that, and of the comedy flavor of "The Trouble with Tribbles." Joseph Pevney, who directed ". . . Tribbles," believes that in some respects STAR TREK found its identity when humor became an integral part of the format.*

RS   The characters were still being taken totally seriously in the first season when I did "This Side of Paradise." I had immersed myself in Arthur C. Clarke, trying to find a hook for me to plug into science fiction, and the idea of comedy kept showing up . . . we kept finding it, and I've always leaned in that direction, anyway. The scene where Spock hangs from the tree . . . was new terrain. It wasn't that they hadn't traveled it yet, but I remember it as being not at all that familiar, and not something that we just fell into. Leonard Nimoy had no reservations about doing it. The scene was originally all set up and ready to shoot with Kirk and Spock meeting in the center of a field. Jerry Finnerman had lit it, and we did a run-through, and it was just dull, with Kirk saying, "What are you doing here?" and Spock putting him off. They were just standing there facing each other. Nothing was working. Something said to me, "I've got to do something more than that." Right out of camera range I saw a tree with a strange limb and I asked Jerry if I could change the setup, which I very seldom do, and he said, "Of course." So we went over and had Spock hang from that tree. Well, they loved it. And I vaguely remember there was a lovely response to the comedy element that Shatner brought into his performance. I do know that when they did the big fight scene later in the story, when Leonard was standing over him with the chair and Bill said, "Had enough?," that was done on the stage, just falling in . . . not so much an adlib as something that was discovered on the set.

AA *The stuntman doubling for Nimoy looked nothing like him.*

RS . . . Those sets were so small that you couldn't get back far enough to make the double work: you were too close.

AA *How much freedom did they give you on "This Side of Paradise"? Did you have casting privileges, for instance?*

RS Oh, yes. "This Side of Paradise" was still Gene Coon. Gene Roddenberry, Gene Coon and, later, John Meredyth Lucas were just sensational. It was a way of working television that doesn't exist today. We were very free creatively, but it wasn't freedom to the point of just turning the show over to us. Everybody worked together.

AA *Most of "This Side of Paradise" was photographed on location. Do you recall where it was shot?*

RS We had great difficulty trying to find a location. We scouted and scouted trying to find a place where we didn't have to build a set: they didn't want to have to build. In fact, we didn't care what the style was. The only place we found that really had it all was the Disney Ranch. And so we just went there and assumed that the people who had settled there had created a community not unlike early America. . . . I think we were scheduled to do three days out there. On the third day we were out at the ranch early in the morning and we received word that Jill Ireland would not be available to come out that day because she had the measles. I think I shot for a little while, finishing up the things that I could shoot around her. We ran out of work and returned to the studio, and then the production department got a call that the Disney Ranch was not available for another day: it was booked and we had another day's work left. So we shot the balance out at Bronson Canyon, which is very close to Paramount. The scenes of Spock's getting hit with the spores and hanging from the tree were shot at Bronson Canyon.

AA *The shot of Spock getting hit with the spores is an upward angle: about all you can see is Spock, the plant, some grass, and the sky.*

RS Right. As long as it was just out in a field. I think they planted the garden down there, too.

AA *There was one shot that looks as though the background is a rear projection: a close shot of Jill Ireland and DeForest Kelley. The background looks static and out of focus.*

RS   It was done with a long lens.

AA   *Your next episode, "Metamorphosis," is one of the most sensitive segments of the entire series.*

RS   That is my favorite . . . I loved doing that show.

AA   *Did Gene Coon visit the set?*

RS   Never. But Gene and I had great rapport, and I had tremendous respect for him, for the material.

AA   *What sort of man was Gene Coon?*

RS   Well, on the inside he was immensely sensitive, terribly professional. I had worked with him on WILD, WILD WEST and he was a real workhorse. He would just simply grind out WILD, WILD WEST. A script would be turned in, and then he would have to make it shootable. He would just sit at the typewriter. He was a marvelous professional, but great to work with because along with professionalism he had the courage, the stability, and the sense of security to not have to hang on . . . to let the next person take over and do his share.

AA   *Was all of "Metamorphosis" shot indoors?*

RS   Every bit of it. We never went outside for that episode. It was short on a very, very small soundstage.

AA   *I recall a shot with Glen Corbett running toward the shuttlecraft, and someone had strategically placed a rock across the top of the set.*

RS   Yes, otherwise we were shooting off the set. The set was just not high enough. It was the only way, and that was Jerry Finnerman's contribution. I was still learning about cameras and the nine millimeter [lens][1] was a new weapon. It's very interesting that they don't stay on that shot too long, when he runs toward the camera, because it would have looked like he had on those magic boots with which you can take a step and every step is a mile. He covers that huge distance in about five strides. Also in "Metamorphosis," Cochrane's house . . . we only had one site in one direction; that is, everything was shot in the same direction. They had to move everything in and out. We'd shoot from day to day. One day they would set up the shuttlecraft in that direction. Then they had the house in that direction, and I had to shoot all of that. When they did the reverse, the shooting away from the house, they had to take the house out and redress the set. In the scene where Kirk and Spock stand and watch Cochrane having his meeting with The Companion, it's all the same site. I did one direction one day, and when I got that I'd go back and do all the reverse, rather than doing it all at one time.

---

[1] A wide-angle lens that distorts the subject, also used in "Is There In Truth No Beauty?" and "The Tholian Web."

AA   *I'm sure that much of the ethereal look of "Metamorphosis" would not have been possible without that lovely purple backdrop that served as the sky.*

RS   I was just going to say that that was Jerry Finnerman's idea to do a purple sky. He just outdid himself on that show. Jerry and I have remained friends through the years. We met on the set of "This Side of Paradise." He has told me that the bond between us was struck the day we did the rack focus shot across the flowers to Spock, where he gets zapped. I put the flowers in the foreground. . . . He felt that my ideas, the things I wanted him to do, gave him extra creative juice and room to be creative. That was the one show that I did at the end of the first season. And then "Metamorphosis" was the second show that was shot the second year, and he just went all out. He also went all out on "Is There In Truth No Beauty?" He taught me the nine millimeter lens, and the day that I was shooting with that, I had to make sure the production department ordered it, because that was not a lens that they carried . . . I used it in another show, too.

AA   *There was also a mist to suggest clouds . . . and pine cones scattered on the ground to suggest the outdoors.*

RS   Jerry did that. Right before every shot they would turn off the fans and they would go through with the bee smoke and just sort of waft smoke up into the air.

AA   *Was it difficult to work with the cast in "Metamorphosis," considering that The Companion was an optical effect not present during production?*

RS   Yes. And we didn't know what it was going to be. But I do remember that they didn't want to do moving mattes. I had to lay out every shot so that all they had to do was just lay it in and they wouldn't have to move it: the camera would move it around in all of those shots.

AA   *They used double exposures.*

RS   It would be a double exposure, but even that is a matte . . . they've done the double exposure with movement involved, like when The Companion moves across the Cochrane. If they had had to move it from its position to just one wide shot, that would have been prohibitively expensive. So what they did was work it out so that they didn't have to do any kind of a matte.

AA   *"Bread and Circuses" is a "parallel world" action story that also comes across as a sensitive episode.*

RS   . . . [In STAR TREK] it was always so important to make "people" stories work. Gene Coon and I hacked out the "son" theme to try to make that work. I remember the stuff we did in the prison cell. He would work late into the night . . . and the day before [it was shot] I went in at six o'clock in the morning to get the pages and lay out the shots. I didn't know he was rewriting them at night. I remember that we had big closeups of Spock and McCoy, I think through the prison bars. I'm not sure. De was marvelous, and Leonard was just sensational. You know, regarding the outtake from the prison cell in "Bread and Circuses" where Ted Cassidy picked William Shatner up and carried him off . . . Ted was working next door, and he came over to our set early in the morning, and we rigged that. That was a setup. We rolled camera, and everybody except Bill knew that Ted was going to come in, pick him up, and carry him off. We staged that, and it survives until this day.

AA   *You worked on THE F.B.I. I guess that accounts for Stephen Brooks' [who costarred on that show] presence in "Obsession."*

RS   That's right, that's right. I did that, and I also did another series [with him in it] later, called THE INTERNS over at Columbia.

AA   *"Obsession" also relied heavily on special effects, although there wasn't much interaction between the effects and the people.*

RS   Yes. Most of the cabin scene, and then the smoke coming over the top of the rock in the teaser . . . we didn't go on location for that. We shot those on their standard exterior planet set. They just moved the rocks around. It seems like they were the same rocks in different positions, and they would change the color of the sky. It gave it more of a science fiction look. The minute you go out and shoot the Disney Ranch or Bronson Canyon, no matter what you do it looks like Scrub, California. You just don't get away from that look. Unless you really want to do a story with a similarity to Earth civilization, like "This Side of Paradise" and "Bread and Circuses," you don't utilize it. In fact, Bronson Canyon is where I shot "Bread and Circuses," in a different part of the canyon than I used when I shot "This Side of Paradise."

AA   *In "Return to Tomorrow" Diana Muldaur was the guest star. You later did "Is There In Truth No Beauty?" with her, and she was also in Gene Roddenberry's 1974 pilot, PLANET EARTH.*

RS   A lot of the guest stars were people I had worked with, who I would suggest: Frank Overton, Diana Muldaur . . . Once I've gotten along with people, I like to work with them again. "Return to Tomorrow" was the last one I did in the second season, after Paramount had taken over. Our shooting schedule was cut down to six days, and we had to quit at 6:12 P.M. each day. . . . Oh, here's a nice story about Diana Muldaur. I had done about five or six shows with her, and suggested her for "Return to Tomorrow." And of course they loved her, she's a beautiful lady, such a good and solid actress. The next year when they were doing "Is There In Truth No Beauty?" we started casting, and they had a self-imposed edict: they didn't want to have a repeat [in casting], and we started trying to cast. The lady we wanted for the role in "Is There In Truth . . ."—I think it was Jessica Walter—was not available, and I don't remember [the circumstances]. So I brought up Diana's name, and they said, "Well, we never repeat." We went through the casting list, and then I asked what would happen if we put a black wig on Diana. Bobby Justman finally relented and said okay. The first day's dailies of "Is There In Truth . . ." was the scene of Diana and David Frankham in her quarters. She was so gorgeous, she came on the screen and after the dailies Bobby Justman said, "I wonder how she's going to look in a red wig?" And had the series gone another year, I'm sure she would have put on a red wig and done another show. John Meredyth Lucas was producing, and Herb Solow was still in charge of production when "Return to Tomorrow" was filmed. I did that episode after I received a last minute request for me to do it. I originally said, "I can't," because there was a conflict: a Jewish holiday fell in there. There was only one day that was a conflict. Solow and Lucas put their heads together, and they worked it out so that I could do the show and go home at four o'clock on that day, and John Meredyth Lucas would come down and finish the day's work for me. He worked it out . . . and for years when I saw Johnny later he would always call himself the Yom Kippur director, my Yom Kippur replacement. David Frankham was just in my house a week ago: he was in "Is There In Truth No Beauty?," and was another actor I'd brought in. When I met him in 1960, we had done a stage production at Pasadena Playhouse, and I'd also done a marvelous TWELVE O'CLOCK HIGH with him.

AA *I believe that the script to "Is There In Truth No Beauty?" was written by someone who had not written any previous television scripts.*

RS I think I knew that somebody who was not a television writer, somebody who wanted to do a script, had done it. . . . In those days a creative person like Gene Coon wasn't afraid to take a chance . . . because he judged the creativity. Committees can only go to a computer and ask, "What has he done?"

AA *Were you happy with the finished episode?*

RS They did some editing on "Is There In Truth No Beauty?" . . . I think that basically they tried to turn it into a monster movie. All the shots cutting back to the box with the ambassador, the light effects . . . they kept trying to build menace with those cuts back to the box. To me they were insulting to an audience. It just curtailed imagination. An audience is smarter than that. . . . It was just a different mentality, treating it as a monster show rather than a subtle picture.

AA *You worked on another after that . . . "The Tholian Web."*

RS It's interesting that I've been credited with it, because I was fired three days into it. I've seen one book that listed me as having directed that. I'm not listed on the screen: I refused to have my name on the screen. Everybody [from the original crew] was gone except for Bobby Justman. Gene [Roddenberry] was still there . . . I worked with him on "Is There In Truth No Beauty?" but . . . I don't think Gene had too much to do with the show creatively in that year. . . . And the pressure from the studio was getting to us. It got me fired. It was getting in the way of creativity and the production end of the show. . . . Gene Coon told me that they averaged about six and a half days per show. And that wasn't bad for television at that time. They wanted to do them in six, but a lot of studios couldn't . . . I think that if they could go back and do it again, the powers-that-be in Paramount would rather have more than the 79 episodes. I bet they wish now that whoever was in charge back then had nursed the show along a little more, and that there were more than 79. At the end of the first day we were half a day behind. The studio and the production department, which I would say was bearing down, were determined that this show would be in under six days or else. At the end of the third day I was called into Mr. Freiberger's office . . . he asked me why I was half a day behind, and I was fired. I think it was significant that "The Tholian Web" won so many awards . . . quite frankly, the good stuff is what I shot. I think that you could probably spot what I shot.

AA *Do you recall what you did shoot?*

RS The nine millimeter footage with Leonard Nimoy was part of it, and I did all the stuff with the silver lamé spacesuits. I think that Gene [Roddenberry] may have been the only person to call me afterward to tell me how appalled he was . . . that he had had absolutely nothing to do with it. . . . And as I explained to Mr. Freiberger, I think I would have finished it in the same three days. . . .

AA *That experience aside, did you enjoy working on STAR TREK?*

RS On "This Side of Paradise" and "Metamorphosis," yes. Desilu was one of those marvelous companies that was like a big family. I'd worked at Desilu before on THE BREAK-ING POINT [1963–64]. That was . . . even *more* contained because it was Bing Crosby Productions, which was a little unit *at* Desilu. It was a marvelous thing.

AA *Can you say why things aren't the same today?*

RS I think it starts at the network. The networks took over, and all of television became so much more committee. That's one reason I think . . . that today's writers are not grounded in the theatrical background as the writers of that era were.

AA *When you were directing your STAR TREK episodes, did it occur to you that people would still be watching them 20 years in the future?*

RS No, at that time we didn't think they'd be watching them now.

AA *Do you have any thoughts pertaining to STAR TREK's longevity?*

RS I do remember that the two Genes, Roddenberry and Coon, had ideas like those of Rod Serling when he did TWILIGHT ZONE. They wanted to do an anthology series with material the networks would not let them do. So, in the guise of making a science fiction series, they were able to do that kind of material in STAR TREK. They did a Viet Nam story . . . One of the shows ["Obsession"] I did was *Moby Dick*. . . . When we did "Bread and Circuses," and the "son" theme that goes through it, we reworked the ending, repeating the Nativity theme so that it . . . would be a dramatic structure, not just narrative storytelling. There was a classic structure to the material that has survived true.

AA *What's your favorite of the STAR TREK episodes you did?*

RS "Metamorphosis." It was a lovely, lovely show, one of those times when the juices got going, with material that gave room to do a lovely show. The material was just rich enough . . . and at the same time it had another dimension. It was another Gene Coon thing. I think he may have been a little surprised at what happened to it . . . it seemed so metaphysical.

AA *In fact, it would have made a great little feature if it had been a little longer.*

RS That's true of a lot of hour television shows that were shot in those days.

AA *A lot of them were edited together by the studios and released abroad. Do you think that would be possible with most of today's product?*

RS God, no. There's no depth, no dimension, no emotional
reality. They get involved with narrative. There were always the words, but then you asked, "What is the thing
really about?" And nowadays in TV production you read the
words and you say, "What is it really about?", and it's about
saying the words. . . .

AA *Had you read any science fiction before you did STAR TREK?*

RS No, but I read a lot of it once I did it. I read an enormous amount, mostly Arthur C. Clarke . . . just to give me
a foundation, to give me a peg to hang on to. I probably
did that reading between "This Side of Paradise" and
"Metamorphosis . . ."

AA *Before you did the STAR TREKs, had you any thoughts
about whether or not you wanted to do science fiction?*

RS I don't think I'd even thought about it, and I don't even
know if I had watched STAR TREK when I did "This Side
of Paradise." I know I was not a Trekkie who was watching
it every week. I do remember, as a television director, that
I usually started watching the [series] shows when I knew I
was going to do one. It was not a matter of sitting down and
watching all the television . . . when I knew I was about to
do a show, I would watch it.

AA *Have you ever spoken at any conventions?*

RS No. I was invited to my first one this past year . . . the
convention was in June. The invitation was mailed in April,
and it took from April to July to reach me. As a matter of
fact, this is really the first conversation that I've had with
anybody about it [STAR TREK] except for the Trekkies
when I go to a party or when I'm with young people. They
find out I've done STAR TREK and they turn around and
they're Trekkies.

AA *I think the attention you would get at a convention, and the
reception you'd get, would amaze you.*

RS The one that they invited me to this year was at the Disney
Hotel. I probably would have gone. You probably have been
to a lot of them.

AA *I was one of the people who put the first East Coast conventions together, starting in 1972.*

RS Do you realize that although I did six and a half STAR
TREKs, you know more about the show than I do.

AA *Thank you very much for a wonderful interview.*

RS I hope this will be of some help. Today I will probably go
down to the bookstore and buy *The Star Trek Compendium.*
. . . I think you've made a sale.

AA *Thank you.*

MARC DANIELS

Pittsburgh-born Marc Daniels attended the University of Michigan before winning a scholarship to the American Academy of Dramatic Arts.

During World War II, Daniels served in a special unit commanded by Willard Josephy, who later became a partner of Lucille Ball's agent.

In 1943, he returned to the American Academy to study and teach, and at this time he took what was probably the earliest course in directing for television. He first used that training directing FORD THEATRE, an early TV series that aired condensed Broadway plays, from 1948 to 1949. After winning the Variety Showmanship Award and working briefly on another series, Daniels' expertise led his former commanding officer Josephy to recommend him as the director of a new series, I LOVE LUCY, that would utilize feature film techniques to produce a series. Daniels directed the first 38 episodes of I LOVE LUCY (he also recommended actress Vivian Vance for the role of Ethel Mertz).

He directed 15 episodes of STAR TREK, beginning in June 1966, with "The Man Trap," and including the additional material shot for the two-parter, "The Menagerie," and wrote one segment of the animated STAR TREK series ("One of Our Planets is Missing") in 1973.

AA *How did you first become involved with STAR TREK?*

MD It was through Gene Roddenberry. I had done some work for him on THE LIEUTENANT. In fact, it was during THE LIEUTENANT that I first made him aware of Leonard Nimoy. I was directing THE ELEVENTH HOUR at MGM, an episode with Fabian, the rock singer, and he asked if he could bring his dramatic coach to the set. His dramatic coach turned out to be Leonard Nimoy. I got to know Leonard, and when I was doing the episode of THE LIEUTENANT I thought of him for the part of the Hollywood producer, so I got him into that show. Roddenberry then got to know Leonard, and was of course taken with his qualities. . . . When he created STAR TREK he remembered Leonard. The rest is history, as they say.

AA *How were the guest stars for the STAR TREK episodes chosen? For instance, Alfred Ryder and Jeanne Bal in "The Man Trap"?*

MD When I cast a segment of an episodic series, I sit with the casting people and ask, "Now, who would be good for this?" They give me ideas, I have my own ideas, and the producer has his own ideas. I make a list of people and say, "All right, let's go for him first." They always try to get a name, and then realize that's a futile process, so I generally retreat to good actors.

AA *"The Naked Time" was an unusual story, and included the first STAR TREK appearance by Bruce Hyde as Lt. Kevin Riley.*

MD Bruce Hyde was my choice for the role because I had done a play called *The Girl in the Freudian Slip,* and he was in it. He was talented, and I thought he would be good.

AA *"The Naked Time" also allowed George Takei's "Sulu" to become a swordsman for a short time.*

MD I had to really, physically restrain him. He got so excited that I was scared to death he was going to stab somebody— not purposely, but he was getting too close . . . I took the sword away from him and had the end of it dulled down. George has a lot of enthusiasm.

AA *"Court-Martial" is definitely a "Kirk" episode, a "Starfleet procedural."*

MD While we were making "Court-Martial" we all felt, "Oh God, this is a dog. Let's get it over with as best we can."

AA *Do you recall why you felt that way?*

MD Part of the problem was that it didn't have too much action in it. Also, Elisha Cook, Jr., who portrayed the main character, couldn't remember his lines. When you're on a six-day schedule, trying to make time, and you've got to keep stopping and going back, it drives everyone crazy. You've got a courtroom scene and you're photographing him one line at a time because he can't remember two. Of course, when you put it together in the editing room, you don't see that because you cut to somebody else and then come back to him. So maybe we all felt, "Thank God that's over with."

AA *You also had Percy Rodrigues, a powerful screen presence.*

MD I like Percy very much.

AA *"The Menagerie" was a novel assignment: a frame for the original pilot footage.*

MD I think there was a little more than that. I shot about an hour of material. A lot of it was in the briefing room where the so-called trial was taking place.

AA *Did you cast Malachi Throne?*

MD Yes. I knew him from New York. I think I got him STAR TREK, and some other things as well.

AA *One of your episodes, "Space Seed," was the basis for the second STAR TREK feature film.*

MD I know that only too well.

AA *Ricardo Montalban was so forceful in both the episode and the feature.*

MD He's a fine actor and a wonderful person to work with.

AA *Michael Forrest was another performer who was perfectly suited for his role, the lead in "Who Mourns For Adonais?"*

MD Oh, yeah. That was terrific. He was a very good actor and a pleasure to work with. We did that episode in six days . . . today we do hour episodes in seven and eight days . . . but six days is not very much time to do an hour show. You could barely get it done if everything went right. Well, if one element goes sour, where are you? It's just incredible and impossible, and the miracle is that anything comes out that's worthwhile at all.

AA *"The Doomsday Machine" has a lot of suspense, and the fine performance of William Windom.*

MD William Windom is a terrific actor, and . . . when you get an actor like that *you* don't get a performance out of him. Maybe you need to steer him in some direction if he's going wrong, but the chances are that he does it himself. Yes. I like that episode, too.

AA *"The Changeling" must have been especially challenging, with a "leading character" that wasn't a living performer, except in a vocal sense.*

MD In "The Changeling" I had to have three different ways to handle the prop. We used it just sitting in a scene when Spock does the mind meld. At other times it was on a wire, suspended overhead for floating and moving about.

AA *And the third one was on a dolly?*

MD Yes, because you couldn't go through a door with the wire, so the third one was on a dolly, and it was kept moving up and down a little bit as it went.

AA *So you also had to adjust the camera angle to compensate for whichever one you used.*

MD Exactly. When it was on a dolly, you obviously couldn't allow the dolly to show. That was a little tricky, but it worked out. All those things had to be figured out before the six days. I did two shows in a row, once: "The Man Trap" and "The Naked Time." It was craziness, but I did it. You usually get one day of preparation for every day that you shoot. And you had to spend those six days in preparation trying to solve these problems. You couldn't wait until you got to the set, starting to shoot, and say, "Oh, gee, how are we going to do this?" because you'd never have gotten it done. Oh, by the way, I'm in "The Changeling." Isn't that the one that has a picture of a scientist? Well, that's me. They also just used my picture in an episode of Lucille Ball's new series, LIFE WITH LUCY, which I fear will never see the air because it was canceled. My photo was used for her dead husband. They always use my picture for somebody who's dead.

AA   *Any recollections about "Mirror, Mirror"?*

MD   I like that one, too. There was a fight in it, and Nichelle Nichols was furious because I used a stunt woman in the fight. She said, "I want to do that. That woman doesn't look anything like me!" I said, "You've got to be out of your mind. This is a complicated stunt. You could get badly hurt unless you know what you're doing, and the production couldn't afford to have you knocked out."

AA   *I guess you heard about the death of Roger C. Carmel.*

MD   Yes, I did read that in the paper. I did one of those with him, not both. I directed the second one, with all the twins, "I, Mudd."

AA   *Those split screens must have been very complex to shoot.*

MD   Yeah, well some of it was trick photography and some of it was just using twins, or photo doubles. At the end we had to do a triple screen, with the wife coming back as three people. She wasn't a twin: we had to do that as a photographic trick.

AA   *"A Private Little War" was shot almost entirely on location.*

MD   That was another good episode. I've always liked it.

AA   *Do you remember where it was shot?*

MD   Yes, out in what we call "Box Canyon," on the Bell Ranch . . . the rocks out there are incredible: those stratified rocks that I tried to put into the picture.

AA   *I thought those formations were Vasquez Rocks.*

MD   Well, that's in the other direction. Vasquez Rocks has a lot of interesting rock formations, but it doesn't have those big pieces of geological strata you find in Box Canyon.

AA   *Are there any special problems connected with shooting on location?*

MD   Location doesn't hurt you. In fact, it sometimes helps, because you don't have to spend so much time on the lighting when you're outdoors: you've got natural light. When you're in the studio you have to light everything.

AA   *Nancy Kovack was wonderfully sensual in "A Private Little War."*

MD   She's terrific, a very good actress. She married Zubin Mehta, and that was the end of her acting career.

AA *While you were working on STAR TREK, do you recall anyone thinking the show would become so popular?*

MD Not at all. We were just engaged in making episodes of a television series, and making them as well as we could. I have always been a science fiction addict. I've always liked it, and I like the science fiction aspects of the show, but I also like the fact that, in the first two years the stories had some genuine dramatic appeal and social feeling about them, and they weren't gimmicky in terms of just being space operas. "A Private Little War" is an example. So is "Who Mourns For Adonais?," which I really like very much. I don't think people who haven't been on a movie set during the making of an episodic television show really understand what goes on, or how it's full of compromises because of the schedule, and how you have to scramble to get it done. It's a wonder you do get it done, and it's a completely insane way to go about it. Anything good that comes out of it is miraculous.

AA *You've mentioned you're a science fiction reader. Who are some of your favorite writers?*

MD Isaac Asimov, of course, Heinlein . . . I don't know, I haven't read so much of it recently, but I do read *The Magazine of Fantasy and Science Fiction* when I get time.

AA *Do you think they'll ever do another series as successful as STAR TREK?*

MD STAR TREK was not a successful series . . . it only ran three years. I just got off ALICE, which ran nine years. M*A*S*H ran ten years. When you're talking about a successful series, three years does not a successful series make. STAR TREK was never really very big in the ratings. They never put it on the air at the proper time, 8:00 P.M., but as a series it is quite unlike anything else that ever existed. It's a series that captured the imagination and affection of so many really loyal fans . . . look at yourself, for instance. You couldn't have been captivated like that by anything else. The reason that you are is the limitless scope of the series.

AA *There have been many other science fiction series on television, but none of them seems to have had that scope.*

MD Because I think . . . no one else had Roddenberry at the start of it. His kind of vision, you see, made the thing work. I once said to him, "When do you think this takes place?" He told me when, and it wasn't very far into the future, and I said, "Well, for God's sake, Gene, this stuff's going to take longer than that to develop." He said: "Stop and think a minute . . . when you were a boy you couldn't fly across the country. There was no television. The geometrical progression of scientific development in the last 50 years has been tremendous—the medical advances, walking on the moon—you can't yet imagine what will be possible a hundred years from now."

AA *Do you have any other opinions regarding the continuing popularity of STAR TREK?*

MD Well, I think the basic reason is they're so far removed from our reality. I think part of the attraction of [STAR TREK] is that there isn't anything identifiable except people's emotions. And that's one of the things I meant about Gene's supervision of the series: you could identify with the characters and the situations they were in, but at the same time they were removed from your own knowledge of everyday life. It wasn't realistic in those terms. It didn't have to be realistic in those terms. If McCoy wanted to give somebody a shot in STAR TREK he didn't have to roll up their sleeve, put some disinfectant on the arm, take the needle and get some drops out of it, and then give the shot—I did a lot of MARCUS WELBY, too, so I know about that—you didn't have to go through all that, and the audience didn't have to see all that. All he did was to take this handy little gadget from his pocket and stick it on somebody's clothes and go [sound of squirting], and then you have it. It's removed from this kind of enslavement to reality, to put it that way. When you're directing a scene you always ask yourself, ". . . Are they behaving normally in terms of their physical surroundings?" You didn't have to worry about that on STAR TREK, because the nature of their surroundings would not matter, and was not reality. You could operate on somebody without cutting them open, you could beam somebody up from a planet to the ship, or beam them down. You did a very simple shot to make the effect.

AA *. . . and you also eliminated a lot of business in the script as a result.*

MD Sure! That has to do with the framework . . . the Enterprise could go wherever you wanted, and could run into whatever situations would make a good story. STAR TREK is removed from our own reality, and from the reality of all those kids who love it. It's what they would like things to be.

AA *Did you find the STAR TREK staff to be a tightly knit group?*

MD A very good group . . . Bob Justman was the line producer. Justman did a great deal for the series, no doubt about it . . . his responsibility was to get the show made. It's all right for somebody to write a script, and say, "Isn't this great?" But then you have to see if you can shoot it in six days. You have to say, "Wait a minute: how are we going to do this? You can't do this, it's going to take three days to do these two pages, and we've got a 50-page script here!" He would block it out with the director: lay out the production boards, and see what you were going to shoot when . . . there are all kinds of complications involved, you know. For example, it costs money to carry an actor. If you have an actor who's seen the first day, and then he has a scene on the sixth day and he doesn't work in between, you have to pay for him all those days.

AA *So you shoot both days consecutively.*

MD Well, you try to, if you can do it, but you don't shoot a picture [television episode] in continuity in any case. You shoot all the scenes on the bridge at one time. You shoot all the scenes on a planet on one or two days. If you're going out on location, you shoot everything that happens at that location, regardless of when it appears in the script. And so there are all those things to figure out. That's a full-time job!

AA *Do you recall what it was like to work with William Shatner and the rest of the regular cast of STAR TREK?*

MD Yeah. Bill's always very conscientious and worked hard, and considering the demands on him and on his time . . . it was very good. All those people were good. None of them were any problem from that standpoint. They all knew they were involved in something they liked, so they all did their jobs. They learned their lines, took direction or differed if they felt different about it, but there wasn't any problem, because that goes on all the time. You come to a meeting of the minds.

AA *What have been your experiences regarding STAR TREK conventions?*

MD I was asked to be on a panel in Pasadena some months ago, and it was amazing. Mike Ansara, for example, was in one show. He went there, and everybody knew him and everybody knew about the episode.

AA *You're very important in the history of television: you were one of the first to work with multiple cameras for television.*

MD I directed the first live hour dramas on CBS in 1948, when we were making up the techniques as we went along. But there were other people at work at the same time, doing the same type of work, like Fred Coe, who was doing PHILCO THEATRE at NBC at the same time. STUDIO ONE came about a year later.

AA *How much television work do you estimate you've done?*

MD . . . I've done maybe a thousand television shows and, frankly, I remember very few of them. After all, I'm 74 years old . . . but I'm still hacking away at it.

AA *For the people who watch the programs and enjoy your work, it's more than "hacking away": it's creating art.*

MD It's more of a craft than an art, but I suppose there's some art that goes into it. Particularly in this medium, the work of the director is so restricted and confined by conditions over which he has no control, like the clock. If you're making a feature, while you still have those worries you do have a lot more time to do what you might call art. But these episodic things are so full of compromise that the matter of compromising becomes an art.

JOSEPH PEVNEY

Born in New York City in 1913, Joseph Pevney entered show business at the age of 13 when he joined a song and dance team. While at New York University, premed student Pevney starred in one varsity show and directed another.

In 1950, Pevney became a director at Universal Pictures. Among the features he directed are The Strange Door *(1951, starring Boris Karloff) and* Man of a Thousand Faces *(1957). Included in his television directing credits are THE ALFRED HITCHCOCK HOUR, BEWITCHED, THE MUNSTERS, and segments of the NANCY DREW and HARDY BOYS series.*

"I love comedy, I love mystery, I'm not very good with car crashes, and that's one of the reasons I don't work anymore," states Pevney. "I don't believe in that stuff. I don't think that's theater. . . ."

People who work with Joseph Pevney, particularly cinematographer Al Francis and actor Walter Koenig, remember him as a relaxed man who knew what he was doing, even with the high-pressure schedule of television. Francis joined the staff of STAR TREK primarily to have the chance to work with Pevney, a close friend.

AA *How did you first become involved with STAR TREK?*

JP Gene Coon was the coproducer . . . we had met very briefly at Universal Studios, when he was a writer and I was a director of motion pictures. Gene brought me over to meet with Roddenberry. Gene Roddenberry had to get to know the people he was going to entrust his dream to. I met with him early in the project and it was very revealing. During one lunch he told me his background; he had been a free-lance writer in New York while he was a pilot flying transoceanic flights. He wrote for pulp magazines, and then he got involved with television . . . Roddenberry and I met, had lunch, we talked, and then I went with the show. . . . It's my conviction, having met and known a number of creative people, that Gene had a touch of genius about him. I believed that about him when I knew him. I don't know how well known this fact is, but he was the speech writer for Parker, who was Chief of Police in Los Angeles.

AA *He also wrote studies regarding drug addiction in Los Angeles.*

JP Did you know that he was also offered the post of Chief of Police? He was on Parker's staff, and he took one of those tests that they give to the Chief of Police. He came out highest in the score, and of course he never took the job, but he could have had it.

AA *At that point I believe he wanted to quit, to become a full-time writer.*

JP Oh, yes, and he did. He quit to go into writing full time. . . .

AA *The first STAR TREK episode you directed was "Arena."*

JP That was one of the first location shows that they'd ever done on STAR TREK. It was shot at Vasquez Rocks.

AA *There was a large set in that that appeared to be left over from an old western feature.*

JP That was an actual set on location, a big fort that was standing there. We found that. Gene [Coon] probably wrote around that particular set so that a sequence could come out of it. We fixed it up a little bit and used it right there. We used the rocks and that set, as I recall.

AA *There were a lot of pyrotechnics in that episode.*

JP And we used a lot of stunt people in the show as a result. As a matter of fact, the Gorn was the son of a friend of mine, a stunt man and horse wrangler with whom I worked on WAGON TRAIN. The son had had a bad accident just before "Arena," and he was resting around not doing anything. I talked Roddenberry into using a stuntman, because the Gorn was a heavy rubber suit: an actor would have been worn out in nothing flat, and I would not have been able to get enough footage without building a fan into the suit. I said, "We'd better get a guy accustomed to roughing it out there," somebody who would be able to go without water for that length of time in order to get enough footage, or we'd be stopping all the time to allow someone to put the

suit on and take it off, over and over. We needed to give him quite a bit of rest, or he would have become dehydrated. I thought he was wonderful in the part, a nice, eager kid, anxious to please.

AA   *"Return of the Archons" came next. The cast included a number of good character people, including Torin Thatcher, Harry Townes, and Charles MacCauley.*

JP   Charles MacCauley was a Pasadena actor. We used him quite often for voice-overs: he had a magnificent voice. But this was the first time we used his face, and he loved doing it.

AA   *He was ultimately in another episode you did, "Wolf in the Fold."*

JP   Harry Townes was thinking of giving up acting at this point, to devote himself to religion. He was a wonderful actor, and I talked him into doing "Return of the Archons" as one last fling. He did it for me, and he gave up thinking about ending his acting career, and went on to do quite a number of other things. He's a truly fine actor.

AA   *You directed David Opatoshu in your next STAR TREK, "A Taste of Armageddon."*

JP   Oh, yes, David. We did a lot of shows together. David is a fine actor, and I miss not seeing him personally, but I never had time to get to know any actors personally except Jeff Chandler. Jeff Chandler and I were very close. Jeff Chandler was a fine human being, and a good actor: a strong personality that came through . . . I named a son after him. . . . David was one of those types I would like to have known, an interesting man who never stopped working at his craft. I knew him in New York City. He was from the Yiddish theater. I was never in the Yiddish theater, but I know some people who came from it, including Paul Muni and Luther Adler. Incidentally, Leonard Nimoy speaks a magnificent Yiddish: it just rolls off the tongue when he speaks it.

AA   *"The Devil in the Dark" was another Gene L. Coon script, and the next one you directed.*

JP   The Horta was "living rock." There again, we had the problem of finding a person to make that thing move, and we finally went with Janos Prohaska, who created the concept. He was small enough so that he could get in the damn thing, and interested enough so that he would be able to stay in the suit long enough. He probably lost eight to ten pounds a day, just from moving around in the suit.

AA   *"Devil in the Dark" was the opposite of "Arena," filmed totally indoors with very restricted sets.*

JP   That was a very difficult show to do. William Shatner's father died during the filming of that episode. Shatner was very close to his father, and it really shook him up, but he managed. He was much better than I was when my wife died: I was impossible. If it hadn't been for the work that I was doing, and the support of my two sons, the fact that I was working so much and so hard, traveling an hour each way to work on the freeway, I probably would have flipped out. Shatner was very shaken then, and Leonard was very good to him at that point; he was with him all the time, and able to give him great comfort.

AA   *I've watched that show many times, and nowhere is there even a hint of his being under any more stress than usual.*

JP   He's a good, solid actor.

AA   *Your next STAR TREK was "City on the Edge of Forever," which most STAR TREK fans agree is one of the best of the series, if not the best.*

JP   Roddenberry was very happy with the end result of that. That was a very intriguing show. That was a pickup period for STAR TREK. The show was picked up, and he was quite convinced at the time that my work had helped. . . . He wrote me a letter which I'm very proud of—I still have it—congratulating me on my work and the extra special contribution he said I made to STAR TREK. The show was intriguing and highly successful. Joan Collins was very good in it. She enjoyed working on that show, and Bill and Leonard were both very good to her; I think that was a tough time in her career. Using her was a good choice. The whole show was interesting: the soup kitchen, and the whole business of hiding the ears. I'm a radio enthusiast, so I remember the business of Spock putting together his memory circuit, which looked like somebody's idea of an old, homemade radio.

AA   *Did you recommend Walter Koenig as "Chekov" because you worked with him in the "Memo from Purgatory" episode of ALFRED HITCHCOCK PRESENTS?*

JP   Yes, that's exactly it. I brought him in from that. I thought he would be an interesting Russian-type fellow. Gene wanted to get an international look. He was thinking of all nationalities, and somebody mentioned a Russian, so I brought him in, and he had a new career. He looks so great. He's got a great face. He has some kind of an interesting accent, but it sure ain't Russian. In any event, who cares? The most Oxford University accent is the Japanese fellow . . .

AA   *Do you remember if Roddenberry interviewed anyone else for the role of Chekov?*

JP   . . . I don't think that he interviewed anybody else. . . . I'm not sure, but I think once he met [Koenig] he liked the idea of the guy and the burning eyes, because he's got great eyes: they're on fire . . .

AA   *Do you have any particular favorites among the cast?*

JP   A permanent member of the cast? I guess Jimmy Doohan. Jimmy was very easy to work with: a good, solid performer, always anxious to do a good job, and always knew his words, inside and out, a good actor, an angel as far as directors are concerned, because he's there and he knows his stuff.

AA   *You did the one episode he really starred in, "Wolf in the Fold."*

JP   I did a lot of those, didn't I?

AA   *You did 14 out of the 79.*

JP   I also brought in the guy who replaced Jerry Finnerman, the cameraman.

AA   *Al Francis?*

JP   Al, yes. I'd wanted to make a first cameraman out of Al for a thousand years. . . . I got Al on STAR TREK as an operator, and he was brilliant. We were very close: we used to go boating together, and as a matter of fact we had sister ships. We were very close, and we had wonderful times. He thought I was a great director, and I thought he was a great operator and should be a cameraman. We just enjoyed each other's company. Anyway, during one of the STAR TREK episodes, and I don't remember which one it was, there was an intricate scene that we rehearsed several times. Just before the take we had one final rehearsal and something occurred on the set which struck Bill [Shatner] as terribly humorous, and he started to laugh. He couldn't stop. It was late, the last shot of the day, maybe 6:00 or 6:30, and his laughter became hysterical, just from fatigue if nothing else. There was no way to stop it. Leonard got into it, then some of the other cast members, and I was looking at the clock, fighting time and trying to get the shot in the can. I stopped everything and I read them the riot act, treated them like small children who needed to be punished, and God, it was so quiet on the stage. They could see that I was upset, being a disciplinarian. I never used to do that. It wasn't my job. I always horsed around with everybody. It was so quiet, and I turned to Al at the camera, he looked at me, and he started to laugh. And, of course, the whole cast started again, and I said to Al, "You, you sonuvabitch, you, my best friend, you . . ." and that made everybody laugh even more. It was a very hysterical situation, and I don't even know if we got the shot . . . It was one of the early shows. I think it was during the second 13, when Al joined the show . . .

AA *The next STAR TREK you did was "Catspaw."*

JP Oh, yes, the magic show.

AA *Robert Bloch, who wrote "Catspaw," also wrote "Wolf in the Fold."*

JP One of my favorite actors was in that . . . John Fiedler. He's such a fine actor, an amazingly good actor; he doesn't look like an actor, doesn't sound like an actor, and he's an excellent actor. I had him in a large role in either FATHER MURPHY or LITTLE HOUSE ON THE PRAIRIE, something a little more challenging than he usually gets. In "Wolf in the Fold" he was very interesting, and quite good. He enjoys acting; it shows all over.

AA *You also worked with Julie Newmar in "Friday's Child."*

JP Just recently, somebody found pictures of Julie, when she was supposed to be pregnant in that episode, and sent them to me. That was a funny show, a great show, filmed at the same location as "Arena."

AA *Tige Andrews was the Klingon in "Friday's Child."*

JP Yes. Tige is a very close friend of Shatner's. That's how he got the role. He came from Canada: that's where Bill Shatner knew him from, so when the time came to cast the role in "Friday's Child," he asked me to "read" Tige and see what I thought of him. And I liked his look, he had a great look, and he worked out fine, I thought. We wanted him to play the Klingon again in my favorite show, "The Trouble with Tribbles," but Tige had something else to do and it couldn't wait. We couldn't meet his schedule, so we put Bill Campbell into it, and he was very good. But Tige would have been exceptional; Tige looked like a Klingon [laughter].

AA *Why is "The Trouble with Tribbles" your favorite?*

JP We had done some comic sequences in STAR TREK, but this was the first out-and-out comedy we had done on the series, and Roddenberry was not in favor of it too much. He didn't cotton to the idea of making fun on this show. I fell in love with the story: it was the first effort of the kid who wrote this to dramatize something for STAR TREK. I loved it, I fell in love with that show. I spent a lot of time with it. I really enjoyed doing it, and I enjoyed working with Leonard and Shatner to make them think in terms of typically farce comedy. The show was successful, and I was very happy about that. I was proven right, that you *can* do comedy if you don't kid the script, and if you don't kid STAR TREK. If you stay in character, you can have wonderful fun with

STAR TREK, and the kinds of things you can do with it are endless if you don't lose the whole flavor of Enterprise discipline.

AA   *Have you seen STAR TREK IV?*

JP   Exactly . . . and that's why it's so successful. I'm right again. Boy, was I right. You can take those characters and you can play comedy, and you can get that much more fun out of it because of their backgrounds.

AA   *Both Shatner and Nimoy have excellent comedy sense and timing.*

JP   They do. Bill is a delicious comedian. He loves doing comedy, too. My only problem was making sure that they never went overboard. Yet Shatner would do a specific thing, and he would say, "Oh, I can't do that," and I would say, "Bill, it's beautiful; do it," and it worked.

AA   *You also had other excellent performers in there, too: William Schallert, Whit Bissell, and Stanley Adams.*

JP   Yes. Whit is another of my favorite actors. Yes, there are good people in that. Stanley Adams was a good comic. And you know, they didn't see him in that role at all. They said, "Oh, my God, no, you're kidding, Joe . . ." Stanley was funny; God, he was funny in that show. A wonderful, broad, heavy humor. Wonderful!

AA   *Did he seem to have fun doing "Tribbles"?*

JP   Oh, yes. Everybody had a ball doing that show. They had fun, and that's what came across. I loved doing that show, and I guess the basic reason I loved doing it was that it was such a change of pace for me, to get humor out of those people. That's the value that STAR TREK has: it made every one of those people recognizable. They were human. Another favorite of mine was the one in which I had Celia Lovsky.

AA   *"Amok Time."*

JP   Remember the gesture Leonard used. I said to him, "We've got to get something special in the greeting, like a handshake or a hello," and it worked magnificently.

AA   *What about "The Deadly Years"—the one in which everybody grew old?*

JP   That was a good premise; very interesting.

AA   *It must have been difficult to direct.*

JP   Very difficult, very difficult, not just because there were problems with the show. The big problems were with the egos of the actors, as I remember. Very difficult. DeForest Kelley was so good: he had little tricks he used, little facial tricks.

AA   *He did something using his lower lip.*

JP That's exactly right. And wouldn't you know that Bill also used it a couple of times? DeForest was very upset, because he had the feeling that this show was his, that he was the chief character in the show, and I was spending more time with Bill than I was spending with him.

AA *He did have the most elaborate makeup.*

JP And he was very good, because he took time doing it. The time that it took to do that show—wow!

AA *That episode must have been too long when it was delivered for editing. There were scenes filmed showing Kirk gradually growing younger as he went from sick bay to the bridge with Spock. But that was all cut, and a scene in sick bay was substituted for it.*

JP As you get older, you slow down your speech pattern, and the footage must have dragged on forever. Nobody figured that a page count to time the script is no longer correct when people are older, because they have to stutter and all that business. All of a sudden toward the second or third day of the show, we began to realize we were going to be way over length. I don't know who did the editing on that show, but it was quite obvious that we'd be overlong. So maybe they just trimmed stuff out.

AA *There was a pickup done, because you saw Kirk in sick bay, and one of the other characters, watching Kirk, says something about his getting younger. And they did something funny. To get the idea across that Kirk's youth was being restored to him, they shot closeups of his groin as this other character said, ". . . The aging process has stopped!"*

JP Are you kidding?

AA *No.*

JP Did they pan down, or just cut?

AA *It might have been photographed as a pan, but it was edited like a cut.*

JP If I had done it, it would have been a pan down. I don't remember it at all. It may have been an added shot. They may have just added it when we were finished with the show. I don't know who edited that. Who was the man who was so involved with all the "tricky" stuff in the series?

AA *Robert Justman?*

JP Bob. I'll bet you it was Bob . . . he's a very talented guy, very creative. Bob is great . . . there's hardly any mention of him regarding the show's development and improvement. I don't think he ever gets the credit he deserves.

GUEST STARS

WORKING ON STAR TREK AFFORDED MANY ACTORS THE CHANCE TO "STRETCH OUT" IN A WAY OTHER SHOWS SIMPLY COULD NOT, AS THE FOLLOWING IN- TERVIEWS AFFIRM.

TASHA (ARLENE) MARTEL

Tasha Martel began her acting career performing in summer stock at the age of 13. Five years later she made her Broadway debut in Uncle Willy, *costarring Menasha Skolnick, Normal Fell, and Harvey Korman.*

Her arrival in Hollywood during the 1950s was the start of a busy television career. She appeared in many television series, including HAVE GUN WILL TRAVEL *and* OUTER LIMITS *(in the episode, "Demon With a Glass Hand," written by Ellison; the assistant director on the show was Robert H. Justman).*

Her long career as "exotic" and "foreign" characters led to her being cast as Spock's wife T'Pring in "Amok Time."

AA *Do you recall how you were approached to work on STAR TREK?*

TM Yes. I had appeared at an audition for another segment called "Catspaw." After I read there was buzz, buzz, buzz, mumbling, and someone said, "Why don't we save her for 'Amok Time?' " I thought, "Oh, God, this is the part I want. Who wants to be saved for 'Amok Time?' What *is* 'Amok Time?' " Anyway, they did keep their word, and I did reappear to read for "Amok Time," never realizing that it would make such an impact on the STAR TREK fans. So they were saving me for something that I was very glad they were saving me for. I'm very grateful that I was contacted for "Amok Time."

AA *Did you have thoughts about the script when you first read it?*

TM Yes. I thought that this would really be a first in my theatrical experience, because before I played T'Pring I had only played women who were very emotional. And here was this woman whose intellect was her center, and perceived and evaluated her life through that. So it was a "first" for me in that sense, of having to use tremendous economy in the role. As much as I emoted the director kept asking me to do less, to make it simpler and simpler, until finally I thought, "Oh, this is going to be so dull that nothing is going to be registering." But apparently it worked.

AA *And yet you managed to inject a very sensuous quality into your character.*

TM [laughs] That was due to the actors teasing me all the way through.

AA *What did they do?*

TM Bill [Shatner] and I were like two kids in school, laughing at the times, at the terminology. It just pressed buttons, tickled them in us, and we went into gales of laughter and giggles. Finally the director came over and said, "Do I have to separate you two, like in kindergarten?" And I'm afraid that's what it came to. I have never broken up on any script or any set, any show as I did in this. It was all I could do to keep a straight face, and my attempt to do that and not laugh contributed to my characterization. Then there was dear Theodore Sturgeon on the sidelines watching, and gazing amorously at me. Every time I would finish a scene he would say to me, "You are my creation." And I would say, "No, you just wrote about me . . . I am *my* creation." We became friends for life: we really hit it off, Theodore Sturgeon and I. He was incredible. He was a nudist, you know. You could count on him answering the door stark naked. He did his thing, and he made no apologies to anyone. He was in great need of approval, affection, and he was a member of our family, a very kind and gentle soul. I still have a photo of him caressing my child's cheek: a very tender and loving man.

AA *How did you feel when you first saw yourself in the makeup?*

TM I fell utterly in love with myself. I had been apologizing for most of my life for looking exotic, trying to look like the girl next door, and I think it was a turning point in my life when I really accepted my own look. I felt much more myself in that makeup than ever before. I felt it came closer to my essence in a strange way. I did much of my own makeup. I don't like someone else puttering around my face, even though I think Fred Phillips, the makeup man on that show, was definitely an artist. In terms of my eyes, I can't have anyone fussing around those, so I did my own. Of course, they did the ears. That was something I couldn't do. I applied my own base, which was green. I look terrific in green makeup. I was very delighted with how I looked. I thought they photographed me beautifully: it was really the way I would fantasize looking in a show. Bill Shatner was a great flirt, which I found so amusing. I had worked with Leonard as husband and wife on a show with Nick Adams where we played a mountain couple—unlikely casting.[1]

[1]In a series entitled THE REBEL, an episode called "The Hunted."

AA   *While "Amok Time" was being filmed, did you suspect that STAR TREK would be so popular years later?*

TM   . . .I didn't give it a thought: I just wanted to do my job well. I'm not sure if it led to more work or not, but I know that I've done parts that I've thought had more impact. That was the one that is remembered. I think visually it was a standout that way, and the fact that it was the first time Spock was experiencing something that showed his sexuality as a focal point is also significant. But I had no idea what it would be. Now, with the new movies, I'd like to see T'Pring brought back.

AA   *What do you think happened to T'Pring after the events of "Amok Time"?*

TM   I thought Stonn was a rather dull character, that they were divorced at this point, and that possibly T'Pring had become the head of some great organization, movement or cause. Who knows: maybe in STAR TREK V there might be an opportunity for that. It would be really nice. Whenever I've spoken at any of the conventions the fans always ask, "When are they going to bring you back?"

AA   *Do you have thoughts on why STAR TREK is so popular?*

TM   I think the opportunity to represent some humanitarian ideas was given the proper vehicle in STAR TREK. Its particular form allowed for expressing very provocative ideas. We seem to separate ourselves: anyone who looks different, or appears to be different from us, is cause for suspicion. There is such paranoia here on this planet, and I think that STAR TREK unified life in a very wonderful way in many of the segments. It also made very clear the motive to create and preserve and support life, including those beings who don't honor that principle. So I think that it defined things for many young people in terms of their own individuality. It was also a show that knew how to entertain well, and I think the characters were very beautifully defined. Many of the early stories were conceptually original. They went through a certain period later where they had monsters and gimmicks. They seemed to have run out of the internal juice. I lost interest at that point. I think the first two years were totally unpredictable. You didn't know what wonderful new point would be brought out, you never knew what chances they were going to take . . . it had a certain element of risk in it. Later they made them predictable and safer, and many of the stories were lackluster after a while. That's my impression.

AA   *Did you read any science fiction before you were in STAR TREK?*

TM   Ray Bradbury. That was about it.

AA   *Do you read any more now?*

TM   More Ray Bradbury, and Theodore Sturgeon. I loved his book *More Than Human.*

AA   *Are you originally from New York City?*

TM   Yes, I went to the School of Performing Arts in New York. I studied with Sidney Lumet there. I graduated with the school's only drama award. I love New York. In fact we [my family and I] want to find a way of being there at least six months of the year. I miss it a lot. I'm very fond of Los Angeles. I'm not part of the league that enjoys putting L.A. down, but New York is my home. I've reconnected with Martin Landau, in fact. He and I met again after bumping into each other at art galleries last spring. Martin and I used to hang out together in the days when I was seeing James Dean. [Dean] was the first love in my life, when we went to the Performing Arts.

AA   *Are you ever stopped on the street by people who recognize you from STAR TREK?*

TM   Yes—in fact, lately, more than ever. It's the strangest thing. Lately I have more of that happening to me at shopping malls and department stores. . . .

AA   *What are some of the other roles you've played on television?*

TM   I played a Spanish flamenco dancer on MATINEE THEATRE. Then came DIVORCE COURT, PLAYHOUSE NINETY, and TWILIGHT ZONE. I did two ROUTE 66's, beautiful Sterling Silliphant stories. One was playing a very innocent 18-year-old Italian girl who thinks she owns the state of Oregon: a soldier in Italy had told her that if he died he would leave her this land. It was a very beautiful story. . . . The shows that I did in the '60s and the early part of the '70s had substance, and were wonderful fun to do. Then going from that, I did the SIX MILLION DOLLAR MAN, and I DREAM OF JEANNIE, THE FLYING NUN and LOVEBOAT and three COLUMBOs. I did a recurring part in HOGAN'S HEROES, played the girlfriend of Bob Crane, "Tiger," who was his French girlfriend, which was totally, totally opposite T'Pring . . . and the trouble was that no one really knew it was me. They'd say "God, was that you? I had no idea." If I had a public relations person, which I never did, he or she would have said, "This week, Tasha Martel is being seen on three shows. On one she's a hooker, on another a nun, and on a third a wife." Much of my career has been so disjointed in that sense. I've done a large variety of roles. If you're not blond and blue-eyed, and you don't look like the person next door, you're cast in these roles, and now what makes it more difficult is that if you're up for an Indian you have to *be* Indian. So it's narrowed down, and for us exotics there are now very few parts.

AA *Except in science fiction.*

TM Exactly.

MICHAEL FOREST

Michael Forest was born in Seattle, Washington, of French and Irish ancestry.

During the 1950s he was under contract at Warner Brothers, and appeared in many segments of their television series, including MAVERICK; his other TV appearances include BACHELOR FATHER, IT TAKES A THIEF, WAGON TRAIN, and ONE STEP BEYOND.

Forest has portrayed Othello several times (he hopes to direct the play now as well); he performed at the San Diego Shakespeare Festival just prior to his appearance in STAR TREK's "Who Mourns For Adonais?" (filmed in May and June 1967).

The actor lived in Rome from 1968 to 1978, where he appeared in 26 feature films produced in Spain, England, and France. During this period he also lent his voice to the dubbing of over five hundred films from Italian and Spanish into English. A true world traveler, he is particularly fond of New York, Barcelona, Paris, and Venice.

AA *How did you first become involved with STAR TREK?*

MF Curiously enough, they were originally looking for a British actor to play the part of Apollo, because of the way in which they wanted the character to be projected. Evidently they were considering some people from the British stage. The actor also had to be pretty well built physically. They couldn't seem to find who they wanted, so they finally called down to the San Diego Shakespeare Festival and asked if they had an actor who could fit this particular role. The artistic director at the time said no, they didn't have anybody there, but he gave them my name, and on the basis of that they contacted my agent. I went in and read for them, and they still weren't sure because they still wanted a British actor. At the time we talked about it, I said that the dialogue really didn't lend itself that specifically to a British actor. I really meant that I didn't want to do a British accent. Finally there was a compromise made that it would be kind of mid-Atlantic, good theater speech type of delivery. They settled for that, and that's really how it came about. That's how I got that particular role. And curiously enough, having done that role, I guess it identified me with that particular part, and I never did another STAR TREK segment.

AA   *Would you have done another, if you had been asked?*

MF   Oh, of course. It was a wonderful part to do, and there was a great deal of attention paid to what was happening, but nobody ever thought that it was going to be that good a segment as this one certainly is. It's very funny because, as you know, the entire series was not that popular when it first played. It was after that that it became such a popular series, a cult. When I was living in Italy during the early 1970s I was standing in line to go into a movie, and a woman came up to me and asked if I was an actor, and I said yes. She asked if I ever did a STAR TREK, and I said yes. She practically fainted dead away, and said, "My God, you're Apollo." At that time I had no idea that the STAR TREK cult had formed. Later on I found out that it had become such a huge success. So it was a big surprise to me. As a matter of fact, last year I went to my first STAR TREK convention, in Atlanta. I didn't know that these conventions are so popular, so widespread around the country. It was an eye-opener to me, because of all the people who were there, and the kind of organization they had.

AA   *Were you pleasantly surprised at the attention?*

MF   Oh, of course. It's always very nice, you know, that people remember. In fact, the people remember more about the part I played than I do. They've seen it so many times that they can tell you the lines, tell you certain things that you did at any given moment in the particular segment, and it's astounding to me to realize that there was such attention being paid by so many people.

AA   *For you it ended after six shooting days, and for them it's still happening.*

MF   That's right, that's right.

AA   *Can you recall any incidents that occurred during the filming of "Who Mourns For Adonais"?*

MF   Leonard [Nimoy] and I were longtime friends before he got into the show, and in that particular segment he didn't have that much to do, but he was on the set a couple of times, and at one point I was sitting on my throne, in my "tutu," and I saw him standing, watching the shooting. I did something like, "Approach and be recognized," that kind of a gag, and he groveled his way up the steps and kissed my foot,

kind of a silly thing. One thing about the show: they worked
very hard, and there was a lot of attention paid to detail, but
they had a lot of fun doing it. It wasn't one of those sets
where everybody was going around so dead serious that
they didn't see the humor. There were things like that. I did
some kind of a little movement with my skirt when I sat
down once, much as a lady might do, and that survives as an
outtake.

AA *How did you meet Mr. Nimoy?*

MF I originally worked with him in the late 1950s. I ran into him
[while] studying with Jeff Corey. Vic Morrow was in the
same class that Leonard and I were in. So that's how we all
met, and I guess the first time we worked together was
when we did *Deathwatch* as a play, which Vic directed. I
think it was in 1963 or 1964 that Leonard and I, Vic Morrow
and Paul Mazurski did the film. It was a noble effort. It's a
strange film, and it just didn't come off. It was close. It
could have been a really dynamic picture, but if you miss
with something like that, then you miss by a long way. But
we tried very hard. One of those things.

AA *The release date is listed as 1966.*

MF I guess it just wasn't released until later on, but we were
doing it in that period of time.

AA *And the movie was coproduced by Leonard Nimoy and Vic
Morrow.*

MF Right, it was.

AA *Do you and Leonard still see much of each other?*

MF As a matter of fact, I saw Leonard two weeks ago at
Paramount. He was ecstatic about the success STAR TREK
is having, and of course they're already looking toward the
next one that Bill Shatner is going to be directing. Leonard
says he's really worn out. He said that he just doesn't feel
that he could direct another one, certainly not at the moment, anyway, he's so tired. And well he might be. It's been
a steady grind for him for the last four or five years. I'd
been living in Europe for ten years, and when I came back I
called him. He was right in the middle of the first film
[STAR TREK—THE MOTION PICTURE]. We talked, and
when I asked how it was going, he said that although
technical things are an integral part of it, it was the human
relationships that existed in the series that made it successful. He felt there wasn't enough of that, that they were
losing a certain amount of what had been successful. I think
he was right. I don't think the first one was that good a film.
I mean, it was successful, but I think the very qualities that
he was talking about were missing. I think it was because of

STAR WARS, and some of the other films that had come out with such tremendous technical pyrotechnics, etc. They felt that in order to be successful and compete on that level that they had to do the same thing. And they found that it was *not* what the audience was looking for. The last one is very much a film of the relationship of people to people, and people to environment. These things are what people really identify with, and that's why it's been so greatly received.

AA *It's a very enjoyable movie. Robert Ellenstein is also in it. Is he one of the old crowd from Jeff Corey's school, too?*

MF Sure. In fact, Bob was in *Deathwatch*. He and Leonard are old friends from way back. We all go back miles . . . I remember Leonard coming in one day, I think while we were still shooting *Deathwatch*. He had just tested for this new series. He said you couldn't believe the makeup they had on him: pointed ears, etc. But of course, it was all so new. Nobody knew then what they know now. When anything is that new, people look at it with a suspicious eye, asking, "Is this going to go or not?," because it's such a completely different format than anybody had seen up until that point. At that time, people were still dealing to a great extent with the westerns; COMBAT was being done at that time; all of a sudden this was something so brand new that I think people were really skeptical whether it was going to go at all.

AA *Do you remember any of Mr. Nimoy's subsequent reactions, after he had become used to the idea of the makeup?*

MF As I recall, in the original pilot he played a rather different character than what Spock later turned out to be. He had more . . . human quality, instead of the characterization that he developed as the show went on. No, I didn't get too much information from him regarding the show. Obviously, as so many actors were in those days, he was happy just to be in a series. I know at one point he had become so identified with the character that he was trying very hard to get away from it, trying to play other roles, and unfortunately or fortunately, however you want to look at it, they didn't want to see him as any other character than Spock, and it was difficult for him to get other parts. He did MISSION: IMPOSSIBLE for a while. I never saw any, so I don't know how they came off.

AA *There was actually some discussion of doing a television series in 1977, called STAR TREK II, without Mr. Spock. A young Hollywood actor had been assigned to appear as another Vulcan science officer.*

MF   I don't think it would have been successful, because if there's anybody identified with the show it's certainly Leonard, even more so than Shatner. I'm sure there's a great deal of rivalry between them. I don't know that for a fact, but just knowing how people are, there is probably a kind of ongoing—how should I say it? I'm sure they're friends, in terms of working colleagues, which would be understandable. I don't think it's anything unhealthy. I think it's good. In fact, if they're both trying to do things that would make the picture or the subsequent picture even better than the last one, I'm sure that Shatner wants to make the last one even better than this one.

AA   *Had you read any science fiction before you did STAR TREK?*

MF   Not really. I've never been particularly interested in it. It wasn't anything that I avoided specifically, but I had not been a big fan of science fiction. As far as STAR TREK was concerned, that particular segment that I did, you can only appreciate from the human qualities that you find within the character. You can't find anything else.

AA   *Or else it would come out a cardboard performance.*

MF   That's right. I felt I had to make him this human within the milieu that we found ourselves. I think that's what anybody would have done. It goes right back to what we were saying earlier, that the only way you can make something believable and palatable to an audience, is to see that there's a reality to it. . . . If you're playing in *Streetcar* you try to capture the character of a Stanley in much the same way as you would capture the character of King Lear, or the character of Apollo. You have to find the qualities of that particular person in that situation. That's all you can do, and then as the actor, extend yourself into it and make it as believable as possible, so they believe you are what you are. Obviously, if you're going to play a truck driver working on a garbage truck, you'd approach the part a lot differently. The dimensions would be different, as all people are different. I think that's why you don't think, "Well, now I'm going to play a god." I'm playing a human, I'm playing a person who *is* this person in this particular situation. Whatever those parameters are, you have to fulfill them.

AA   *Did you have any difficulty with the scenes in which you were acting alone with just a partial set in front of a blue screen?*

MF   No, you just have to believe what you're doing, what every actor does . . . just put it in your mind and let your imagination do it for you, and fulfill whatever it is that they want you to do at that point, however big or small, as the moment calls for.

AA *Do you have thoughts on why STAR TREK is so successful?*

MF I guess the only thing I can say is what I said before, that there was a relationship between the people and the environment that people identify with. I guess there's a certain kind of universality in the series that took a while to grow on people, because of the format, and because it was so new: nobody had ever done anything quite like that before. I think it took a while to catch on. But there is this universality about it, and I think that's what makes anything successful: that the people who read it or see it can identify it as a kind of human experience. I think that if they'd done SHANE in a space setting the basic relationships that the people had would still have made it successful. Why are pieces like *Oedipus Rex* and *Hamlet* still successful? Although they're in the past, and Mr. Roddenberry's talking about the future, it's the same thing because basically you're talking about human relationships, which are not going to change that much. If it has universality, then it will be there, whether it is five thousand years ago or five thousand years in the future. I think that STAR TREK had that quality that people could identify with.

TECHNICAL CREW

THOUGH THE PEOPLE IN FRONT OF THE CAMERA GET THE NOTORIETY, THEIR WORK WOULD BE IMPOSSIBLE WITHOUT THE CONTRIBUTIONS OF A TALENTED BEHIND-THE-SCENES CREW. CASTING DIRECTOR JOE D'AGOSTA WAS WITH THE SHOW FROM THE BEGINNING. PEOPLE LIKE DIRECTOR OF PHOTOGRAPHY AL FRANCIS, ART DIRECTOR WALTER M. JEFFRIES, HELPED MAKE THE 23RD CENTURY LOOK REAL NOT ONLY TO THE STAR TREK ACTORS BUT TO ITS AUDIENCE AS WELL. JACK FINLAY, JOSEPH SOROKIN AND DOUGLAS GRINDSTAFF GAVE A VOICE TO THAT WORLD: EVERY SOUND ABOARD THE STARSHIP ENTERPRISE AND ALL THE OTHER VESSELS AND WORLDS SEEN IN THE SERIES HAD TO BE CREATED FROM THEIR OWN IMAGINATIONS. EXCEPT, OF COURSE, THE WONDERFUL MUSIC OF COMPOSERS LIKE GERALD FRIED AND GEORGE DUNING. MUSIC EDITOR ROBERT RAFF WAS ULTIMATELY RESPONSIBLE FOR DETERMINING HOW THAT MUSIC WOULD BE USED IN A PARTICULAR EPISODE. FINALLY, IT WAS UP TO FILM EDITOR FABIEN TORDJMANN TO ASSEMBLE THE COMPLETED PIECES OF THE PUZZLE.

THE FACT THAT SO MANY OF THE SHOWS HOLD UP SO WELL AFTER SO MANY YEARS IS A TRIBUTE TO ALL THESE MEN AND THEIR VARIED TALENTS.

JOSEPH D'AGOSTA

Joe D'Agosta first worked with Gene Roddenberry when he was casting THE LIEUTENANT at MGM in 1963. The following year, when Roddenberry was casting "The Cage" at Desilu, D'Agosta was working at 20th Century-Fox. He helped to cast "The Cage" and later "Where No Man Has Gone Before" working after-hours and on weekends.

After leaving 20th Century-Fox Television, D'Agosta went to work at Desilu, casting both STAR TREK and MISSION: IMPOSSIBLE. His ability to find the best and most interesting looking actors for the most unusual roles helped to make STAR TREK and MISSION: IMPOSSIBLE so popular.

Mr. D'Agosta is still a Hollywood casting agent.

AA *How did you first become involved with STAR TREK?*

JD I cast THE LIEUTENANT for Gene Roddenberry. We began to trust each other and like each other, and because he was somewhat of a novice producer at the time he ended up going on my word on many things, and they worked out on that particular series. So when he got STAR TREK, he called me and said he had no casting director and asked if I could help him. At that time I was at Fox. Gene said, "I gotta have you," and I cast it on the phone by just suggesting films to look at and what actors to see, and I relayed all this through a young man named Morris Chapnick, who was Gene's assistant.

AA *Do you recall your contributions regarding the casting of Jeffrey Hunter?*

JD Jeffrey Hunter was the first captain, and that was a selection made from the name list given by the network and the studio. I was not even involved in that. Perhaps the casting of that character was important to whether the show was a "go" or not, as the correct casting of the lead is in many shows. On the Spock character, the only guidelines I had were that he had to be thin, and a good actor who could act with no emotion. He was a cold, calculating, logical person. Humor was not even considered at that time.

AA *Do you recall how Leonard Nimoy came to Mr. Roddenberry's attention?*

JD   Leonard Nimoy was an actor I had been well aware of for a long time. I'm not sure I'd ever used him, because I was a rather young casting director at the time, myself. But I was very familiar with Leonard because he was on the actors' circuit. He was just one of a number of people to meet and look at film on. Since I was casting long distance, I wasn't even there when they responded to him, so I have to give all of that credit to Gene Roddenberry and his vision. I really do believe that Leonard was slated to be a featured actor who worked occasionally who you could always depend upon to fill out a multiple group. He was mainly in the gangster/reporter area, you know.

AA   *Do you recall who any of the other candidates for Spock were?*

JD   No. Gosh, I'm afraid I can't.

AA   TV Guide *reported that Martin Landau was considered.*

JD   It's quite possible, though I believe the casting of Martin Landau [for MISSION: IMPOSSIBLE] came almost simultaneously, because they did the two pilots at exactly the same time. Bruce Geller was very close to Martin Landau. As a producer he used to attend Martin's classes to learn something about how to deal with actors.

AA   *I remember Martin Landau as a heavy in* North by Northwest.

JD   . . . Somehow that performance you just mentioned stuck in people's minds. That's usual. The only thing people usually remember about actors is the impression. You remember that more than the story, and whatever first impression you got, it always hangs in. As to DeForest Kelley, he was a long-time friend of Mr. Roddenberry's, and I don't even know if the doctor was going to be the major character that emerged. Gene was just very interested in getting him in, because he had worked with him at Ziv on some of those early cheapo cop shows on which Gene Roddenberry had cut his producing teeth. I believe that Gene was a technical advisor for the police department. I don't know going in whether I would have had the foresight to cast DeForest Kelley, because I really did look at him as less of a country doctor, which was the concept: a country doctor in the future, and I'd always looked at DeForest Kelley as rather a streetwise reporter/detective type. So again, I have to give that credit to Gene Roddenberry.

AA   *The doctors in the first two pilots were portrayed by John Hoyt and Paul Fix.*

JD   You've just jogged something. I just said something I didn't even realize. John Hoyt and Paul Fix are probably who I would have cast as a country doctor, and probably did. That means that I was directly involved in the DeForest Kelley casting, but I know that came from Gene, because Gene knew him for so long. That would have been closer to my image, talking about those kinds of guys, because I had worked on GUNSMOKE and RAWHIDE, and those were the kinds of characters I would have thought of for those shows: Milburn Stone, you know? The lovable country doctor. Now, again, Gene is the one who thought of DeForest.

AA *What about the casting of James Doohan for the second pilot?*

JD Scotty was originally such a minor role that I cannot tell you the concept except that he was supposed to be a highly intelligent, skilled engineer. Just to show you the difference between casting directors' minds and producers' minds, I would probably have cast a less likable, homey character, an engineer of the Brooks Brothers type, the modern engineer. Gene wanted everybody on that show to be lean and healthy looking, because by then they would have figured out the correct nutritional system and proper exercise, so everybody had to be in physically perfect condition. Now again, I would not have thought of DeForest Kelley or James Doohan. James Doohan could have come from Jimmy Goldstone, who has a great eye for casting. I would not have thought of them in that vein. . . .

AA *I know that Lloyd Haynes was cast as the communications officer in the second pilot. Nichelle Nichols didn't enter the series until "The Corbomite Maneuver" was being cast.*

JD She was also mine. I had found Nichelle in a scene that she did, and cast her in a major role in THE LIEUTENANT, which she has never forgotten: she's always forever grateful for that. When STAR TREK came up, I turned to Gene and said, "What about Nichelle?" She had done such a good job in THE LIEUTENANT: it was her first job, and it was a major lead. So we'd had that great experience with her ability before. The major casting I got involved in with the regulars was Walter Koenig as the young Russian, Chekov. Walter earned it because he was a good actor, and he wasn't the hunk of today, or the hunk of those days which was the Warner Brothers "Bob Conrad" type of guy. I did a movie with Walter. It was a small movie in which we were both actors, and we had become friends. I knew he was highly intelligent and had ability with accents.

AA *There was a wonderful succession of actors on STAR TREK and MISSION: IMPOSSIBLE. Did you have a list of such performers?*

JD I'm the worst kind of casting director, because I don't just work from lists. I always start every show from scratch. I might have lists in books that I refer to, just to look at, but I don't have an "I'm going to use this person" list. I'd start every show brand new, and then I'd go through the directory, then through lists I'd have, books, magazines: anything I can, as though it was the first time I'd ever seen anything. I've always been very good using the agents who supply the pool of talent. I spend endless time with them, talking about people they have, and if they try to sell me ten, I try to narrow it down to the two who are really good actors, just in conversation, using challenging remarks or considerations. I would see a number of people myself, and then bring a number of choices to Bruce Geller on MIS-SION: IMPOSSIBLE and Gene Roddenberry on STAR TREK, and they were always the best. If I brought five actors per role, they would usually select one of those five, and from three they'd usually select one of those three. Very rarely did I have to go back and show them ten people or one hundred people. That's the way they work today. They want to see everybody before they'll cast somebody. I'd just rely on the people out there, and feed people every week. I'd have my list over here of actors who I liked, and my list of actors I didn't like; I'd always have that stack to go to.

AA *You cast a lot of actors with distinctive faces: William O'Con-nell, Reggie Nalder . . .*

JD We probably go back to some of the people who we rely on. That's really my answer. MISSION: IMPOSSIBLE was a little easier than STAR TREK, because basically we needed good, theatrical actors who could be foreigners of some sort. It just depended upon what country they were in. They had to have either light or dark complexions, and they all had to be classical, powerful actors. On STAR TREK, every part was a different challenge because every episode involved different kinds of characters. They were either gangsters from New York or Chicago, or they were cow-boys, aliens, or very beautiful women. Beautiful women: I really had a corner on them [laughs]. Many times I would find an actor, use him, and then years later say, "Did I cast that person?" We approached everything very fresh. And the great thing about it was that these guys were very open, particularly the Roddenberry group. When an actor came in, we didn't really consider the fact that he had done a lot of work. That always helped, of course, but it was considering how that person fit the role, and then the next judgment was whether or not he would be professionally able to handle it. We didn't have as many of those old-line "traffic directors." Joe Sargent, for instance, was a very creative, inventive man: fresh. He approached every picture as though it was the most important picture of his life. But there are those directors in television to whom it makes no difference what they're directing: they take their masters, their two closeups, and then they move on. "Traffic cops," I call them. We just didn't have a lot of those guys. We had people who I guess were hungry for careers, and inventive, on both series.

AA   *Were you ever asked to cast any of the STAR TREK feature films?*

JD   No. I may not have been asked because I got out of casting for a while and went into producing. I was also head of casting at various places: Paramount, Universal, then MGM. That may be the reason . . .

AA   *Why do you think STAR TREK is so successful?*

JD   The topics were so current, and they were hidden behind this gauze of the future. I set that aside from the use of humor, of sex and all that. It's a rather cartoony show if you look at it, particularly now. But the subjects were so current, and whether it was prejudice, the Viet Nam war, or women's independence . . . I remember they used to attack important subjects the same way Archie Bunker used to: STAR TREK wasn't just an adventure show. We knew it then. I guess that's why it was successful.

AA   *Did you think it would still be watched so many years in the future?*

JD   No, I didn't, quite frankly. I thought the Trekkie thing was going to die out. They did fight to keep the show, and it didn't work, and so I figured this was maybe two years of all these guys running around and Gene Roddenberry selling off scripts and pictures: his wife formed Lincoln Enterprises, and they'd send scripts and film clips out to people. I gave it two years, and thought it was a smart idea to market the stuff while you could, but I didn't think it was going to last.

AA   *Were you ever recognized because of your work in STAR TREK?*

JD   My brother had a customized motorcycle, and I once had to pick it up after I had borrowed it and it conked out on me on the street. I wanted to put it in somebody's yard, until I could get back with a trailer to tow it. Anyway, I left a note. When I got back there was another note: "Are you *the* Joe D'Agosta?," and I turned around and there was this 13-year-old staring at me, saying, "Oh, my God, it really is you, isn't it?" And I'm going, "What?" My name is only *that* big in the credits, a little tiny thing among all those other names. That kid gave me a little moment of what it feels like to be a movie star.

AL FRANCIS

Al Francis, a native Californian, helped photograph science fiction films long before he became STAR TREK's director of photography. After joining Universal during the 1940s, he assisted John P. Fulton, head of the studio's photographic effects department (who would later work at Paramount). When Fulton left Universal, David Stanley Horsley became the head of the department, and Francis was one of his camera operators. "He was a mathematician," Al remembers. "Everything he did had to be done on a slide rule." Francis worked on such films as This Island Earth, Tarantula, *and* The Incredible Shrinking Man.

It was Al's friendship with director Joseph Pevney that led to his association with STAR TREK. "I met him in 1947," Francis recalls, "when I was an assistant cameraman and he had just come to Universal . . . I always thought that he is the most outstanding director I've ever worked with. I love him as a friend, and as a person. He's the most honest man I've ever known. . . . Just before I did STAR TREK," says Francis, "I was asked to work as a camera operator on The Graduate, *and I turned that down to go with Joe Pevney on STAR TREK."*

AA   *How did you become involved with STAR TREK?*

AF   I was going to do a feature, and Joe Pevney called me to say they were having a little problem with STAR TREK's camera operator, an older man who wasn't giving them what they wanted. Joe said that if I would take over as the operator that in a matter of months I would be the first cameraman. I said, "All right, I'll talk about it." He had Gregg Peters come in with Gene Roddenberry and one of the producers. . . . They said Jerry Finnerman was going to leave the [series] and that when he left they would make me first cameraman.

AA   *This was during the series' second year?*

AF   Yes, I think it was the second year.

AA *How did you find the STAR TREK company to work with?*

AF They were all excellent people, well-qualified professionals. I just stepped into it. Fortunately I'd had a lot of experience. Gene Roddenberry called me into his office right after I had started, and he said, "I don't want you to be afraid to do anything. Use any kind of colors in the background, or anything else you feel might enhance the picture, and I will back you. We all make mistakes," he said, "but give it everything you've got and do anything you want to do. If you think it will work and that it will be different, let's do it." So I went crazy with colors on the backgrounds. . . . Everybody seemed to approve because when I finished STAR TREK I was really in demand. I had so many offers to go to other places that it was unreal.

AA *Did anybody ever tell you at any time that they wanted you to feature the same values that Mr. Finnerman introduced into the show?*

AF No, nobody ever mentioned that at all. Of course I had been on the picture for several months, and I didn't want to change the photography very much. I did change it a little bit, but not so that it would be noticed, except by anybody who was in the business. I just smoothed out some of the things that Jerry did. They suited him all right, and there was no criticism of them, but I thought that closeups and other things should be done a little differently.

AA *It seems that you cut down on the soft focus.*

AF Yes, I made it a little bit harder. Not to an extreme, just a little bit harder.

AA *Your episodes also look brighter.*

AF I believe that, too. I went in for a little bit more contrast than he had, so that would make it just a little brighter.

AA *Less muddy.*

AF Right. And then I asked them for the stuff to be "printed up."[1] I didn't like the "dirty" look that I sometimes saw in the dailies, and I would ask them to bring it up to look natural and clean. That was my way of doing it.

AA *Some of your episodes have angles that were not seen in earlier segments, for instance the camera shooting closeups of people on the transporter.*

AF Yes, I would talk to the directors, and since I was familiar with the sets by then, I would try to change a little of the regular routine, and sometimes that changed the setups quite a bit. I think I made more dolly shots. I tried keeping

[1]To bring up the contrast of the film in the lab.

the camera moving, so it wouldn't look like a set, so that it would look more like we were on a ship.

AA *That must have been very difficult, because a lot of those sets were very small.*

AF There was room to dolly in on the main control area [the bridge]. I worked the guys a little harder: I'd have them pull out walls . . .

AA *That's why the bridge seemed bigger toward the end of the series, because that was in "wild" sections, and permitted you to do that.*

AF Yes, we did a lot of things like that.

AA *Why weren't such things done during the earlier episodes of the series?*

AF Well, everybody has his own ideas. When I do a picture I like to put into it what I think is right, and that's why I usually have pretty close relationships with the director and the producers: I make suggestions like this where a lot of others don't. I had also had more feature film experience than Jerry, and I had never worked much in TV. I'd been on features, and features were a lot different from TV in those days. Now they're getting closer together, but in those days features were perfection, and TV was just a secondary thing. Well, I tried to carry that experience over when I started doing TV work.

AA *I remember a shot in "The Mark of Gideon" with Kirk and some others sitting at a glass table. The camera appeared to be under the table.*

AF I don't remember the room, but I remember the shot.

AA *I've always wondered why there were no almost subjective camera shots in STAR TREK. You used a "fisheye" lens a couple of times, when someone was supposed to be going crazy, but other than that I don't recall anything along that line.*

AF You see, at that time the cameras were all changing. We were making a lot of trick shots, such as the transporter footage, that required the cameras to be tied down. And of course, at that time we were going from regular cameras with finders on them to reflex cameras like they're using today, where you look through the camera itself, eliminating the finder. You have no parallax or anything else, so it's much easier to do those things with the trick camera.

AA *What you saw was what you got.*

AF That's exactly right.

AA *You worked with some excellent directors, too, on STAR TREK: Vincent McEveety, Ralph Senensky . . .*

AF . . . I remember that Ralph Senensky was replaced on the last episode that he did. Herb Wallerstein came in and took

Ralph's place, and he was really uptight and he kind of let me lead him through the picture. I'd known Herb some years previous to that. He had only been directing off and on. The rest of the time he had been an executive in the production office. When he came in, I volunteered my help and he said, "Give me all the help you can give me. I'll watch the actors, you watch everything else." And that's the way we finished it. . . . The people in STAR TREK enjoyed each other. . . . I raced motorcycles. Shatner wanted to ride motorcycles, and so I would take him out on the weekends and I would give him some instructions about what I knew about racing motorcycles. We became very close friends.

AA *Do you have any specific memories of anything funny that happened on the set?*

AF There were enormous numbers of things. I'll give you some examples. Joe Pevney was directing one of the episodes. I had worked with Joe for many years, and we had a signal: if everything was all right I'd just nod my head, and he'd say, "Print it." If I shook my head no, he'd say, "Well, let's do it again." Bill Shatner and some of the others were clowning around on the set. Joe was having a little problem with that, and he really barked at them. He told them that they were going to have to settle down, and he didn't want any more noise on the set. I was looking through the camera at the time, and I could see Shatner's eyes go over to him: here's a guy who really means business, and he'd better be quiet. I burst out laughing. Joe said that of all the people to start laughing when he'd gotten everything under control, it would be me. And, I'll tell you, it was hilarious, because then everybody just broke up. Also, in one scene in "The Trouble with Tribbles," these things started coming out this chute. They would come out, we'd just get rolling, and then they would stop. We were doing this thing over a dozen times. Finally we started, and none came out. We were just about ready to shut the camera off, and then they came out, all over everything: camera, hall, every place.

AA *I imagine there was a fair share of practical jokes played, too.*

AF Always. Someone would take someone else's script and hide it, and then the place would be in turmoil for a little while, then everybody would have a good laugh. In one scene the entire crew was having dinner and cocktails. Their drinks were always blue or green, or some exotic color. The prop man, Irving Feinberger, had gotten a blue liqueur to use in the scene. I don't remember the name of it, but it's real blue and real strong. They started drinking that, and the first thing you know everybody got silly. From that time on, I think they used other things.

AA   *Did you find there was any change when Desilu was taken over by Paramount?*

AF   There didn't seem to be any change . . . there may have been some things I didn't know about, but there didn't seem to be. All that happened was they cut a hole in the fence so we could get from what had been the Desilu lot into Paramount. That's the only thing I can recall that happened. We were on what at the time was Desilu's lot.

AA   *Following Gene Roddenberry's initial encouragement, was the STAR TREK staff receptive to all your ideas?*

AF   I never had a problem in the world. I would go in and talk to Gene, and it was a big family. That's the way I saw it. It was the closest relationship that I ever had while making a picture, from the producers right down to the crafts servicemen. Everybody enjoyed working with everybody else, and when the series ceased production, I think that everybody was a little unhappy. I know I was unhappy, and I know the crew that I had was very unhappy about it. Paramount said they didn't want me to leave the studio, so I went from STAR TREK to LOVE, AMERICAN STYLE. On the first year of LOVE, AMERICAN STYLE I did every other show, and then I did THE IMMORTAL for them, followed by LONGSTREET.

AA   *What do you think of today's television, as opposed to the television of STAR TREK's time?*

AF   I think that they have a lot more to work with today than they had then. You've got much better special effects as far as film is concerned in the lab part of it, the opticals.

AA   *Do you think cinematographers use these new opticals techniques as best as they can?*

AF   No, I don't. I think that the breed of cameramen who are working today are lacking in experience; they're an operator today, and tomorrow they're a first cameraman, or they're an assistant today and tomorrow they're an operator. They don't have the opportunity, to my way of thinking, of working with the variety of cameramen who really knows what he's doing. When I was starting out, I worked with Jimmy Howe on *Yankee Doodle Dandy* when I was 20 years old. Then I did *The Hard Way,* and *Air Force* also with Jimmy Howe, and then *Across the Pacific* with Ted McCord. I'm not in any way putting down the cameramen of today because they do have a lot to contend with, such as schedules and budgets. But I think there are a lot of shortcuts they could take that they don't know how to take. . . . I think that if they had a better knowledge of lighting sets, they could do better, and I don't like the style of photography today. I think that they're doing away with the natural look of TV, and they're showing the photography and not the actors.

AA *What do you think of STAR TREK when you see it now? Does it hold up as quality entertainment?*

AF I look at them occasionally, and of course, you're your own worst critic. I see flaws and things I would do if I had it to do all over again to make the shows better: some of the camera moves I made, better angles, and things like that. But I'm happy with it. I'm not ashamed of my name being on it. You know, I did a feature for Paramount called *Paper Moon.* There was a different type of photography.

AA *It was very soft, wasn't it?*

AF Yes. What I tried to do was to keep the color in it, but subdue it. And so I had 25 people call me from all different parts of the country, wanting to know how I did it. When I first went in and talked to them about doing the film, I had read the script and knew that it was supposed to be back in the 1920s. I asked for enough money to make a test, and I went with an assistant and made a series of tests in different ways, showing them what I could do to subdue the color but still give the actor the appearance and prestige he should have.

AA *And you did this without using filters?*

AF What I did was to "flash" the film.[2] I would underexpose it and then flash it. Everybody loved the test, and I made the picture that way.

AA *Did you receive any assignments because of your STAR TREK work?*

AF Oh, sure . . . when I finished STAR TREK I had so many offers I couldn't keep track of them. Everybody wanted me to come in and do something. So I knew that I had done the right thing. I knew Jerry Finnerman when he came into the loading room at Warners. His dad, Perry Finnerman, was also an excellent cameraman. Anyway, he left and that's when I took over the show. . . . He gave them some sort of ultimatum, and that's when they called me in and told me that I would have the picture. Of course, I would never have taken it, because I was getting so much more money working on features that it wouldn't have been worth my while, but inasmuch as Joe Pevney was there and we were such good friends, I did.

[2]To expose the unprocessed film to a carefully controlled amount of light in the lab. This flattens the contrast.

AA   *If you were asked to appear at a STAR TREK convention, would you go to speak?*

AF   Oh, sure . . .

AA   *Do you have anything you'd like to say to the fans of STAR TREK?*

AF   Yes. I think the STAR TREK fans are very loyal. I don't think there are any fans of anything who are more loyal.

AA   *Do you think their loyalty is justified?*

AF   I do. I really do. The only way I'd say that it wasn't justified is that we should have continued the series. But at that time I don't think anybody, including Paramount and the network, realized the following that it had. When they both realized that they made a mistake, it was too late. The fans resisted its cancellation, and afterward there were many people who traveled miles to see the STAR TREK actors. You know, I took my name out of the phone book because I was getting calls all the time. I still have many of the STAR TREK scripts left, and I'm saving those. I have the scripts to the first episode that I shot, and it's signed by all the actors with their congratulations and wishes for success. They wrote notes and everything in it, so I never got rid of them. I'm saving them all to pass along to my family.

WALTER M. JEFFERIES

When the first STAR TREK pilot was being planned during the summer of 1964, Walter M. Jefferies' background made him the perfect choice to design the U.S.S. Enterprise. Jefferies had worked on the designs of another outer spaces series, MEN INTO SPACE (1959–60). In his honor, the access conduits aboard the Enterprise, constructed from his designs, are referred to as "The Jefferies Tubes."

Following his work on STAR TREK, Jefferies chose to return to simpler times as art director of LITTLE HOUSE ON THE PRAIRIE, beginning in 1974. He stayed with the series through its entire run, designing the log cabins and larger structures needed for the series.

AA   *You worked on THE LONG HUNT OF APRIL SAVAGE, a western series pilot for Gene Roddenberry. Was filming on that completed?*

MJ Oh, indeed it was. I did three pilots in a row. I did the STAR TREK pilot, then the MISSION: IMPOSSIBLE pilot, and just as soon as that was finished I went immediately into THE LONG HUNT OF APRIL SAVAGE. They were all shot, and, as you know, two of them sold. APRIL SAVAGE was penciled in; it looked like it was going to sell. It hung for six to eight weeks, and then the network decided not to do it.

AA *Do you remember anything specific about it?*

MJ Bob Lansing starred, and one of the heavies was Bruce Dern. The whole thing was shot up at a Boy Scout camp outside of Big Bear. I built all of the sets, then took them up there and set them up. We built a complete little cabin, made it in a mill, and dressed it. I walked Gene Roddenberry and Herb Solow into it at about seven o'clock one night and it was lit with two kerosene lamps and a fireplace. And they bought it, we undressed it and put the dressing on a truck, took the cabin apart and shipped it out to Big Bear by truck at about four o'clock in the morning.

AA *You worked on other shows at Desilu, such as THE UN-TOUCHABLES, which had nothing to do with science fiction. When you were first assigned to STAR TREK, how did you approach your research?*

MJ Basically, Roddenberry outlined what the ship had to be. I got everything I could find: "Flash Gordon," "Buck Rogers," and everything I could get from NASA, and said, "This is what we will *not* do." So that defined the envelope. Other than that, I was wide open.

AA *You wanted to avoid doing anything that was familiar to the public?*

MJ That's right.

AA *Did your knowledge of manned flight designs come in handy when you were designing the starship Enterprise?*

MJ No. We had other, more profound reasons for coming up with what we did, such as requirements of lighting and photography.

AA *Were you in agreement with Roddenberry about the final design of the ship?*

MJ Oh, yes.

AA *When and why were the modifications made on the miniatures of the Enterprise during production of the series?*

MJ There were modifications made all the way through. The primary reason was that television was going from black and white to color, and we were having a lot of problems with how it appeared on film, compared to how it transmitted electronically. Consequently, we were constantly making changes, because the whole electronic broadcast setup was changing, and what worked great this week might not have worked the following week. We had to keep pace and experiment along with the changes in broadcast technology.

AA   *I recall that Pato Guzman and Franz Bachelin worked on the first pilot.*

MJ   That's right. Franz was the art director, and Pato was his assistant. I was the set designer on it.

AA   *So you actually designed the bridge.*

MJ   I designed the bridge, and the Enterprise, and they took care of the other sets. When the second pilot was done, I had all of that.

AA   *Were you also in charge of refurbishing the sets for "Where No Man Has Gone Before"?*

MJ   Refurbishing, redesigning, and restructuring. The bulk of the sets from the first pilot were set up so that they could only be shot from one angle. We had to broaden those aspects, so that if the second pilot sold, the same sets could work for the series.

AA   *Was that when you made the sets "wild"?*

MJ   That's when we made them wild, but we also had to add more to them, so that they could be shot from a number of different directions. What you could nail off for a pilot is far from adequate for a series. There had been so much money spent; we knew that if it sold they wouldn't give us anything with which to build additional sets, so we had to make sure the things would work serieswise when we did the second pilot.

AA   *Did you have any sort of guide when you were designing the standing sets for the series?*

MJ   That was all just what I felt was right. It was designed to be functional. It had to be.

AA   *How many stretches of ship's corridor did you have in the series?*

MJ   Only one. There was a long, easy curve, and one very short leg.

AA   *There were times when you dealt with civilizations that were not futuristic. And your work on LITTLE HOUSE . . . indicates you have quite an interest in historical designs.*

MJ   Oh, yes. Absolutely. As far as I'm concerned, to design anything you have to have a certain amount of logic behind it. You've got to define your design envelope, and work inside of that. If you want an example, you can design fancy sportscars until the sun comes up, but unless you harness those pretty sketches to actual physical requirements, the human body and the car's power plant and how it's driven, those sketches don't mean anything.

AA *Do you think that the believability you put into the sets contributes to STAR TREK's acceptance?*

MJ I certainly like to think so.

AA *Do you have any other opinions regarding the success of the series?*

MJ There were good stories, and excellent character definition. The story definition and the character definition were *the* tremendous parts of it, I think.

AA *Do you recall anything regarding the designing of the phasers and the other hand props?*

MJ The phasers, definitely. I did all of that, all the way down to the final engineering drawings of them. My brother John was also a craftsman who worked for me. He did quite a bit of the final engineering drawings on the phaser weapons.

AA *They all looked like they did something along the lines of what they represented.*

MJ I never liked the phaser rifle. But you've got to satisfy directors on it. Somehow or other, a weapon to them has to look like a weapon as we know it. They want it "jazzed up."

AA *What would you prefer to have been done?*

MJ Oh, something much smaller, much simpler.

AA *Whose idea was it to have the hand phaser and the pistol-grip phaser combine into one weapon?*

MJ That was my idea. Which one they used depended upon the requirements regarding power and range.

AA *Was the communicator also your design?*

MJ Vaguely, yes; in substance, but not in detail. I don't recall who worked out the final details. I was involved in so many things at that point, to try to get the show going, that I just couldn't take care of all the little details.

AA *As the art director on STAR TREK, were you also responsible for the design of the optical paintings?*

MJ Yes, for the basic layout of them. They were designed in conjunction with any set components we built for use with them.

AA *What did you use as your inspirations for your designs of the futuristic cities and specialized installations?*

MJ Oh, I used to climb the wall looking for ideas. We utilized anything.

AA *Including photos of oil refineries and industrial complexes?*

MJ We utilized anything like that. There are certain things that over the years are not going to change much in spite of technology.

AA *What was your usual deadline for designing an episode?*

MJ To design and build it is all part of the same thing; anywhere from three days to a week, and sometimes less because we only had the two stages to work in. Consequently, whatever building had to be done on the set had to be done while the company was shooting on the planet stage.

AA   *And you were responsible for everything?*

MJ   Everything the camera caught, except the people. We were shooting one episode, painting and dressing on one, and designing another, so we were working on as many as five shows all at the same time.

AA   *So if anybody asked you what was current, your answer depended on what stage of development they were interested in.*

MJ   Right . . . that's the way television works.

AA   *Would you say that you were usually satisfied with the end result, or was it mostly a series of compromises?*

MJ   It's a compromise for everyone. I never got what I considered to be the ideal. I don't think Jim Rugg did. I'm sure Gene Roddenberry didn't; the directors felt that way and so did the writers. Everybody has to give somewhere at some time. Nobody ever gets the optimum. After all, it's a team effort to come up with the final product.

AA   *Have you watched any STAR TREK episodes recently?*

MJ   I pick one up every now and then, yes. Three nights ago I stayed up late . . .

AA   *Is there anything you want to say to the fans of STAR TREK?*

MJ   Hang in there. I'm still amazed at it all. Really, I think at the time we were doing the show and the basic designing, if we had had any idea at all that it was going to be memorized and studied and everything as much as it has, we'd probably never have been able to definitely make up our minds about what anything would look like.

JACK FINLAY,
JOSEPH SOROKIN,
DOUGLAS GRINDSTAFF

Jack Finlay, Joseph Sorokin, and Douglas Grindstaff are all long-time, sound professionals. Finlay headed the sound effects department at CBS for 15 years, working on GUNSMOKE, HAWAII FIVE-O, and other series before accepting the difficult assignment to assemble the sound effects for the first STAR TREK pilot in 1964.

Joseph Sorokin, who assisted Finlay on "The Cage," had worked at the old Hal Roach Studios, and is one of the few surviving members of the AMOS 'N ANDY production team. He also worked on the MISSION: IMPOSSIBLE pilot in 1965, and after Finlay's job on STAR TREK was done, Sorokin took the original pilot's sound effects, combed the country for other existing sounds, then put together some of his own. The results of Sorokin's work form the bulk of the sounds heard throughout STAR TREK's three production seasons.

Sorokin brought Douglas Grindstaff into STAR TREK, and when Sorokin left the staff Grindstaff became the head of the sound department for the series.

Jack Finlay is now in retirement. Sorokin and Grindstaff, good friends for years, still work together in the industry at Lorimar Pictures, where Doug is now Joe's boss. The two still can't say enough about each other's professional abilities and personal virtues.

JACK FINLAY

AA *How did you go about getting the sound effects assembled for "The Cage"?*

JF It wasn't that easy to get. In those days the major studios wouldn't give you what you wanted if you wanted it for television production. I called a friend over at Paramount and got some stuff from *War of the Worlds* [1953]. I had seen it, and my friend over there had worked on it . . . I got that stuff, and whatever else I could scrounge from around the town. I went to the libraries and got out every possible thing that might work to put together. I ran those sounds backwards, slowed them down, and did whatever I had to do to them so they would work for us. . . . Joe Sorokin was my best boy [second in command]. . . . We had some other kids working on it, but they didn't stay. They wouldn't do the long hours that were necessary to get the job done when it was needed and it boiled down to Joe and me. Trying to get the work done on time was the big thing, because that's the name of the game in television: "deadlines." They didn't give us a lot of money to get the stuff together, but on one occasion I told Gene that I needed a full night on the sound stage to play back what I had, just to see what was there. . . . Joe and I worked all through that night compositing everything I had, listening to it, changing it, eliminating some things and adding others. I came up with a large assortment of things that I probably used 20 percent of, but it was at least a nucleus of interesting stuff with which to get started. . . .

AA *Do you remember how you produced any specific sound effects for "The Cage"?*

JF The photon torpedo sound, the "twang," came from *War of the Worlds*, and was obtained by striking a stretched length of cable. This was used with another effect over it to create a "popping" type of sound. . . . The things that I was really concerned about were the ship itself and the door openings. The sound of the ship [as heard from inside] wasn't that hard. We just got in some jet stuff and fooled around with it. Gene felt that the doors were airtight hatches . . . so I put in a couple of compressed air pops. Darrell Anderson first showed me the transporter optical, and I came up with an interesting sound there. The composer, Alexander Courage, had some interesting ideas, but it wasn't enough to do the job. We needed sound effects to do it rather than musical effects. . . . I think I had 10 or 15 types of generators with which to generate sounds, some low and some high. One component of the transporter sound, the high-pitched hum, was a generator which I used for the backup of quite a few sounds. The moving, mechanical grinding sound [in the transporter sound effect] was either a ski lift or a cannery machine that I used . . . and there are a couple of other elements in there, possibly another generator, but these are the predominant effects in there, out of a total of four or five sounds. The low hum that builds up at the start [of the transporter effect] is the laser cannon effect I put together, which I sped up on a variable speed recorder. The original laser cannon effect was done over at Paramount, prepared on one of their stages and left over from *War of the Worlds*. Those sounds were put together from Paramount's sound effects department here at that time, and Tommy Milton and Gene Garvin, the head mixer. . . . We also did a sound effect by rubbing things against dry ice then putting the sound on a variable speed recorder. . . .

AA *How did Gene Roddenberry regard "The Cage" after its completion?*

JF As I recall, Gene was happy with the original pilot. He wished he could have gone farther with it, but there has to be a stopping point. . . . I thought he was very happy with what he had. . . . He kept fighting Darrell with the opticals. Gene had something in mind, but he couldn't tell Darrell what it was, so he just told Darrell, "Do it." It was trial and error. . . . Gene was very happy with Robert Butler's work; I've always thought Bob is an excellent director. . . . When I first saw "The Cage," I thought it really had a lot of possibilities, and I'm not a big science fiction fan. When I saw it, and the interesting characters he created, I was flabbergasted. I thought it was a great project, except that I knew that NBC would probably think it cost too much money. . . . Gene was very proud of "The Cage" after it was completed, but I think he'd probably still be there making it if they allowed him to do that. He'd never know when to quit. . . .

JOSEPH SOROKIN

AA *What was your earliest experience regarding STAR TREK?*

JS When I was working on THE UNTOUCHABLES, the STAR TREK script was already in the works but they did not yet know what the ship was going to look like. Walter M. Jefferies, a dear friend of mine who just retired, is a pilot. I've been a flight instructor for the better part of my life, and since we both flew . . . he called me over one dark night when we were both working late and said, "Joe I've got something to show you. This is my conception for what I believe the Enterprise should look like." He unrolled this godforsaken pastel drawing of the Enterprise. It had a twin tail, very much like a P-38. I remember leaning over his bag and saying, "Matt, is this what you're going to show Roddenberry in the morning?" He said, "Yes." I said, "He'll never buy it. I just don't think it looks like what this huge, totally futuristic vessel should look like." Anyway, the rest is history. It shows how wrong I was. Roddenberry took one look and he flipped, and that became the Enterprise.

AA *How did you become associated with STAR TREK?*

JS I was working at Desilu with Jack Finlay, who was the supervising sound editor at the time, when Gene Roddenberry came aboard and formed his own company, Norway Productions, and Norway and Desilu, in conjunction with NBC, were to do the first pilot. . . . I'll never forget, after I found out that we were going to do a second pilot, I was talking with Roddenberry one night and he said to me, "Joe, I'm either going to make Desilu or break Desilu . . ."

AA   *How long did you have to do all the sound effects for the first pilot?*

JS   If my memory serves me right, it was probably about eight days . . . I believe Jack and I did it ourselves. I still remember doing the sound effects for a huge giant. . . . I also remember that working for Gene Roddenberry was quite an experience. There are so many big producers who do take sound for granted . . . who aren't cognizant of the tremendous amount of time, sweat and energy that goes into completing a show's sound effects. Putting music in is simpler, since you're only dealing with one score, once it's all been put together, but sound editing is tremendously complex and diversified.

AA   *Are most of the sounds that we take for granted in a film actually put in during postproduction, things like street noises and footsteps?*

JS   Some of what we use is shot with the show, but more often than not a lot of it is put in. For example, suppose Allan and Joe were eating in a restaurant in New York. You should hear all the noises of the dishes, and there has to be a uniformity in the murmur going on in the background. If we're walking in Central Park in the daytime you want to hear the birds, the wind, people talking and laughing, dogs barking, distant traffic noises—all the things that would be attendant for Central Park in New York City.

AA   *Therefore you, the sound editor, have to be aware of all the layers of sound going on at any one given moment.*

JS   . . . I don't want to sound corny, but a sound editor has to have lived life a little bit to know what it is that goes into a product.

AA   *Then how do you handle something like STAR TREK, that includes routines and experiences that you can't possibly live through in today's world?*

JS   Well, that is exactly what made doing the series so difficult: we knew what we wanted, but nobody could put their finger on it. Everybody knew what they wanted verbally, but physically nobody could say, "Here it is, use this." All those sounds had to be manufactured for the series before they could be added to the soundtracks. I put the entire STAR TREK sound effects library together during one summer after we did the pilots, and a young man named Jack Fagin helped me. I obtained all the sound effects from the Air Force Library at the top of Lookout Mountain. Some of these sounds are rather hokey and corny now, but you have to view it in the context of the past. At the time that we were putting STAR TREK together, the existing sound effects were like something out of "Flash Gordon" or "Buck Rogers." So we had to come up with something else. Authenticity was very important to Gene Roddenberry. Now, authenticity for something that we know about is one thing, but you have to *create* the authenticity for something that you *don't* know about. Roddenberry gave me full rein and a little bit of money. I taped the Air Force Library, went to Ryan International down in San Diego and taped their library, and I also taped the libraries of Douglas and Boeing in Seattle, Washington.

AA   *Then all of the sounds that we hear of accelerating engines in the series are really accelerating engines?*

JS   No. A lot of those sounds were made on soundstages. Some things were real. . . . The bridge of the Enterprise was kind of a joint effort between Jack Finlay and myself. We had about seven or eight loops going, perhaps as many as a dozen, and from that we made various combinations until we got it all down to one.

AA   *Who arrived at an approximation of what sounds and how many were needed?*

JS   People like myself and Doug Grindstaff . . . I was the department head when I brought Doug in. Then, when I left, Doug took over. . . . Originally we tried to synchronize the sounds with all those flashing lights built into the bridge, but that was a never-ending, totally ridiculous situation. So after a while we just got hold of a half dozen to a dozen different loops of various sounds that we decided at a meeting were going to be the particular sounds for the Enterprise bridge. Doug Grindstaff, I might say, is perhaps one of the most able, competent men in the business. . . .

AA   *What do you feel now when you watch an episode of STAR TREK?*

JS   My daughter's at school at the University of Victoria in Canada, and every now and then she'll tell me, "Daddy, all the kids got together in the dormitory and watched STAR TREK, and I was so proud because there was your name!" When I see the shows on the air, sometimes I cringe at the cornball approach in retrospect. Here we are in 1987, and it is somewhat amateurish 20 years later, but in the main, I'm tremendously gratified and satisfied that I was able to be a part of STAR TREK.

DOUGLAS GRINDSTAFF

AA *What are the responsibilities of a sound editor?*

DG Briefly, we handle the entire dialogue track. We have to smooth it out.

AA *In other words, anything that appears on the soundtrack?*

DG Anything that appears on the soundtrack, other than music, from footsteps to subtle movements of clothing, picking up a pencil and putting it down . . . all of the various things you take for granted we put in and make sure they're set up correctly for the mix. Then we add anything we have to, including special effects.

AA *You were the sound effects editor on STAR TREK for three years.*

DG I worked on every episode.

AA *Including the two pilots?*

DG Yes. I don't think that there were many of us who did that.

AA *How did you become involved with STAR TREK?*

DG When they did the first pilot, they asked me to come over and work on it.

AA *That entailed getting the sound effects recorded and edited into the film?*

DG What happened was, we assembled a whole library of various sounds originally, and then we made the stuff on the scoring stage. We didn't have synthesizers like they do now.

AA *Do you recall any specific problems that occurred when you were doing STAR TREK?*

DG Many. It was very tough, very hard work, and like I said we'd have to create a lot of the stuff, spend hours working on it. Gene would come up to the cutting room, and I'd run something for him, and explain, "This is what we're doing," and he'd say, "Yeah, that's it," or "Maybe you should take this direction." I'd have three or four sounds that I'd develop to a certain point and then I'd have him come up to take a look at them and ask, "Which way do you want to go?" Gene had a knack for pulling in people creatively. All of a sudden you were just sucked into it, and you couldn't let go. It was a seven day a week total commitment. But it was just such a pleasure working with Roddenberry, Bob Justman, and Eddie Milkis. They were just great, the three of them

. . . [Roddenberry] does pull it out of you. I'll give you an example. I remember I got an 11-page typewritten memo on one show. Now that's unheard of, in all my 30-odd years in the business. If I were to give one of my sound editors that many notes on one show today, they'd freak out. I just sort of looked at it as though it was nothing.

AA *Since you were on the series all three years, can you tell me if the relationships of the production people changed at all during that time?*

DG In the last season Gene got mad at the network when they didn't give him the time slot they had promised him. He moved out of his big office and across the lot. There was this little fire escape outside, and I could walk up to talk to him through the window in the little office where he isolated himself. There were times I used to get upset and go running into his office, and he'd give me a lecture on how I couldn't have everything my way, and that even he had had to give in. But the overall relationship was good. The first year was probably the wildest. It was just sheer bedlam trying to get the thing out. We had an American air date and a Canadian air date to meet. Every room aboard the ship had a sound, and every planet had a sound. It was a monumental thing. Gene Roddenberry once told me to think like a painter: he wanted a "painted" sound, which I'll never forget. My concern was that we were sometimes getting too cartoony. I tended to want to be more realistic, to try to stay away from getting too corny or too cartoony, but he was pressing all the time to "paint it with sound." And that's what we tried to do on it. And then, of course, we had a big debate on whether or not we should have sound out in space. So, in some of the early episodes, you hear the ship go by and hear the engines, and in some you don't. The sound of the ship was originally a cymbal crash which we then had to edit in with the sound effects every week. But then they dropped it, so it was there and then it wasn't. They were trying to feel their way to find out what would work and what wouldn't, and the debate would go on.

AA *In most productions you'd be dealing with sounds that already exist: you just go someplace and get the sounds, or recreate them in controlled environments. But where do you go to get a phaser blast?*

DG That's true. Then you've got to create something, you've got to use your imagination. What does it sound like? Nobody knows. What you had to do was create the sound effects ahead of time, before we would get the actual show. So a lot of times I would talk with Gene and find out what he had in mind. He would call me up and tell me a script was being written, or stop by with a prop: for instance, a tribble. He showed it to me, and we talked about how we should go soundwise with it. It had to make a very pleasant sound, it had to rear up when somebody approached and it didn't like him. There had to be a sound for one individual tribble, another for several tribbles, then a few more, then more than that, and eventually the sound had to fill the whole ship. I found a dove "coo," I flipped the track over, and shaved off part of it with a razor blade. I then made a loop out of it, put it on a variable speed machine, and changed the pitch of it to different frequencies. Then I chose those frequencies I liked the best and decided which ones I would use in each spot. I then went to a screech owl for the sound of the tribble rearing up, took the screech owl and played with it and got variations of it. Then I took a bunch of little balloon sounds, where you'd get a balloon and rub it, and we mixed that with other little squeaky sounds that we had in the library, playing with all these at variable speeds, mixing them and making new sounds out of them, and putting them all together until we came up with the various composite sounds used throughout the whole show. When the editors got the show, all I had to do was hand it to them and say, "Here you are." The bridge background must have been made up of over 20 different backgrounds. Gene wanted a very busy, active bridge.

AA   *There were always voices in there, too, saying unintelligible things.*

DG   Yes, and those were all added later, on different tracks. The bridge itself was pure, without any voices in it.

AA   *Did I hear the sound of an accelerating train for the ship's engines?*

DG   No, that was actually a generator-type sound that I turned around and again put on variable speed, changing the pitch until I got what I wanted. It's hard to explain. Sometimes I'd combine stuff and play with it until I got just what I wanted. I'll give you another example. I had the "warp power" sound, and then they wanted it to go to Warp three, four, five, etc., and I had to make variations of one sound once we had decided on it. Then we also had the sound of the ship in trouble. I put the warp sound on a recorder, stuck my finger in, and pushed up and down on the loop and it sort of warbled, and that's how I got the sound of the ship straining. Jack Cookerly had an old organ all rigged up to do electronic sounds. I brought him in one time, made up picture loops of various things, and played the loops. He looked at them and we talked to him, and then he made certain sounds to fit the pictures. I took those sounds and played with them: cut them, edited them, slowed them up or combined them with some other things to get what we wanted. He also made a bunch of what I call "raw material," which we used in different things. It was a real old organ which he had rigged up to do this; it was not one of your modern synthesizers. All that came in later. I remember Yamaha came out with some organ that was supposed to do a lot, and it wasn't that great at the time. But I'd get in on the tail end of a scoring session and get sounds from an electric guitar, a drum, or some other instrument. One time the whole orchestra tuned up, and I reverberated it and used it as a fogged planet background.

AA   *Was STAR TREK the most challenging thing you ever worked on?*

DG   Yes. We did the MISSION: IMPOSSIBLE pilot, which was also a challenge. We tried to give the Enterprise the feeling of a big ship. You may have noticed the Bosun's whistle and the alarm system. Gene Roddenberry wanted it to have the feeling of a big nautical ship. The red alert, for instance, was a signal used aboard ship. In almost 99 percent of the cases we would take something like that and slow it up or do something to it so that it was still recognizable. On ["Amok Time"] I remember we had a big gong, a Chinese-type gong on Vulcan. We got on the scoring stage and recorded a nice gong, then we turned it around and recorded twangs on the electric guitar, and combined everything to give the gong a distinctive quality. We had to do stuff like that.

AA   *There were wind chimes in that show, too. I guess all those sounds were added during postproduction.*

DG   Yes. We had to make all those sounds and put them in. There was one time when I brought in a two-and-a-half ton truck filled with dirt and dumped it on one of the stages so that we could record spears going into it. People started to think we were crazy.

AA   *When you were doing the series, did you think that people would still be watching it today?*

DG   No. I can honestly say I didn't realize it then.

AA   *After all these years, what's it like seeing an episode?*

DG   It's almost like it was done yesterday. Sometimes I won't remember, but then I'll start to watch it, and I'll say, "Oh, yeah, I remember that, and this is what I did there." If I'm looking at it, then it comes right back. After we finished STAR TREK, Eddie Milkis took over the editorial department, and I came back and ran the sound editing department for Eddie for several years after STAR TREK. Then I left the business, and came back and ran the department at Columbia. Now I'm over here at Lorimar running the department.

AA   *Do you have any favorites among the STAR TREK episodes?*

DG   . . . Of all of them I probably like the original pilot best of all. I thought that was really imaginative . . . it just made me tingle.

GERALD FRIED

Born on February 13, 1928, in the Bronx, New York, Gerald Fried began his professional music career in 1948, spending eight years associated with the Dallas Symphony Orchestra, the Pittsburgh Symphony, and the New York Little Orchestra.

Fried has scored episodes of more than 30 television series: everything including westerns, comedies, dramas, and more exotic projects such as LOST IN SPACE (1965), THE MAN FROM U.N.C.L.E. (1965), IT'S ABOUT TIME (1966), T.H.E. CAT (1966), MR. TERRIFIC (1967), and THE SIXTH SENSE (1971). His unique blend of jazz and symphonic music is also heard in many episodes of MISSION: IMPOSSIBLE and, of course, STAR TREK.

AA   *How did you become involved with STAR TREK?*

GF   It was just another TV job. I was doing other shows, I got a call, and I did them. Nobody knew this was going to turn out to be a major cultural phenomenon. It was just a TV series— no, it wasn't, actually. They took it more seriously, and the stories had more substance. There was a quality that I have not experienced too much in movies and television. When I worked on ROOTS, there was the same type of attitude. They were doing something special and wonderful. So it really wasn't just another TV show, I take that back. That kind of infected us, and it was exciting to work on. We still didn't know that it was going to have a life of its own.

AA   *Was it Wilbur Hatch who first brought you in?*

GF   Possibly. I forgot that name, but I think it was . . . Jack Hunsaker was the music editor when I was doing these shows. Now he's the head of music at Paramount TV.

AA   *You composed the scores for five episodes: "Shore Leave,"*
      "Catspaw," "Friday's Child," "Amok Time," and "Paradise
      Syndrome."

GF   They also tracked my music into a lot of episodes. People
      tell me how much they enjoyed my music in a lot of shows I
      don't even know about.

AA   *You did some beautiful music in "Shore Leave." There was*
      an Irish tune . . .

GF   Oh, yes, when he was fighting his Academy friend . . .

AA   *Did that come from any specific source, or was it a completely*
      new melody?

GF   It was based on a lot of Irish folk tunes I knew. Certainly
      the idiom was based on original folk material, but it's easier
      to write your own, rather than copy a folk tune which may
      have a copyrighted arrangement. I'm sure it was original,
      although it sounded like a lot of other things.

AA   *The next episode you scored, "Catspaw," was very different*
      and called for an eerie, sustained sound.

GF   That's the one with all the bass clarinets. I don't even have
      the scores. For some reason Paramount and MGM used to
      be the same way. They wouldn't even let us keep copies of
      our own scores. And we said, "What the heck, so we don't
      have scores," and we didn't have tapes of them, either. We
      were so busy. We went on to the next thing, and we didn't
      think that there may come a time when you'd want to sit
      back and listen to these. Now, fortunately, at least in the
      case of STAR TREK, we get a chance: they've been rere-
      corded. Fred Steiner and John Lasher are doing them. "The
      Paradise Syndrome" was recorded, and I think so was "Shore
      Leave." I hope "Amok Time" was, too. That is my favorite.

AA   *It also has one of the most important musical pieces in the*
      series—Spock's theme, played by bass guitarist Barney Kessel.
      What was your intent in composing that?

GF   Well, it had to be a theme that had some lyrical pretensions,
      and yet it had to be special: it had to be a Vulcan theme, so
      the choice of instruments, a bass guitar—which was not
      very common in those days, and it's not much more com-
      mon now—came to mind. And I tried to make it angular, as
      if it's trying to be expressivo, but because of the nature of
      Mr. Spock's emotional makeup, it would never be a senti-
      mental thing. So I tried to get all those factors into one
      theme.

AA   *Did it take you long to compose?*

GF   Nothing in those days took you long, because you had no
      choice. You had to finish a score in five or six days. It was
      madness. Of course, STAR TREK may have given us a

little more time than others, say, MAN FROM U.N.C.L.E. There was one MISSION: IMPOSSIBLE for which I had to write 18 minutes of music in one night. That, of course, is hardly composing. It's just using tricks to get by.

AA   *Your Vulcan music had a lot of percussion in it.*

GF   I was drum-happy in those days, and to some extent still am.

AA   *You used a drum very effectively in ROOTS, too, as I remember.*

GF   Sure. In fact, I wrote what was perhaps the first all-percussion score, for Stanley Kubrick's *Paths of Glory*. Except for the opening La Marseillaise and a few Strauss waltzes in the ballroom scene, it was an all-percussion score.

AA   *I guess that helps to heighten the tension.*

GF   Yes, it was a military theme, and a fresh sound was also a motive. There aren't many ways to get fresh coloration into a movie, and considering the theme of that movie, it was appropriate.

AA   *The "Amok Time" score reminds me of another score you did, for* The Vampire.

GF   Oh, for God's sake, I have no secrets from you [laughter].

AA   *I even remember* The Curse of the Faceless Man.

GF   Oh, my!

AA   *All of these were such interesting scores that I've remembered them through the years, even if some of the movies weren't as interesting as the music.*

GF   Yes. Oddly enough, when you get those monster movies the industry permits you to do more interesting composing than some of the bigger budget things I've done since.

AA   *Do you enjoy that additional freedom?*

GF   Sure. Do you remember something called *I Bury the Living*? That I like. I did a harpsichord fugue with the "Dies Irae." You don't get a chance to do that in other kinds of work.

AA   *Your music to "The Paradise Syndrome" is perfect for the episode.*

GF   Yes, my Indian thing.

AA   *Was that music actually based on any native American musical idioms?*

GF   I did a documentary for CBS around that time, called "Gaughan in Tahiti, the Search for Paradise," and I did a lot of research into ethnic music then. I think I used some of that research in the music for "The Paradise Syndrome."

AA   *Since they were discussing the "Tahiti Syndrome" in the episode, it was very appropriate.*

GF   Kind of, yes. That CBS documentary was my first Emmy nomination.

AA   *Were you ever nominated for a STAR TREK score?*

GF No. But I think I picked up three Emmy nominations for ROOTS, and I won one.

AA *I remember the TV movie* I Will Fight No More Forever *has music that sounds a lot like the score for "The Paradise Syndrome." I guess that was the product of the same research you mentioned earlier.*

GF Probably, yes. I actually did some American Indian research, but some of those things flowed so nicely that I probably just did variations of them. And sometimes at three or four o'clock in the morning you don't remember if that's a sketch, or if you actually did it before. A lot of the times when we composers repeat ourselves, we don't mean to, but we're not sure and who has time to think at that time, "Did I already do this?," or "Is this something I thought about five minutes ago, or did I write it ten years ago?" So I don't think we're really not sure. Have you ever talked to a composer in the middle of a 20-hour-a-day schedule?

AA *No, but I've spoken to writers in the middle of a 20-hour-a-day schedule, and I've had some of those myself.*

GF You probably forget how to hold a telephone.

AA *Your mind has to be on your work, and only on your work. What was your impression of the people who worked on STAR TREK?*

GF They had a vision of a certain kind of humanistic excellence, I think. The only two I got to know personally were Lenny Nimoy and Bob Justman. I also worked on another movie with Lenny Nimoy, called *Deathwatch*.

AA *Were you given any directive, in reference to your STAR TREK assignments, to compose a specific type of music?*

GF I don't think so. The producers were so pressed . . . I dealt primarily with Bob Justman. I think he talked to me for a few minutes, found out that I had some reasonable threshold of intelligence and musical background, and he said, "God, just do it, man, we've got other things to worry about." I think that's basically the way those conversations went. And then we were just on our own. You know, the pressures in TV, as you're finding out by doing these interviews, are really horrendous. And all those things, in retrospect, that you think were carefully planned with balanced aesthetics that were discussed and mulled over for months—it didn't happen that way.

AA *One of the directors, Marc Daniels, described it to me as a series of compromises.*

GF That's not altogether a bad way of stating it.

AA *Did they invite you in to show you each episode?*

GF　It was the standard procedure. We'd go in and we'd see it once, and I don't remember if Justman or one of the other producers was there, arguing about whether music should go there, and if so, what it should do, but usually that's the way it works. Sometimes they just said, "You figure out where it should go," and I would be alone with the projectionist, yelling, "Could you roll back a second? I want to see this again." They'd figure out where it starts, and where it stops, what has been called "spotting." You'd spot the places where the music should go, and then you'd go home and figure what the music should say, and how to say it.

AA　*Watching the series now, do you still think it holds up?*

GF　I haven't seen it, except in passing. While I'm switching channels, maybe I'll see some of it. But I haven't really sat down and watched it. My first family is too old to have seen it, and those in my second family are too young.

AA　*How does it sound, listening to your own music so many years later?*

GF　I love it. I'm usually surprised that it's that good. I have almost disparaging feelings about it. I feel almost ashamed of the way I just ground it out at four o'clock in the morning. I don't remember what I wrote. When I hear it, by God, it's kind of nice. Most of the time I'm very pleased. A couple of times I wince, but not as often as you would think.

AA　*Do you have any theories about STAR TREK's continued popularity?*

GF　It touches something mythic, a combination of mythic values and human values, in a way that I don't think anybody else did. TWILIGHT ZONE was very mythic and fantastic, and most dramas are based on human values. STAR TREK bridged both values. It also came at a time when a lot of the baby boomers were at an age when they would take such things seriously. I've never seen this identification with characters anyplace else. It's really quite remarkable. Maybe it's that split that did it, the combination of real human drama and the mythic element. The scripts were also thoughtful. They tried to understand what was really going on, instead of trying to titillate and frighten people.

GEORGE DUNING

George Duning was a trumpet player in Cincinnati, Ohio, and a music director for radio and television orchestras before he began his film career in the 1940s.

Following his World War II term in the Armed Forces Radio Service, Duning joined the staff of Columbia Pictures as an orchestrator. Making use of his jazz and symphonic training, Duning soon attracted the attention of studio music department head Morris Stoloff, who gave him the opportunity to compose his first score.

Among the hundreds of scores composed by Duning are Down to Earth, My Blood Runs Cold, *and* Bell, Book and Candle, *and the television movies* Black Moon, Terror in the Wax Museum, *and* Beyond Witch Mountain.

His most famous television music is his main title theme for THE NAKED CITY.

Duning scored the STAR TREK episodes "Metamorphosis," "Return to Tomorrow," "And the Children Shall Lead," "Is There In Truth No Beauty?," and "The Empath."

AA *How did you first become involved with STAR TREK?*

GD I was still working at Columbia Pictures as a contract composer, and Robert Justman had become one of my fans through my motion picture scores. He called and asked whether they could borrow me occasionally to do STAR TREKs, which were also a lot of fun.

AA *Do you recall the procedure that they used when you scored an episode?*

GD They'd call me in, and I'd see the picture with the music editor. On a theatrical picture, I always run it at least once without anybody sitting alongside, no producer or director, to get my own feel of the action, the dialogue, the sense and mood of the picture. Then I would sit down with the producer and director and we'd start discussing where there should be music or there shouldn't be. With the television shows, you never had that time. I would run the picture, say, nine o'clock in the morning, we'd have one screening and then they'd turn it over to me and my music editor, we'd stop the picture, he would start timing the cues on his moviola in his cutting room and I would go to my office and start working out ideas for the music. By the end of the day I was already getting timing cues, so that I could start writing the actual cues. That's the way it is in television. Never enough time, really.

AA *It's amazing that so much beautiful stuff gets done.*

GD That's true. I think it's a great credit to the boys that they were able to do this, to all the people like Freddie Steiner, Jerry Fielding, all the boys [who] have done these shows. I think it's a very admirable thing that they can work under such pressure.

AA *How long did you have to compose each STAR TREK score?*

GD . . . Between six and ten days was the average. Everything was deadlines, but I've found over the years some of the best things I ever did for both television and theatrical movies was when I was fighting deadlines . . . the pressure seems to goad you on, and scores usually turn out very well . . .

AA *Had you ever seen STAR TREK before you began writing for the series?*

GD I've been a fan for years. I still watch the shows occasionally. When I have the time and I know there's one on, I usually turn it on, 'cause I was a space buff when I was a 15-year-old kid. I was very interested in space and that sort of thing, so I've always been a science fiction fan.

AA *Do you still read any science fiction?*

GD Oh, yes, quite a bit: Asimov, Fred Pohl, Arthur Clarke and . . . oh, I love science fiction. As a matter of fact, if I could come back in a reincarnation, I would probably become an astronaut. . . . I don't know whether you remember, but the first science fiction magazine was Hugo Gernsback's *Amazing Stories,* and I would spend my quarter allowance that I got at that time buying a magazine. I remember when my parents discovered I was reading it, they would ask, "What are you reading all that impossible trash for?" Well, I've lived to see it all happen, you know, the trips to the moon, all that sort of thing, I've seen it all happen.

AA *Did you find yourself defending your being a science fiction fan?*

GD Yes, quite often, to a lot of people. Not any more, though. . . . I think [science fiction] is the ultimate solution to all the problems that seem to be confronting the future generations. I know I often worry about not only my own three daughters who are all grown, but their kids and what they're going to have to face after the year 2020. There are going to be a lot of problems which I think will only be solved by technology.

AA *Do you have any theories as to why STAR TREK is so popular?*

GD . . . I can't quite pin it down except there must be a lot of people and young kids like myself when I first became interested in space. That's the only way I can account for it, and I think the shows were all very well done technically: production on the show was always excellent.

AA *Ralph Senensky, who direced "Metamorphosis," indicated that if it weren't for your music and Jerry Finnerman's cinematography, that episode would not have worked out nearly as beautifully as it did.*

GD Well, that's nice to hear, very nice to hear.

AA *When I wrote the first edition of* The Star Trek Compendium, *my first fan letter was from Fred Steiner. He said that no prior book had mentioned the STAR TREK music.*

GD That's true. That's very true. Freddie's a great guy [and] he's one of the finest musicologists I think I've ever run into. The time that he has devoted to things like this [is] to be greatly admired. . . . He's very active now with the society that was formed about a year ago called The Society for the Preservation of Film Music. They recently had an awards dinner for Alex North, one of my old buddies. . . .

AA *When I was interested in soundtracks in my teens, I found that very few of them were ever recorded. I remember ransacking stores trying to find anything by Bernard Herrmann or Miklos Rozsa.*

GD That reminds me: I just recently had a lovely fan letter from a young man in Brooklyn, New York, who has a collection of everything of mine that's ever been recorded, and one of the special mentions he made was about STAR TREK . . . [letters] like that always make me feel good, particularly at this point in my life when my career is over as a professional writer—I've been retired now for three years due to a major operation I had—but I still keep up. I'm working on an album of songs about New York of all things, speaking of Brooklyn . . . [my lyricist and I] have done 15 songs and are now in the process of getting demos made on it and then [we'll] see if we can get some recording company to get an album out for us. . . . I guess you probably know that last year three of my STAR TREK scores were rerecorded in London with the London Philharmonia.

AA *What did you think of them?*

GD Oh, I have to tell you, it was a real thrill to hear that music again after all these years. Now, when I recorded those scores originally in Hollywood, I was limited by budgets to fairly small groups . . . maybe six or eight violins, three or four celli, and a violist if I was lucky, but in London, one score, I think it was "The Empath," had sixteen violins, eight cellos, six violas and three basses. To a composer, that's the ultimate sound.

AA   *So at last you heard it as you always wanted to hear it, and as you always wanted others to hear it.*

GD   Right.

AA   *Some of the music that you did for* Devil at Four O'Clock, *Camille's theme, reminds me very much of the theme you did for "The Empath."*

GD   [Chuckling] Oh, yeah, well, I've stolen from myself quite often.

AA   *Did you find that the people on STAR TREK had a respect for you as a musician, as a composer?*

GD   Oh, definitely, very definitely. I never had any problems with the music people, or with the people who worked for Bob Justman. Bob, particularly, is just great to work with. No, I had no problems at all on those STAR TREKS.

ROBERT RAFF

Chicago-born Robert Raff studied music at Chicago Musical College. He entered the film industry as a mail clerk at RKO-Radio Pictures, advancing to that studio's film shipping department, which he describes as ". . . the entree into the editorial department" (where he worked for a short time assisting Robert Wise). By 1945 he was an assistant in the RKO-Radio music library. Following his promotion to music editor, he stayed at the studio for approximately ten years.

At Desilu Studios, Raff edited the music for THE UNTOUCHABLES, MISSION: IMPOSSIBLE, MANNIX and, of course, STAR TREK.

Following his work at Desilu and Paramount, he moved to the feature films division of 20th Century-Fox, and then to Lorimar Productions, where he still works.

AA   *What was your earliest involvement with STAR TREK?*

RR   I did the pilots.

AA   *Do you recall anything about the creation of the series' main title theme?*

RR   Sandy [Alexander] Courage did the thematic material, the pilots and several episodes. When we went down to the dubbing stage to record the main title music, it was great. It was a very unusual concept using that . . . because with that type of show everybody expected some sort of triumphant march, or some mechanical sounding thing, and it was quite a clever innovation. It was rather daring, because it was a departure from what you would expect. You know, the opening visuals of the ship zipping by in the main credits were originally silent. There were no sound effects; it felt empty. So Gene asked the sound effects guys to put in some rocket ship noise. They did, and he wasn't happy with it. The sound didn't quite make it, so he turned to me and asked, "What can you do?" I said, "I don't know. Give me a day." What I ultimately ended up doing was taking an effect called a cymbal shimmer, where the musician will hit the cymbal very softly with a mallet, and it will go "Ddddjjjjj . . ." Laying the cymbal shimmer against the visual image didn't sound unique: you could realize what it was, and I knew Gene wouldn't buy that. So I took a cymbal shimmer hit, where the musician had struck and then rolled off to dimuendo, and I ran it backwards in the rerecording room. Then I shaved the impact off, so ultimately we got that "fffffffssssshhhwwwwt" noise that you hear on the screen now when the little ships run by. In hindsight it looks very easy, but it was an experiment and I was very nervous about it. I didn't know what Gene would say. That ended up in the picture, and it was my one great, creative contribution to STAR TREK [laughs].

AA   *Do you recall who made the determination whether or not the episodes would have an original score or be tracked?*

RR   There was a union contract that called for a certain number of hours to be scored. . . . After we had gotten into two or three episodes, Gene Roddenberry and Robert Justman would sit in the projection room and ask me if we had material that would cover each episode. Looking at the picture we'd "spot" the show each week. Gene [Roddenberry] was usually too busy, as I recall, so it was mostly Bob Justman and myself. The head of our music department would sit in, and the decision would be made whether we would track the show or score it. If it was scored, it would be the usual team . . . and if it was to be tracked, I'd take the picture in the back. You can tell if they were tracked or scored by the credits on them at the end: "Music written by," or "conducted by." There's a clue there. If it doesn't have that, if it only has the editor's name in the credits without the composer, other than the credit Sandy got every week as the composer of the theme, then you can tell which ones were tracked and which ones were scored.

AA *Taking into account the time involved, and the lack of budget, it's amazing what was done.*

RR Yes, it is. . . . I ended up as head of the music editing and sound effects department about midseason, working basically for Bill Heath. I don't remember how many episodes I did, probably the first 13. After that, I decided that I would go back to work cutting music. I didn't like being an executive in charge of sound effects and music. It really wasn't my cup of tea. I ended up with both situations. It was just too much work and too much aggravation. . . .

AA *I've heard that Desilu was like a small family.*

RR Oh, it was. It was a marvelous place to work. I had a great time over there. Gene Roddenberry is one hell of a guy. He kept his office open to all of us. We worked long, hard schedules on that show, because of the amount of work that was involved. During some long nights we would pop in on Gene to have a drink with him. He had a living room suite where he stayed, writing in his office. He had a bedroom and a kitchen, and he actually lived there for days on end, he'd get so involved in the show.

AA *You also had some of the best composers available then for television work, including Sol Kaplan, Gerald Fried, George Duning, Jerry Fielding, and Joseph Mullendore.*

RR Sol Kaplan was, in my estimation, by far the premiere composer. He didn't do many, but he was a master musician. Gerald Fried has a percussive sort of style. I used to call him "the Ping-Pong player." He's a good composer, he makes a living, and he does a good job. . . .

AA *Do you recall anything about the system for filing each music cue when episodes were tracked?*

RR I would classify music cues by type: tension cue, or mysterioso, or what we call a "bridge"—a short piece that would go from a dissolve. I would have discs made. Each disc was categorized as to the particular emotion, such as "chase" or "right." Accumulated on the disc was all the material related to that particular emoton, so that when I viewed the film, and after we spotted it, and they needed fight music, I could go to the disc which had maybe eight or nine fights on it. I'd select the one to three that were appropriate, and then knit them together into a single piece to match the action or the mood. The guys had labels on all their effects: for "interior noise," "exteriors," and "the doors." All the sound effects were standardized as they were categorized . . . we put the library of material that the composers did on disc, and we had the masters on film.

FABIEN TORDJMANN

Born and raised in France, Fabien Tordjmann came to the United States after studying film in Paris, then found he had to start all over again. Tordjmann, an energetic man who speaks with the exuberance of a child and the disciplined experience of an adult, worked hard for his second start. He often worked late into the night to finish a project. His ambition did not go unnoticed. He recalls, ". . . In America there's a wonderful thing: when they see that you're courageous, you don't mind working and you want to learn, then people will give you help and credit."

Among the STAR TREK episodes he edited are: "The Enemy Within," "Charlie X," "Bread and Circuses," "Obsession," "The Enterprise Incident," "For the World is Hollow . . . ," and "That Which Survives."

AA *How did you become involved with STAR TREK?*

FT I worked with Gene Roddenberry on THE LIEUTENANT at MGM. I'd also worked on another MGM series, DR. KILDARE, with the director Jim Goldstone, who's a wonderful fellow, and was also going to direct "Where No Man Has Gone Before." So Gene knew me, and then Jim Goldstone brought up my name. They really liked what I'd done at the time on KILDARE; that's why they invited me to work on the pilot.

AA *So you were the film editor on "Where No Man Has Gone Before"?*

FT No. At that time, I did not yet have enough time in the union, so I couldn't do the pilot, but the minute it sold they said, "We want you," which was very nice of them. In the meantime, I was going on call to do THE MONKEES. It was very different but I had to turn it down as I was committed to Gene. I think I was one of the few, if not the only one, who stayed with STAR TREK the entire three years.

AA *THE MONKEES must have been very interesting, because of all the crazy visual things that were constantly happening in these episodes.*

FT Yes, it was very tempting. When I finished STAR TREK's second season, I started ROWAN AND MARTIN'S LAUGH-IN, another show that had quick cuts. I needed that as relief, to do something with comedy in it.

AA *That was also different because it was tape, wasn't it?*

FT Yes, partly on tape and partly on film. But we did everything: I even shot some stuff, and I was *in* it. There was a whole group doing it, and that was a lot of fun. My mentor in France is a wonderful man . . . a master of comedy, Jacques Tati. I rarely worked with somebody as worthy as that. I was lucky, early in my life.

AA *In comedy you learn a lot about timing.*

FT Yes, definitely. It's easier to edit drama than it is to edit comedy. In comedy you either have it, or you don't, it's either funny, or it isn't, and if it isn't funny there's nothing you can do about it. Editing is like a second chance at directing. Particularly in television, there's so little time and they shoot so much more than they would normally shoot, and there's more of a choice to make.

AA *Do you recall how much time you had to edit each STAR TREK episode?*

FT We had about three weeks, usually alternating three editors: one editor would pick up a show that would shoot for six days, sometimes seven but usually six, and then he'd start putting it together while the second one was shooting. By the time the third one was shooting, we should have been through with that first one. But, of course, it took some time. It was often delayed, because it takes longer to edit than to shoot, and so by the end of the season it was pretty tight. There was also a hang-up with opticals, especially during the first year when everything we were doing was new. We were improvising, and working with imaginative optical houses. We really had to do it all with a low budget, using our imagination very much, and that was a lot of fun.

AA *Would there be two assemblies, one before the opticals came in, and another afterward?*

FT The opticals would trickle in, but what we did was cut in the reactions to those effects that were still being completed, and when they came in we had to change very little. All of us had to have pretty strong visual imaginations, and stick to it, trying not to make a mistake.

AA *Was the airing order of the episodes influenced by the post-production problems?*

FT No, because we had to make the deadline. But the networks, as they still do, prefer to run what they consider stronger episodes at certain times during the season to raise the ratings. For example, at times they would prefer [that] the eighth one shot should be the fifth one completed, and then we'd have to scramble to make it. Sometimes we couldn't.

Of course, conversely, at times, we would have a break because they would have a pre-emption. Then we could have a breather of a week, which would help all of us. It's still the same thing in television, I believe, but I don't do too much television now.

AA *Was there anyone other than the editors who had a say in the editing process?*

FT Oh, yes. Normally, we put it together first. This is the procedure in America, to do it that way. In other countries it's different, but I believe it's the best way. We'd talk with the director, then we'd talk to the producer, and they'd tell us what they wanted to do with it, and of course we'd have to consider the film being shot, because a lot of imponderables happened during the time of the shooting. New things happen: acting is different, lines are changed. So we'd put it together and then we'd look at it with the director, and I believe also with the producer, and the director would work with us to try to make our work as close to our vision as possible. The director would leave, and we would show it to the producer again, and he would try to adjust it to his vision, too. So it was a compromise. And sometimes we'd also fight for something we'd think was right. We were usually closer to the director, because we had the same type of background; however, the producer and the network have the last words, so at times we had to make some changes. Gene Roddenberry, Bob Justman, Eddie Milkis, and Gene Coon all had some wonderful ideas and we all worked together to achieve the best possible results in the amount of time allotted to us. So it's really a collaboration. Film is a collaborative medium, on any level, whether it's television, features, or documentaries. The amateur theory is not quite true. It's good to have a guiding light in the author, and especially in America the script is paramount, but the script comes alive on the screen, and that's what you have to judge.

AA *So everybody is dependent upon everyone else in the business?*

FT Yes, we all work together. But I must say it was all quite a wonderful adventure. I haven't had something like that in a long time.

AA *Was it a close-knit family?*

FT Yes, we liked each other very much, and Roddenberry was fine. He was very picky, and sometimes we'd chafe under that because we'd have to deliver a film, but on the other hand we'd recognize that he was right in trying to do the thing that would correspond more to the new way that this show was being done. It was not like LOST IN SPACE, with just gimmicks. And, above all, I think that all of us were concerned about human beings, following Gene's lead. He has been proven right. The human element is often lost nowadays. It imparts a quality to a series that goes on, because it's like a family for the viewers who keep looking at it. That idea of a close-knit family is, I think, what Gene Roddenberry felt. That's why he was very keen on getting the people who had enthusiasm and could put life into the project. We've all gone on to other things. I did some features, and I traveled a lot. I worked in Europe and Canada. All the STAR TREK movies that they've done since have been fine. I think this time [STAR TREK IV] seems to be a longer TV episode, but it was fun. In fact, they picked up on one show that I did and that you may have seen, one of the only real comedies they ever had, directed by Jimmy Komack ["A Piece of the Action"]. I had a lot of fun working with Jimmy.

AA *Did you ever want to do things you were unable to?*

FT Yes. I was fascinated with "Shore Leave" because they talked of being in a place where all your wishes are fulfilled, and the flowers are beautiful. They shot with two cameras, and the director was Robert Sparr, a wonderful man who's since passed away. . . . They had a second camera that picked up very beautiful, out-of-focus images of Kirk's hand holding flowers as he talked to a woman . . . It was so beautiful that I stuck in one or two shots of those out-of-focus hands with the flower behind them. They kept telling me to please take them out. I fought with them, and they said, "No, no." Every time I went to a screening they expected to see it taken out, but I was younger then and I wanted to leave it in. In the end they said, "Come on, you have to take it out," so I took it out. But I was upset. I recognized their point of view but I had mine, too, and I felt those out-of-focus scenes fit in and helped to achieve some measure of beauty. Often we screened TV film on a bigger screen, so it was really very effective.

AA *That's very odd, because there were a lot of soft-focus scenes in STAR TREK.*

FT But this was *really* out-of-focus. I went into surrealism that time. Also, in that same segment we didn't have time to finish the sequence where the man [Finnegan] is taunting Kirk. I didn't know how to put that thing together. It was really a problem, and 20 minutes before the first screening I decided how to do it: to literally have him popping in everywhere, taunting Kirk and talking to him over Kirk's shoulder. And they loved it. They kept it that way. When I saw the episode recently, I was disappointed. It's much more "cutty" than I thought.

AA *It also adds to the theory that Finnegan is not real.*

FT That's right. I felt that was just right. That they loved. The minute I brought that in they all said, "Oh, that's terrific!" It was done in a linear way. The guy runs, Kirk turns around, and he goes somewhere else. I had to put them all in, but it was really very wild. I remember another one that I liked very much: the one with the "Horta" ["The Devil in the Dark"].

AA *Did you ever have an experience where a director didn't provide you with enough material, with sufficient footage?*

FT Of course. If you don't have enough, you can be creative, but you can't always make it work. Gene liked to change things all the time. We'd move things from the beginning to the end of a scene in order to make that scene more valid. It's good to be with somebody with whom you can agree and disagree. It's fruitful.

AA *Did the series change much in the last year from your standpoint?*

FT I really don't think so. There were different producers at the helm. Gene Coon was terrific, and I think Fred Freiberger was pretty good, too. I think sometimes that the requirements of the network may have been different. I think they may have had more money at the beginning, more of a lure to attract real science fiction writers. Some people who were good science fiction writers went into it, and I think that perhaps there was less of that quality of writing later. Bob Justman was very involved in the series, and I like him very much. He's very wonderful. He was very tough in the beginning with me, but I was very resilient, and we developed a very good relationship.

AA *What do you think makes STAR TREK such a popular series?*

FT STAR TREK was about the future, so no matter what was happening at the time you could escape safely. It was reassuring, but in a good sense, because American television is often *too* reassuring. It doesn't give us the idea of what's happening in the real world. That's just my own humble opinion.

THE MOVIES

ALTHOUGH A FEATURE FILM IS BY NATURE VERY DIF-
FERENT FROM A TELEVISION EPISODE, REQUIRING VERY
DIFFERENT TALENTS TO COMPLETE, THE PEOPLE WHO
WORKED ON THE STAR TREK MOVIES SPOKE OF THEIR
EXPERIENCES IN MUCH THE SAME WAY THAT THOSE
WHO WORKED ON THE ORIGINAL SERIES SO LONG
AGO SPOKE OF THEIRS. FOR THEM, THAT WORK BE-
CAME A TRUE LABOR OF LOVE

ROBERT FLETCHER

Iowa-born Robert Fletcher attended Harvard and studied archeology until he discovered the stage, first as an actor and then as a costume designer.

Fletcher provided the costume designs for many plays, operas, ballets, and television presentations before he landed his first feature film assignment, STAR TREK—THE MOTION PICTURE. He has since designed the costumes for STAR TREK features II through IV.

AA *How did you become involved with STAR TREK?*

RF I was the third person hired to do the first movie. The first person was Bill Theiss, who did the TV series. Then he left the film and they saw everybody in Hollywood. I was interviewed at that time, after Bill was no longer on the picture. Then they hired another man who worked for two weeks and made some samples. On the day that he showed the samples he was fired. . . . The director, Robert Wise, had liked my work in the theater and wanted me to do the film, but he had been overruled because I had not done a film before. . . . After the debacle with that second designer, he called me and said, "Can you come over in 15 minutes?" I went over, and he asked, "Would you undertake, for a fee, to make some sketches for a week?" I said, "Yes," brought them in, and passed the test. People seemed to like it, and I was hired.

AA *How do you go about choosing the fabrics to be used? Do you find new and exciting things, or old and exciting things?*

RF . . . I used a great deal of the stock that I found at Paramount. It has now been practically used up. All that stuff represents things that will no longer be made because they don't fit into the economy.

AA *How was all that stock stored to keep it in such good condition?*

RF It was stored in the dark. Light is the general enemy of most things. There was an interior storeroom with no windows at all, and that was the reason most of it survived.

AA *I can imagine how you felt when you first went inside and looked around.*

RF Like a kid in candy store. There were all these thousands of yards of things, which you couldn't buy. Most synthetic fabrics are very difficult to work with. They don't cut, they don't drape and they don't sew very well. The stuff resists. You can't shrink it on the hand or manipulate things the way tailors and seamstresses have done for centuries in order to get a thing to look well, and that's why most modern clothes, to suit the manufacturer, are made very loose with no construction.

AA   *When you designed the wardrobe for the officers, did you permit yourself to think about them as individuals, or did you think of the service as a whole?*

RF   Both. There was some feeling of individuality, particularly in STAR TREK—THE MOTION PICTURE, because we had more varieties of uniforms in that: off duty, on duty, leisure suits, sports suits, and formal wear.

AA   *Considering the number of hours in which that film is supposed to be taking place, it seems odd to have all those people in different changes of uniforms.*

RF   Yes, but remember they're doing different things on the ship. If you go into a big navy ship today, you'll find people wearing all classes of uniforms, depending on what they're doing: whether they're on work detail, standing inspection, launching or flying the fighter planes, on the command deck, or in the hospital. If you'll examine modern armies and navies, you'll find that you don't get inducted and have one uniform. You have class A, B, and C . . . barracks hats, foul weather gear, etc. That was the reason for it. They wanted a little visual variety.

AA   *Were the shoes and the trousers one piece?*

RF   I call that "Fletcher's Folly." I'll never try that again. . . . That was the hardest thing in the world to fit . . . it had to be exactly right. You couldn't alter it.

AA   *How did the belt buckles come about?*

RF   I felt I visually needed something in that area to break up the waistline, so I invented a belt buckle, and I invented a reason for it. They were meant to be biorhythm monitors that when pressed would give you your reading for the day. Theoretically, "Bones" could adjust it to perk you up.

AA   *Were there two different sizes of buckles, one for men and one for women?*

RF   Right. That was taking into account their skeletal structure. Everybody liked the idea of the belt buckles. Gene said, "Ooh, I'll write in something about it," but it never happened. There's no reference to it.

AA   *Who spoke to you about what kind of look they wanted for the first film?*

RF   Everybody. Wives, agents, actors . . . oh, there was plenty of input. I simply had to try to figure it out, try to balance everybody. I'm not sure that I was happy with the final result on number one. It seemed to me to be too much committee . . . Robert Wise wanted it to be military, but relaxed. Gene Roddenberry wanted it to be nonmilitary. The actors, I felt, wanted things that were as becoming as possible. The original clothes were pretty good for younger actors, but when people got older that very soft, clinging kind of style from the TV show was not at all flattering. . . . They were tight and nonconstructed, almost like tights or a dance costume, essentially a T-shirt. So I tried to put a little more construction in it. The second group of costumes for II, III, and IV were done in order to please another director who came on, Nick Meyer, who wanted things more military with a little more color.

AA   *What, if anything, did he ask you to design in addition to that?*

RF   His only remark was he liked *The Prisoner of Zenda* and if you will remember, Douglas Fairbanks, Jr., in that film wore . . .

AA   *. . . That beautiful Russian silk shirt . . .*

RF   . . . With that turned-back double flap. It's really based more on that than on the British naval uniforms.

AA   *Why were those lengths of chain sewn into the flaps on the STAR TREK II jackets?*

RF   I put those in there because being in the 23rd century one can presume some mysterious new means of closing.

AA   *So they are there to hide the snaps?*

RF   . . . It was to hide the snaps! It was just put in for that device. . . . Actually, people have been using hooks and snaps and buttons for a thousand years. The zipper is the only new means of closing that we've had since before the birth of Christ. They had a form of safety pin in the Roman Empire. I don't actually imagine that by the 23rd century there will be many new things invented to hold your clothes together.

AA   *Do you have any personal favorites out of all the designs you've created for STAR TREK?*

RF   I like the clothes for Sarek and the High Priestess, and I was very happy with the Klingons. I would love to make some changes in the basic uniforms, now, but I never know from one movie to the next whether they're going to ask me to do the next one. . . . If I were to do another STAR TREK film, I would like to make some additions to the standard uniform, just to keep people entertained. I think people like to see a little something new. I don't mean an entirely new design, but when I introduced the slight, short leather jacket for Scotty, everybody was very pleased with it, and I get a lot of calls from Trekkers asking about it: what it's made of, and so forth.

AA *How does it feel, being creatively involved in a myth, a part of the world's culture?*

RF It's a privilege. It's special, something that I never expected to be involved in, although as long as STAR TREK has been shown, I've always been a fan. I was never a "rabid" fan, but I certainly watched. I don't know that I've seen all of them, I've seen a great many of them, and I've always loved them. I was very happy when they started to make the films. I had no idea I was going to be a part of it. But I enjoy my part in it, and I'm proud of it, and I like to contribute. I feel so very lucky to have been allowed to do it, because I get a lot of pleasure in designing for theater, but you rarely get a chance to do anything on such a scale with the required imagination and the use of color. There's really so much freedom in creativity.

JAMES HORNER

James Horner began studying piano at the age of five. A few years later he went to England and studied music at the Royal Conservatory. He lived in England for ten years, studied composition, returned to the United States and earned his B.A. and M.A. degrees at U.S.C.

He began to teach at U.C.L.A. while working on his doctorate, but soon became disenchanted with the academic world. When he was asked to score a movie for the American film Institute, he remembers that, "It was like a stepping stone. I knew what I wanted to do with composition."

Stopping work on his doctorate, Horner gave up his teaching position and began ". . . struggling in the movie world. Then Roger Corman gave me my first job." Among the films Horner scored for Corman's New World Pictures are Battle Beyond the Stars *and* Humanoids from the Deep, *and the underwater sequences of* Up from the Depths.

The following interview was conducted during the summer of 1982, shortly after the release of STAR TREK II. During our conversation,

Horner mentioned that he might possibly score Krull. *The film is interesting; Horner's music is exquisite.*

Horner's subsequent scores include Something Wicked This Way Comes, Brainstorm, The Name of the Rose *and, of course,* STAR TREK III.

AA *Who first contacted you about scoring STAR TREK II?*

JH . . . The head of the music department at Paramount, Joel Sill, had been watching my career, trying to nudge me in there. The producers were originally talking to big name people and it was hard to sell me, being a nobody, basically. . . . Except for *Battle Beyond the Stars*, I had nothing but horror or very sensitive, small orchestra stuff. Joel was in large part responsible for introducing me to Harve Bennett and to the director, Nick Meyer, and I met with them and we seemed to hit it off very well and then they asked me to do the film . . . about two weeks before they were finished wrapping the film. Because of the schedule, it was being edited as it was being shot. They would simply stick in sequences and then fine-tune them, so there was no three-month editing process after the film was shot. I was hired about four weeks before I was to start writing music and I had basically four and a half weeks to write the score before our first scoring session. We had our first batch of scoring sessions around the middle of April, four days of scoring, and then we arranged to have a day at the end of April, as well, to cover any last-minute changes. . . . Basically, I couldn't start until they had finished as much cutting as possible.

AA *Did the film have a temporary music track when you first saw it?*

JH Nicholas had put in a temp track during the docking sequence—I forgot what film it was from, but it was a great, jaunty, jolly kind of seafaring thing. . . . When I first heard it, I looked at him and he kind of smiled because he knew I didn't like it. . . . Anyway, it stayed in all through the thing, and finally it was taken out. . . . There were a few things that they kept in temporarily that I knew were coming out. Nicholas and I discussed the score at great length and we became very good friends. . . . He's a very musical person, and sometimes that can be very dangerous, when you work with a filmmaker who thinks he knows more than you do. That didn't happen with Nicholas. He gave me free rein. He told me what he wanted in terms of the feeling—something seafaring, nautical, flowing . . .

AA   *The smell of the breeze . . .*

JH   The smell of the breeze, the sails, the whole thing, as well as something very exciting, and we agreed on the concept of a large orchestra.

AA   *Had you ever watched STAR TREK before you scored STAR TREK II?*

JH   I had not watched it [from] week to week, but once every month and a half I'd switch on and there would be some episode of STAR TREK. At one time or another I have probably seen 15 episodes.

AA   *Did you ever form any opinion on the music that was used in the series?*

JH   I had never thought about it because it had never occurred to me that I'd be involved in this whole thing. . . . They had a lot of people working on it. You know, some of the things in hindsight I don't like. Other things I like very much . . . I'm always interested in the endings of films. How you leave the audience is very important, and some of them are really wonderful. There are a couple of episodes [with] touching endings where Spock would say, "For the first time, I was happy"; you'd cut to outer space, and the music would do something wonderful . . . Those are wonderful, those touching moments, and that was a quality of Spock that I really liked but we rarely saw. That was something I was trying to elicit. That was one of my favorite sequences. . . .

AA   *Did you do much listening to the tapes from the original TV series?*

JH   None. I didn't want to. When I was first hired . . . they asked me, do I have any ideas. I said that you have certain "givens" in a STAR TREK. You have the Enterprise. If you redesign the Enterprise—unless it was blown up and rebuilt—the Enterprise is a given: Spock, Kirk, they're givens. The bridge is pretty much a given. Costumes you can change as an update, but there are certain givens and as far as music went in the previous movie, I never felt there was a musical given and I think you need that. They said, "We'd like you to use, if possible, something that would relate it to the series, and at first I was against the idea. I thought I could create something different. And then I had the idea of using the fanfare, the first part of the theme, very much like the beginning of *2001*, where you don't even have to do more than three notes and you know exactly what the film is. . . . You know, people have asked me, "Well, doesn't it bother you that you put somebody else's music in your score?" and I think, in this case, it was a terrific decision because it has such a galvanizing effect, right away. It's like you know you're seeing STAR TREK, and it's a given. So, I used the fanfare motif, or bits of it, in about four or five cues throughout the film, primarily through the first third. After about the first third, I slowly phased it out and we never have a reference to it again until Spock dies. It works very well. It's like the common thread of STAR TREK as far as the sound goes. . . . It happens in the main title and the next time we hear it is when Captain Kirk is aboard the shuttle and Sulu is sitting there . . .

AA *Your theme for Kirk is an interesting one.*

JH . . . The theme was actually built in two parts, the theme of Kirk and the theme of the Enterprise, like a ship under sail . . .

AA *Your theme for Spock is also unusual, in terms of its musical structure.*

JH I wanted the music to have a slightly ethnic sound, and I didn't want it to be really in tune, so what I did was use a Pipes of Pan as well as a very weird kind of Renaissance recorder. The two of them were slightly out of tune with one another, and when you combined them with the percussion instrument, it was just enough to give it that kind of quality. I wanted to give Spock a very human quality. . . . We [also] had a tremendous amount of battle scenes, and one nebula scene, but I decided to play that quiet, absolutely stilled, with the sounds of the ships.

AA *Nicholas Meyer brought up the analogy of a submarine-type fight.*

JH Yes . . . we talked about it. When I first saw it, I said that looks like one of those great submarine movies like *Run Silent, Run Deep* or *The Enemy Below*, and that's the sound we wanted. After all this noise of the battle we wanted to create the effect of spookiness. Absolutely no sound in a movie theater does not work. What you always have to do is create the *impression* of no sound, putting in sound very skillfully.

AA *How did you regard Spock's death, in musical terms?*

JH . . . When Spock dies in the film I wanted to give the impression that it was more than Spock dying. Something epic was happening. It was the end of something. . . . It was world-ending in terms of this movie, in terms of the STAR TREK audience. One of the favorite characters is gone, and I had had so little time to develop Spock's theme throughout the movie. The only place for Spock's theme is really in that scene where he and Kirk talk in Spock's quarters.

AA   *You couldn't use it in the radiation chamber because there's so much going on there.*

JH   No, right. I used it earlier in the sequence where they leave drydock. Spock says, "There's a first time for everything, don't you agree, Admiral?" But nobody registers it's Spock's theme there. . . . When he dies I wanted to give the [impression] that Kirk is losing a very close friend who is actually much closer than we all suspect; I mean, they were really like brothers. I also wanted to give the feeling that something awesome was happening . . . from there to the end of the film. The music that I use to set up the Genesis explosion when we first see Genesis, when Kirk is walking down that tunnel and we see the first matte painting . . . that music is very abstract in terms of those chords. . . . When the Genesis device explodes, as Kirk's running down the corridors after you realize Spock has left his station, you hear this wonderful Genesis music, because we're forming a planet; at the same time you hear this very pulling theme of Kirk running down the halls because he knows what's happened and up high, very high, Spock's theme is woven into that. At the end, when Kirk makes the entry in his log, and talks about Spock, you hear Spock's theme and then the whole thing transcends and you cut through the clouds on the planet and you weave together the Genesis theme and Spock's theme and it becomes really very pulling. . . . When I [first] looked at that last pickup scene, I knew what I wanted to do. . . . Harve was very nervous about the scene; we were all nervous. It looked so beautiful and so pretty, we were afraid it would be like you were waiting for a perfume commercial or something. . . . I remember Harve standing out there. I was rehearsing; nobody had seen it [with the score] and it's a big sequence. I said, "Okay, let's rehearse it with picture . . ." We finished the cue, I said, "Thank you," the orchestra obviously liked it, but Harve came up to me and embraced me. He was crying and he just . . . It was just wonderful. . . . I've never been in that kind of a position. . . . Harve was crying during the dubbing, I mean, it did something for us all. It put an end on the film that, with visuals and the music, just did exactly what we wanted it to do. It made it bigger than these two people, made it something really awesome that had happened.

HARVE BENNETT

Chicago-born Harve Bennett began his show business career in 1941 as one of radio's QUIZ KIDS. He remained as a regular on that series for five years, specializing in questions about United States presidents.

While he was a student at UCLA he wrote a column for the Chicago Sun-Times from 1944 to 1948, edited a department store magazine and wrote several industrial films. Bennett earned his B.A. degree in theater arts and motion pictures before serving in the army from 1952 to 1955.

Back in civilian life, Bennett became an associate producer for CBS Television, then graduated to producer of that network's remote specials. In 1962 he ended his affiliation with CBS and worked for a year as a producer for television station KNXT.

Joining ABC in 1963 as manager of program development, Bennett became vice president in charge of programming before leaving to produce MOD SQUAD, a series he had helped to develop.

He joined Universal Television in 1971 as a writer and producer, and became executive producer of THE SIX MILLION DOLLAR MAN for the series' first five years, a position he repeated in 1976 for THE BIONIC WOMAN, and the miniseries "Rich Man, Poor Man."

In 1977, he became president of Bennett-Katleman Television Productions at Columbia Studios.

His television work has won him the Edgar Award (the mystery equivalent of the Academy Award) for a MOD SQUAD script, a Golden Globe Award for "Rich Man, Poor Man," and 26 Emmy Award nominations.

In 1981 Bennett began his association with the STAR TREK feature films as executive producer and cowriter of STAR TREK II.

AA How did the shooting script of STAR TREK II evolve?

HB After considering other writers, I found out that Jack Sowards, a great "movie of the week" writer, was a great STAR TREK fan. We talked, and he clearly knew more about STAR TREK than I did, so I hired him. He worked out a story and wrote first and second draft scripts. . . . It was very flat, in my humble opinion, and I brought in Sam Peeples, who had done outstanding work in other areas when I was at ABC. He had done two pilots that I had been involved with, and I thought he could write robustly. So I brought him in, he read the script and I said, "Sam, you know more about STAR TREK than I do. I want you to fix this." He said, "I know just what to do." The result was his script. If my memory is not failing me, which it sometimes does, he introduced Saavik, and that was the sole contribution of his draft that we kept. . . . I went right back to Jack's script, inserted Saavik, and did a quick rewrite of my own, just to get everything together. Enter Nick Meyer. When I saw *The-Seven-Per-Cent-Solution* I was so impressed with the screenplay that I went out and read the book, and I was even more impressed with the book. . . . Nick read my rewrite of Sowards and Peeples and said, "This has promise. What if . . ." He signed on and said, "You write it, and I'll rewrite you." In 15 days, not counting five days of [preliminary work] I wrote furiously, 10 or 12 pages a day, and a messenger would take them from me and send them to Nick's house. The next morning I would get back 8 pages from Nick, substantively the same, but they were Nick's pages and they were beginning to sound terrific . . . I reached the end of the script, went over his pages, and then he went over mine.

AA *What was the first you heard regarding the success of STAR TREK II?*

HB I knew when it continued to do business after the fifth and sixth weeks that we had a good movie. I knew after the reviews began to be filtered back to us, and I really knew when Janet Maslin of *The New York Times,* not a patsy critic, began—and I should frame it somewhere, maybe on my tombstone—"STAR TREK II—Now that's more like it." That's the highest praise I have ever received for what I feel I brought to STAR TREK.

AA *Did you have any other reactions at the time?*

HB I felt as scared as when I first took it over, maybe more. . . . In the nature of our business, or in the nature of any business, success breeds fear because you say, "I'll never do it again, I'll never be successful again, how am I gonna pass the test again? How am I going to make another great movie?" . . . So, my feelings at the end of STAR TREK II were, "Whew! Let me go on to something else," 'cause [it takes] such energy to do that well. . . . That's why the NBA basketball teams rarely repeat two seasons in a row: You get yourself hung-up on, "What if I fail? What if I don't make the last shot? . . . [filmmaking's] no different: concentration, forgetting the winning and the losing, forgetting the importance of expectation. I'm not a meditative person, but I do believe that concentration on the road is the critical thing in what any of us do.

AA *The only difference is that making movies is a slower game.*

HB Yeah, well, slower certainly, in relation to television . . . It's interesting. I was thinking recently that television for me is a medium in which [if] episodes three and four might not be good, episodes five and six may be good. You have a time continuum, hard as it is, to make episodic television. It's like playing a season, not playing an individual championship. . . . I pepper my life with sports analogies because sports is the highest drama of all time. That's why people watch it on television: it is an analogy to what we do. There is conflict in success and failure. How you deal with those things is what life is all about. I walked away from STAR TREK II with an enormous sense of accomplishment. . . . I had an actor who now not only wanted to *be* in STAR TREK III, but also wanted to *direct* it!

AA *How and when was it decided that there could be a STAR TREK III?*

HB The events that led to III were in clusters. Cluster one was that the original ending of II was considered by the studio to be a downer. Nick wanted to keep it the way it was, feeling that, "We said we'd kill him, let's kill him." I disagreed with Nick because in our early screenings there was a gloom over the picture, and people were weeping when they walked out. It was a hopeless, hopeless ending. So in some controversy, and with some [initial] objection from Nick, I went to the typewriter and did a series of adjustments . . . [including] "Remember," which was designed not so much to help the ending, but to make the death ambiguous. It occurred to me that if Spock did a mind-meld with an unconscious McCoy and said, "Remember," it could be taken at the very least to be "Remember *me*," and at the very most to be something more profound to be discovered. Then there was an additional scene with Kirk at the helm, leaving him behind, saying, "There are always possibilities." That was not in the original script. Then we sent a second unit out to Golden Gate Park and we said, "Let's see the casket has landed. Let's just see that. That's an option for us." The only thing we had from ILM was the shooting of the torpedo. I then put it together without the final casket discovery scene, and Nick okayed it. . . . When I got the shot back from the second unit, I didn't show it to Nick right away. It was a beautiful shot.

They did 19 takes, and about take number 17 it was just unbelievably good. Nick was off doing something, so we didn't do it behind his back, but he wasn't there. We put music on it, put it into the picture, and showed it to Nick, and he cried.

AA *How did you go about working out the screenplay for STAR TREK III?*

HB As you know, I was the sole writer on that, so I didn't have to consult with too many people. It would be absolutely false to say that I had preplanned it. . . . I had to make a story out of the following "givens": One, there is a casket on a planet that has been created by the reformation of life forces, and life has been created from death. Two, "There are always possibilities." Three, before he died Spock said, "Remember." Remember what? The puzzle was solved so easily that I think 17 other people could have written the script to STAR TREK III. . . . If you end a film with a Genesis device that can in one "poof" create life where there was lifelessness, you have created an enormous story device that can not be ignored. . . . Now the fans would be justified in saying, "Well, why not just create a planet as a plot solution?" Or, "What would happen if the Klingons got hold of this? They wouldn't use it to make a planet, they would destroy a planet." Therefore, the final puzzle-solving was the denial of the validity of the Genesis device. That was—as "The Lord giveth, the Lord taketh away"—necessary, or we would have so expanded the borders of STAR TREK, even subliminally, that it would have had the same impact the A-bomb had on the 20th century, so as to make conventional things no longer viable. That's fine, but who needed to restructure STAR TREK on that basis? Also . . . we did not feel that the character of David was a viable character upon which to build further stories. We didn't set out to kill him. We didn't even set out to use him, but when I got to the crisis and came up with the idea, "I'm going to kill one of them," then, with an eye to plot it, [it] became obvious which one I would have to kill, because it was the one I didn't need. I had no idea what the future of Saavik might be. Clearly, I couldn't kill Spock a second time or the picture would be over, and David was extraneous then. It wasn't the actor's fault so much as [that] the character just didn't make it. It was like the [Decker] character in the first movie: it was a good try, and it is very interesting to see the number of tries to bring "new blood" into "the family." It's hard, and I don't know the answer to that. I've given up trying. I have no desire to bring in new commanders, and all that stuff. I don't think the fans want it, particularly.

AA   *To what do you attribute the remarkable success of STAR TREK IV?*

HB   In my opinion, what made the movie work was the 20-day rewrite Nicholas and I did together. I did an incredible amount of work in acts one and three. Nicholas did passionate and funny [things with] the middle part of it which set the tone. And we were racing along new channels, asking, "Do you think it's going to be funny? Do you think people are going to laugh?". . . I was influenced more by the irreverence of Nick Meyer on STAR TREK II, which had proven to me, against my kicking and screaming, that you could have fun with STAR TREK without losing its sting. That was the lesson that turned me on to him, and when he was available to come in and do the rewrite, I cherished the fact that his irreverence, which exceeds mine, would literally help to pick it up off the floor. . . . STAR TREK IV was as totally irreverent as any of [the movies], and yet it wasn't. You compare the illogic of STAR TREK IV with, let us say, "City on the Edge of Forever." And here's Kirk saying, pure Nick Meyer, "My friends, we are about to enter a strange valley. People here are primitive and you will encounter many strange customs, violence, this, that and the other thing, and you have your phasers, keep them handy." Is this a speech that a man would make who has already been back to Earth in the 20th century three times? No, no, but it *is* the speech of a guy who says, "Well, we're into something new here, and I'm the Captain, and most of you guys haven't been here before, so let me tell you what we're about." And, would there ever be any logic or justification for a line like, "Everybody remember where we parked"? No, there is no justification for that, and yet I have never been told that this line is not STAR TREK. . . . If you ask anybody what STAR TREK IV was about, they will say, "They came back to Earth to have a lot of hysterical fun." . . . We swapped: I rewrote Nicholas ten percent, and he rewrote me ten percent. Without Nicholas I don't think I could have imparted the sense of buoyancy and irreverence. That was a great gift because it was my responsibility to get the people to come to the movies, and to give them what they want. Nicholas made it possible for me to see that they got what they wanted, plus what *he* wanted. Each movie has increased through that. Not accidentally. The audiences have increased because we have been less slavish to the core audience, and more aware of people who have never had STAR TREK experience, and how it might be fun for them. It's good material. Why not spread it around? . . . [But] the greatest, proudest achievement of STAR TREK IV, which is why it's the best movie, is that it's not about good and evil. In a curious way, it has no evil in it. It has shortsightedness, it has nonunderstanding. Name the "heavy" of STAR TREK IV. There is none. And there's a reason for that. I was under the clear injunction for STAR TREKs II and III, "Who is the heavy? Who is the black hat? We won't make this picture unless there *is* a black-hat heavy." You know the solution the writers and producers came up with for II: Khan. I had been watching the STAR TREK episodes, and I said, "Okay, where's my heavy?" Montalban, especially now that he's become "Mr. White Suit," is the best heavy there ever was. It's great! Great reverse casting, and it works. I had to manufacture a heavy in STAR TREK III, which is the fault of III. I had to take Kruge out of nowhere and make him into a devil.

AA *In STAR TREK III, I think it is more than implied that Saavik and Spock . . .*

HB Yes.

AA *Was there ever anything planned for IV to follow up on that?*

HB Yes. I had a section of the rewrite, and I was very teasing about it. In fact, there was a scene about which Leonard was always very uncomfortable. I'm not sure why, so I would only be guessing, whether it was Leonard the actor who was uncomfortable at being burdened with a romance that he didn't think was appropriate to his character, or whether it was Leonard the director, saying, "I think that's corny." All I know is that he wasn't comfortable. He said, "Do we really have to explore this?". . . I think the opinion was split. I think Gene didn't like it. And I think there were some who read it and said, "What a great idea. We could keep this going forever." On the other hand, what I did do for it was this simple: the mechanics of IV made it impossible to bring Saavik along, because when we finally evolved the story we had enough bodies, and Saavik in the 20th century would have become yet another ear to hide. That would have become complicated, and if there is anything I like to do in storytelling, I like to keep things simple . . . too many movies fail because they are complex. . . . On the Saavik pregnancy I wrote in two scenes, a piece of which is in the movie. There is a scene, filmed, in which just before Kirk sees Spock on the mountain, Bones shuffles off surly because Saavik comes down the steps from within the ship, and she says something like, "Everything is ready, sir." Kirk says, "Thank you, Saavik, for everything, for all you've done." She says, "You're welcome, sir." He says, "You'll be well cared for, here. This is where you belong." She says, "I feel guilty," and he says, "Don't feel that way . . ." It was pretty explicit.

AA *It also explains why when the ship takes off she's standing with Amanda.*

HB That's the third piece, and that's interesting. We put that back. That was the final "given." I said, "Put it in. Let people talk about it." When Spock comes aboard, with that scene out it no longer has the same impact. . . . Oh, there's another line. "Does Spock know?" "No." I threw in everything . . . and I figured maybe, even if we get just one line in, "Are you all right? You'll be well cared for here, here's where you belong . . ." The combination of the whole scene, and then Spock's entrance, "Good day to you, sir," "Saavik," "Live long and prosper," is powerful because it is STELLA DALLAS. It is, "I bravely leave you now, to bear your child, and you don't know it." And then she goes out and we have the third element, "Mother and daughter-in-law." But all that remains in the movie is, "Have a good day, live long and prosper," and she's there with Mother. Those who wish to read it will read it, and those who don't see it, won't. I haven't seen a lot of reaction to it. . . . By the time we reached the crisis of "Is she pregnant, or isn't she pregnant?," I gave it my best shot. We shot it, we cut it. Leonard cut it, and I didn't ask for it back for a lot of reasons. First of all, overall time was a consideration, and it wasn't doing anything for the picture. It was purely TREK-studded. It was Christmas stocking presents to the fans, which I feel responsible to do whenever possible, up to the point of injuring a story: the tribbles in the bar in STAR TREK III. That's, "Hey, kids, you came to see the movie, here's a treat, it's our joke." But this didn't add anything to the movie, so I have no quarrel with the fact that it was not in the movie. Ultimately, it will be in the expanded cassette. We've got to save something, don't we? We probably cut about three minutes out of it. . . .

AA *Wasn't there a scene planned for STAR TREK IV involving Sulu meeting his great, great, great, great grandfather?*

HB You know about the scene that I wrote for George in IV but did not shoot? We wrote the scene, cast the actor, we spent the money. . . . We gave it our best shot.

AA *Was there a scene filmed showing Sulu stealing the helicopter?*

HB No . . . I was really upset with that scene. If the scene of George with the helicopter pilot had been filmed as written

. . . Leonard did a lot that day. In one day he did the entire plexiglass sequence. . . . The helicopter was waiting outside in the plexiglass yard. The scene as scripted . . . Sulu is discovered checking things out. He looks, he sees, p.o.v. helicopter, guy working on helicopter, Sulu smiles, he starts forward, enters the scene. "Hi," he says. "Huey 204, isn't it?" The guy says, "Yeah, do you fly?" Sulu says, "Here and there . . . in my Academy days." That's funny, too. The guy says, "Then this must be old stuff to you." Now, this demands a closeup, and George says, "Yes, but interesting . . . do you mind if I ask you a few questions?" Cut. That's the scene. What you see on screen is a master shot including a helicopter and two figures, with a closer angle when Sulu gets in to look at the dials. . . . That scene could have been charming, and it was written to be very flashy for George. It was further written to set up the scene, which is now kind of flat, of George flying the helicopter. . . . Now you say that it doesn't matter how he got there, he knows how to do it, except that he doesn't. He throws a switch and the windshield wipers go. That's funny, but it's only funny if you have set up the first scene. . . .

AA   *What was your reaction to the reception of STAR TREK IV?*

HB   STAR TREK IV may have been the most enjoyable postmortem experience. It will not say that it was the most enjoyable while happening. I think I had more fun on II and III. STAR TREK IV was enormously challenging and difficult. It was the most complicated picture, and Leonard was the most stressed because he had the most enormous task, and there were both personal and creative challenges. . . . I think that's behind us, but at the time it was difficult. . . . When it was over, I never had more fun in my life. . . . From the first preview, there were no adjustments to be made: a few tweaks here and there. The first full-paid audience was magnificent, people who had waited in line, people who love our material, and then a week later it went to Hawaii and I saw it, and I saw it in various places. . . . and I'm going to see it again next week in Moscow. And I will be fascinated because there's the ultimate "edge of the universe" in terms of, "Will it work there?"

AA   *Where is it actually being screened in Moscow?*

HB   It's being screened twice in Moscow. Once for what is called the Union of Cinematography, which I suppose is the equivalent of the Directors' Guild, the Writers' Guild, and the Academy of Motion Picture Arts and Sciences all rolled into one. [Then] we're screening at the American Embassy for the Diplomatic Corps, Russian and international, *specifically* in conjunction with the International Wildlife Foundation and its successful campaign to get the Russians to sign a moratorium on whale hunting, which they have already done. This will help publicize the fact that they have done it. The picture has been prescreened, obviously, and highly approved by those who saw it as a fine international, spirited, good-will picture. There was no censorship . . . but there was a suggestion. The question was . . . translating the subtitles, which will be in the Cyrillic alphabet, of course, but the picture will be in English, and this is, I think, of some interest to STAR TREK students. You will recall that in the picture there was a thematic statement that begins in II with the death of Spock, which Nick Meyer wanted and which I expanded. "The good [or 'needs'] of the many," says Spock, "outweighs the good of the few . . . ," and thus saying, he dieth. In STAR TREK III everybody else risks life, limb, career, and all that, to go back because they think there's a chance that he might be there. And when Spock asks at the end of the film, "Why would you do this?," Kirk says with a smile, "Because the good of the one outweighed the good of the many." In STAR TREK IV that line is reiterated, with Spock trying to grasp the meaning of such things as feelings and logic. You'll remember at the beginning of the picture his mother asks, "Now, don't you understand?," and Spock says, "I would accept that as a truism, that the good of the many . . . ," then she says, "But, in this case," and he says, "Humans are very illogical." The Russians asked if we could translate the line to read, "The good of the one *sometimes* outweighs the good of the many."

AA *It's a much better compromise than I expected.*

HB Not only is it better compromise, but as the writer analyzing it, [I can say] it is the line I should have written for Kirk. No one is saying that, either, is a hard and fast rule. One is saying that there are occasions when all of us will sacrifice because someone's in trouble.

AA *It also ties right in with Kirk changing the rules of the Kobayashi Maru.*

HB That's correct. So, ironically, that which might be interpreted by some as censorship is, upon analysis, a humanistic statement which belonged in the picture and, as Anne Frank said in her diary, "They put me to shame."

AA *It's almost as if you got a paper back from the Soviet government saying, "Kirk should have said this!"*

HB Yes. Isn't that fun? If analyzed from a cliché point of view, you say, "Of course, the good of the one outweighing the good of the many is absolutely antithetical to Marxist doctrine." But, analyzed in terms of human behavior, it is correct. So I'm very anxious to see if this same glow that I've had ever since this picture began playing to people persists in Moscow.

AA *I wonder how the Soviets will react to the character of "Mr. Chekov"?*

HB That's interesting. I don't know. There's an interesting technical question: how does "nuclear wessel" translate into Cyrillic? My friend at Harvard who's the head of Slavic languages wrote to the translator with some suggestions as to how to make it sound like an accent in Russian. In other words, we would say "wessel" with a "w," and there is an equivalent to that in Russian to indicate to the Russians that he is speaking English in a Russian accent. We'll see. . . . Anyway, although STAR TREK IV was not the best experience for me when it was still working . . . It's a terrific thing to have done. It's over, and you can sit back and say, "Well, it works." And more than that it gave me a perspective. . . . When I hesitated to do V, my attorney asked, "Why don't you want to do V?" And I said, "I think I've done a trilogy . . . I think I've succeeded, why do I have to . . . I mean, I can't top IV." STAR TREK IV is the culmination of a progression of stories. . . . Why should I do STAR TREK, THE MOVIES, PART II? . . . Curiously enough, as we discuss STAR TREK V and its possibilities, I feel more confident that we can make this one work. . . . Because I know that I can count on DeForest Kelley to save my tush: no matter what happens I can think of one-liners, such as, "Of all the times to ask," and that becomes one of STAR TREK IV's great moments.

AA *William Shatner mentioned maintaining the fine balance of including humor in the STAR TREK feature films, without detracting from the scope and seriousness of their formats.*

HB The difference between the series and my films—I believe this stylistically as well as editorially—that word is *reality*. Character reality. This is not a value judgment. I just feel that stylistically we have placed a value upon character reality/credibility in II, III, and IV. What would these people really do and say, as opposed to a more operatic style of drama? The loosest moment in STAR TREK—THE MOTION PICTURE is, "Where would you like to go, Captain?" "Um, thataway." But even "thataway" is not believable, it's operatic.

AA *Did Leonard Nimoy tell you what he wanted to do with that sequence, addressing McCoy and stating that as long as the Doctor was remaining with the ship, it appeared to be Spock's* *duty to stay to inject some logic into the day-to-day routine of the Enterprise crew?*

HB Yes, he did. Leonard's instincts there were pulling in the same direction that my instincts are pulling in subsequent pictures. . . .

AA *Do you feel that this direction is along the lines of that preferred by the majority of STAR TREK fans?*

HB The difference between the people who make STAR TREK and the people who regard STAR TREK from a very serious standpoint is that, like all devotees of anything, be it literature or art or tennis, they begin to formulate dogmatic rules. And when you violate these rules they say, "Wait a second. These are not the rules of the cosmos. This is not the universe, and I will tell you why. See, the logical thing to do here. . . ." and from there it's like lawyers going on in a case history. "This was established as precedent in this episode." Well, precedent has nothing to do with drama, first of all because there is no one in this whole world . . . who knows everything about STAR TREK. . . . I became a student of it, and culled that which was necessary and consistent about it, as opposed to that which is extraneous. . . . On top of that, there is another [point] the fans have confused terribly, and that it took me a long time to sort out, and that is real dogma vs. superimposed dogma. By superimposed dogma, I refer to the novels, the fanzines, the animation episodes, you name it—another body of literary dogma that is superimposed interpretively on the original stuff. As I began to realize early on what this was about, the story that came to mind was about Sigmund Freud, who, in an apocryphal story, was on his deathbed and was asked by a reporter, "I can't understand the inconsistencies between what you wrote when you were 22, and what you wrote [later]. There are contradictions here, and this doesn't make sense." And Freud [responded], "Why are you asking me? I'm not a Freudian!" And I'm not a "Trekkie." And no one is.

AA *There's another layer of unintentional dogma there. Marc Daniels observes that TV directing is a series of compromises, and that some STAR TREK fans have assigned the most profound reasons for things that he remembers were done because of simple expediency, due to requirements of storytelling and to limits of money and deadlines.*

HB . . . Absolutely . . . I'm sure that if you could ask Van Gogh about the origin and germination of the thick palette, he would probably say, "I couldn't use a brush," or, "I wanted to get my fingers dirty. That was my statement." Fine. *A*

Man and a Woman made [Claude] LeLouche a cult filmmaker. It was filmed partly in color and partly in black and white. The changeover seemed to be random . . . you could not puzzle it out, you could not say that it was black and white or color for a flashback, there was no sense of order to the choices. And the debate raged like STAR TREK canons are raged in "Interstat" or "Starlog." Well, one day I was watching "The Johnny Carson Show," and the guest was Claude LeLouche. Carson asked the first question: "Claude, how come . . . ?," and LeLouche looked at him, really quite puzzled, and said (imitating a French accent), "Well, I do not understand all this discussion. What it is, is that I have made many commercials for the Ford Motor Company, and I have 100,000 feet of color stock left, and I shot it, and when it was all over I had no money so I bought the cheapest things I could and finished the picture." Thus do commerce and art meet. . . . I have a very dear friend who is head of critical studies at UCLA. . . . I respect him enormously as a scholar, but he knows that I don't respect the function of critical studies because as an artist it's taken me over 50 years not to feel guilty using that word; I'm at last comfortable saying I'm an artist. That's very interesting and very profound. There is such a premium placed on the word "artist," and it is a premium caused by critical studies: by reviews, by critics. The fact of the matter is that every man and woman is an artist of sorts. Some achieve immortality, and some do not. Most do not, and everybody has an expressive, artistic nature. [Whether] it is the hammering of a nail or a water-color made when you're five, you're an artist. Society has it all screwed up. A man who bowls 300 is an artist. As I once read in the obituary of a handball player in London in 1921, he does, "better the thing that many seek to do." Kareem Abdul Jabbar is an artist. Fine. I mean, in the loosest sense if people do things that are human endeavors and they do them well, then they're artists. . . . The act of creating something where nothing existed before is art. To then take that and subject it to a measure of dogma or canon of any kind is a destructive act. I guess I've grown very adamant about that, not because I'm personally injured. I don't care about what people write about my stuff. I think I told you already that the highest praise I ever got from the STAR TREK movies was from Janet Maslin, in the illustrious *New York Times,* saying that STAR TREK was "Well, that's more like it." . . . Now, I think that it's fair to say of art, "This is art, but in my opinion it is not art that will last into the next century. . . . This is really esoteric, there are about six people who will like this . . . ," but to imply success or failure, which are like the measurements of a basketball game, to human creativity is devastating. It has caused too many suicides. Moreover, it is false. I really now have reached a point where I read comments by fans on inconsistencies and philosophical mistakes and madness and all that stuff, and I get the giggles, because part of the art is their perception. Part of the art is their participation, and that's the redeeming grace of criticism, that the person who is criticizing is an artist expressing himself in response to you. The final balance for me is this: It is very easy to coach from the stands. It is very easy to criticize a mistake made by others in the act of passion, it is very easy to say, "You played a lousy game," and it's very hard to stand from ground zero and play the game. Therefore, I think that artists have to learn to try not to listen to the dogma. STAR TREK has so much dogma you get a tremendous lesson from that . . . When people say, "This is, or this isn't STAR TREK," whoever they may be, then I say they ought not to be in the stadium with us because they themselves have not perceived what STAR TREK is, which is diversity, which is expansiveness . . . I think that if I were writing the critique of my movies after having lived STAR TREK and studied it, I would say something that no one has ever said in self-criticism. I would say, "Bennett's movies are small compared to Roddenberry's series vision," and that's an ironic statement because my movies are big. They're on a big screen, they have stereophonic sound, they have epic special effects . . . but the thematic material of the series was big and very difficult, allegorical. The thematic material of STAR TREK the movies is simpler and smaller. It is not unprofound. Life, death, life is not chopped liver, but I am not dealing with "cosmos," I'm dealing with the family. And that is my STAR TREK . . . At last I recognize . . . that I am not Gene Roddenberry. The STAR TREK movies are not STAR TREK: they are the STAR TREK movies. They have an identity, they have a statement that is their own, that is in a true sense based on the television series created by a great man. It is time for me, as well as for him, to recognize that they are cousins, not identical twins. . . . Anyhow, I sit here today realizing with some confidence that I have been through three movies, and I never emerge from the shadow of the legend any more than Gene Coon did. . . . My STAR TREK is: these are fascinating people, and I am obsessed with [the fact that they] are now in the middle ages of their lives as I am. This is what I identify with, this is what the first movie did not have, here's where the riches are. So from that you take step one, and it is followed by all the other steps. And suddenly you find yourself writing a trilogy . . . [of which] it can be said, "Wow, it sure doesn't have much to do with Gorns, and it doesn't have much to do with guys with black and white faces," and I say, "Correct." And you are in a different world now. You are in STAR TREK—The Middle Years, as opposed to the original series or STAR TREK—THE NEXT GENERATION.